STEAMY SECRETS
OF SENSATIONAL SEX

—The one thing that never fails to supremely pleasure a man

—How to make sure you are the sexiest woman he knows

—Intimate quizzes that reveal what kind of loving he really wants—as well as your own personal prescription for bliss in bed

—The fantastic fun of being a sexual flirt when you both know what the ecstatic outcome is going to be

—A sex-dream dictionary that details the entire language of lustful love from A to Z

—The uninhibited personal testimony of women and their men who have discovered that anything goes when it comes to what they do and enjoy together

—Becoming a woman of erotic skills and astounding passions

HOW TO MAKE HIS WILDEST
DREAMS COME TRUE

HOW TO MAKE HIS WILDEST DREAMS COME TRUE

Graham Masterton

A SIGNET BOOK

SIGNET
Published by the Penguin Group
Penguin Books USA Inc., 375 Hudson Street,
New York, New York 10014, U.S.A.
Penguin Books Ltd, 27 Wrights Lane,
London W8 5TZ, England
Penguin Books Australia Ltd, Ringwood,
Victoria, Australia
Penguin Books Canada Ltd, 10 Alcorn Avenue,
Toronto, Ontario, Canada M4V 3B2
Penguin Books (N.Z.) Ltd, 182–190 Wairau Road,
Auckland 10, New Zealand

Penguin Books Ltd, Registered Offices:
Harmondsworth, Middlesex, England

First published by Signet, an imprint of Dutton Signet,
a division of Penguin Books USA Inc.

Portions of this book first appeared in *Woman's Own.*

First Printing, April, 1996

10 9 8 7 6 5 4 3 2 1

ONE

Are You the Sexiest Woman He Knows?

Be honest, now. Are you really confident that you're the sexiest woman he knows?

Or can you think of other women who always seem to turn your partner's head? Women who always make you feel threatened and jealous; and who always have you clinging possessively onto your partner's arm?

That woman at the office, perhaps, the one with the sassy smile and the blouse that always seems to be open one button too many. Or how about his old girl-friends? Is there a name that comes up time after time, and always makes you feel that you're slightly less than first best?

And what about your partner's ideal lover ... the type of woman who would have him sitting up to beg? Blonde? Brunette? Big-breasted? A compliant, long-legged creature who looks as if she's just stepped out of a *Playboy* centerfold via the last episode of *Baywatch*?

And are these women, past and present, real and imagined, very much sexier than you?

If you've silently answered yes to that question, you're not alone. More than 70 percent of the women with whom I talked when I was preparing this book felt that they weren't as sexy as other women, and that their partner had sexual fantasies about women who were much more willing.

"Bob always says that our lovemaking is fantastic, and that he's completely satisfied, but the truth is that it's nothing out of the ordinary ... and I don't believe him. The point is that *I'm* not completely satisfied. I know there are things we could be doing ... things to make our sex life much more exciting. Yet I don't know how to suggest them without sounding as if *I'm* dissatisfied. What should I do?"

That was from Janice, a 30-year-old insurance broker from Baltimore. Janice had been married to Bob for five years, and she was facing a problem that afflicts literally millions of long-term sexual relationships all over the world ... a problem that so many couples suffer in silence.

When compatible couples first meet, their lovemaking is usually passionate and uncritical. But then, if they stay together, they become sexually familiar. In many ways, this can *improve* their sex lives, because they learn how to stimulate their partners in the ways they like best. But there's no doubt that when two people live together for quite a while, some of the electricity goes out of their physical relationship. The feel of her breast against his arm no longer stirs up an instant erection. His kisses become sporadic, and less meaningful, and don't moisten her panties anymore. But at a time when a couple should be thinking about refreshing their sex life, they usually have far too many other distractions confronting them—children, finances, career. Gone are the days of making love on the kitchen table, or under a blanket on the beach. Once it was urgent and all-important; now sex drops lower and lower on the list of priorities, until it runs a poor second to meeting the boss for dinner or attending your twice-weekly fitness class.

Domestic security and financial interdependence bring caution into any relationship. There are few greater dampers on passion than the joint bank account. To be really exciting, sex should have risk, and danger, and letting-go. Sex should be dirty, and thrilling. Forget about his high-interest bonds: turn around and let him take you from behind.

So often, however, lovemaking becomes a routine chore, or so infrequent that a couple can hardly be defined as having an ongoing physical relationship. Because women are usually afraid of hurting their husbands' feelings, and of risking their security, they rarely speak out and say that they're bored, and dissatisfied, and they'd love some more loving attention. For their part, men become sexually lethargic—at least as far as their wives are concerned. Having conquered, tamed, and domesticated their partner, they often fail to see that she still has strong sexual desires, and a need to be frequently stimulated and satisfied.

It is this combination of embarrassment, anxiety and—yes—sheer laziness that leads to more marriage breakups than any other single contributory cause. I have talked with dozens and dozens of men, and they all give virtually the same response: "After we'd bought the house, and had the children, I didn't think that Joan was all that interested in sex anymore." "We were man and wife . . . we'd been married for 11 years . . . you don't do kinky stuff with your *wife*."

Men tend to have two conflicting views about their partner's sexuality. They want a partner who is sexually willing, but at the same time they want a partner to be respectable and faithful. In fact, according to my own survey, "faithfulness" and "respectability" were the top two values that most men are seeking in a long-term partner—far above "sexual inventiveness" and "passion."

A relationship is always at its most vulnerable when it has reached this stage of complacent sexual routine. Lovemaking continues, but it loses much of its thrill. Gone are the days of tearing off each others' clothes as soon as you open the apartment door, and making love among the Safeway shopping bags. Gone are the days of surreptitious hands-up-the-skirt and cock-squeezing in taxis. Both man and woman start looking outside of their relationship for that sexual frisson that first brought them together. In the 1950s they called it the Seven-Year-Itch. These days, we can call it the Three-Year-Deadlock. Couples have been so busy establishing their careers and their financial security and constructing a family that they have forgotten about sex.

Although they may limp along for another two or three years or even longer, most relationships that suffer sexual problems begin to fall apart after the first three years. So after two-and-a-half years together, you really should take a good honest look at your love life, and see what you can do to improve it ... not just tonight, but tomorrow night and every night for years to come.

Now, careers and sex are not mutually exclusive, by any means. They should be complementary. What's the point of having a beautiful home and a healthy income if you don't have a loving partner to share them with? And not just an ordinary loving partner, but a red-hot loving partner. The best years of your sex life are comparatively short: don't find yourself looking back in later years and thinking to yourself "... if only ..."

This book is written specifically for women who want to change their sex lives ... not by changing partners, but by electrifying the partner they already love. Based on scores of real-life experiences, some of them not-so-successful, some of them very successful, and some of them downright explosive, it will show you how to transform yourself into that woman whom your partner always turns around to ogle.

In other words, it will show you how you can make his wildest sexual dreams come true.

First of all, of course, you have to find out what his wildest sexual dreams actually are. You may think you know your partner well. You may think you know your partner *very* well. But I can guarantee that you don't know the deepest, darkest sexual fantasies that he plays out in his mind. This book will tell you how to discover what they are ... and then how to bring them to life.

Provided you're prepared to be brave, and uninhibited, and do some things that might have made you blush when you were younger, *you can completely and dramatically transform your sex life tonight,* and that's a promise.

Discovering your partner's secret sexual fantasies isn't as difficult as it sounds, because male fantasies fall into several distinctive categories, and it usually isn't hard to determine which one arouses your particular partner. This book will show you what signs to look for in his manner, his responses, and his personal behavior. It will give you a chart to his sexuality which will enable you to become more than the woman he loves . . . the woman of his wildest dreams.

Several women asked me, "Why should *I* be the one who transforms our sex life? Why can't *he* do it? After all, I thought that men were supposed to be in charge, when it comes to sex."

Well, the notion that the man is supposed to be "in charge" is hopelessly outdated. I believe that a man should make it his business to be skilled and knowledgeable in sex, because every woman deserves all the satisfaction that a man is capable of giving her. But these days, women know more about sex than they ever did before, and they also know what they're entitled to.

What they're entitled to is proper stimulation, exciting and imaginative lovemaking, and full sexual satisfaction. There is so much sexual information available that no man has any excuse for that clumsy and hurried sex that left so many generations of women feeling bewildered and frustrated.

All the same, just because you're *entitled* to exciting sex, that doesn't mean that you can lie back and expect your partner to do all the work—particularly since *you* are the one who holds the key to making your love life so much more thrilling.

Not only should you learn as much as you can about sex and sexual responses, you should start on a program to build your sexual confidence and to say goodbye to your inhibitions. Ask yourself these questions now: do you have any objection to your partner opening your legs and exploring you in the full light of your bedside lamp? Do you shrink from kissing your partner's penis? If your partner wanted you to wear high-heeled shoes in bed, would you refuse? Would you mind if your partner watched you on the toilet?

If you said yes to more than three of those questions, then you still have some way to go to overcome your sexual reticence. But this book will show you how you can do it . . . how you can bring out the good bad girl in you, and never feel embarrassed about anything sexual, ever again.

Although your sexual knowledge is a hundred times more comprehensive than it was, say, 20 years ago, lovemaking is still a complicated and difficult subject to deal with, because technique is inextricable from emotion. When you teach golf, you can teach grip and swing and stance: you don't have to worry about encouraging your student to overcome shyness, or inhibition, or embarrassment.

When you discuss sex, however, it's no use pretending that many people don't find some aspects of it shocking, or embarrassing, or "dirty"—especially when you start talking about advanced sexual techniques such as oral and anal stimulation, or variations such as bondage or rubberwear.

You can compare golf strokes quite openly. But there are very few opportunities to compare your lovemaking with anybody else's, unless you regularly attend orgies, or you watch porno movies every night. Even then, people behave differently at orgies than they do in private: and people in porno movies are being paid for what they do (unlike you!).

But the very first thing you'll learn in this book is that when it comes to sex, absolutely anything can go. There are only two limiting factors. One, it should be safe. Two, you should both enjoy it. Apart from that, the only other limiting factor is your own imagination, and I'm sure that you can think of some pretty wild things to do in bed without much prompting from me.

Men may be skilled and strong when it comes to

sex (that's if you're lucky). But it is women who hold the power to effect immediate changes to their sexual relationships. This is because of the radical difference in male and female sexuality. Men have a very quick sexual response to *visual* stimulation. They can be quickly aroused by the sight of a sexily dressed woman—even a woman they don't know. They can become highly excited by photographs of female breasts and genitalia—even if they can't even see the faces of the women they belong to.

They can be stimulated by sexy clothes, by erotic underwear, by semi-nudity and nudity. They can be even more stimulated by provocative behavior out of its normal context—in other words, by discovering in the middle of shopping that you're not wearing panties; or seeing you do your household chores naked. Jane, a full-breasted brunette from Chicago, told me, "On Saturday mornings, I never dressed. Not a stitch. I brought him his coffee, I tidied up the apartment, I cooked lunch, and I never wore anything. Phil couldn't wait for Saturdays. I never managed to do much housework. He couldn't keep his hands off me. He was always fondling my breasts or sliding his hand up between my legs."

Apart from dressing sexily and undressing sexily, we'll also be looking at more than 50 things you can do to turn him on tonight—things he'll remember for the rest of his life. But you don't have to do something sexually outrageous every day ... most of the sexual techniques I describe will be quite enough to keep the stimulus level in your relationship raised for several weeks.

The secret of arousing men and keeping them aroused is not just to stimulate them physically but to give them a feast of memorable visual images. That time you greeted him at the front door wearing nothing but a wide cinch belt and high-heeled boots. That time you lay sleeping(!) with your nightgown lifted so that he could sit there for as long as he liked and look at your exposed vulva. That time you pushed him back on the pillows and gave his erection a lascivious exhibitionistic licking that he'll never forget.

Never forget that your partner is turned on by *looking* at you—especially if you give him the opportunity to do it openly. If men weren't turned on by looking at naked and semi-naked women, then Hugh Hefner and Bob Guccione would have gone out of business years ago.

Remember, too, that erotic contrasts are very arousing ... for instance, if you sit astride the arm of a black leather couch, with your bare vagina pressed against the smooth surface ... if you walk around your apartment bare-breasted with long strings of pearls around your neck ... if you wear a huge warm turtleneck sweater and thick woolly socks but nothing else, not even a wisp of pubic hair to keep you warm ...

You'll have to be more than broadminded. After all, you're raising the excitement level in your sexual relationship way beyond anything you've ever done before. Even the most extreme techniques that I will tell you about are completely harmless, but they do require nerve. This book will show you how to acquire that nerve by creating a Sexual Character for yourself.

Scores of women of different ages and backgrounds have already tried it, and so far the response has been tremendously encouraging. Creating your own Sexual Character helps you overcome almost all of your sexual inhibitions, and allows you to explore the wilder limits of sex without feeling nearly so cautious or embarrassed. Charlene, a 26-year-old Memphis woman, used her Sexual Character to change herself from a "mousy homemaker" who would only make love with the lights off to what she called "a brazen temptress." "After only a week, I was lying on the bed with my legs apart, giving my husband a demonstration of how I liked to masturbate myself. He didn't know what had hit him, but he loved it."

Many women find it difficult to "come on strong" to their partners because they're embarrassed. They find that they're tongue-tied when it comes to talking about sex, and they shy from showing themselves off. Creating your own Sexual Character is a first step toward those daring, exciting moments that you're going to love.

Melanie, a 24-year-old cosmetician from Denver, describes herself in her late teens and early twenties as "painfully shy, especially when it came to sex." She had only two boyfriends before she married a college friend, Dean, and "to say that I knew nothing about sex was an understatement." Although she had an exceptional figure, she was what she called "a towel and bathrobe girl . . . I never walked around the apartment naked, and I didn't like making love on top of the covers."

After Melanie had acquired her own Sexual Character, however, her attitude toward nudity and sexual display changed dramatically. So did her willingness to try new sexual techniques.

"When Dean came home, I made sure that I was on the couch, watching television. I was always on the couch watching television when he came home, but this time I was wearing this little yellow pleated skirt and I had it raised up right around my waist, so that my cunt was exposed. I was watching television and playing with my cunt, fingering myself. He came in and said, 'What are you doing?' He was obviously shocked. I said, 'Waiting for you.' He put down his briefcase and knelt down in front of me. He took my hand away from my cunt, and said, 'Don't you know that's my job?' He started to finger me, slipping two or three fingers up my cunt. Then he couldn't resist it, and he started licking me, and kissing me, and in the end he had his whole face buried in my cunt, and his tongue right up inside me, all stiff and wriggling. His tongue wriggled all over my cunt until I couldn't help coming. I didn't think I was going to, but it suddenly swelled over me, like a huge dark wave. Then he climbed on top of me, and opened up his pants, and his cock was huge. I held it in both hands and sucked it. It tasted delicious. In fact there is nothing like the taste of cock. I sucked him and sucked him, tugging his balls and digging my fingernails into his ass. He wanted to fuck me. He kept trying to take his cock out of my mouth but I wouldn't let him. In the end he suddenly came, and my mouth was full of it, thick sticky sperm, it was even running down my chin.

"That night we made love three more times, which we'd never done before. Dean didn't know what had hit him, but I did. I lay awake till morning, thinking about my new life. I'd done it. I'd actually had the guts to do it. From now on, I was going to have sex whenever I wanted, and as much as I wanted, and in any way I wanted."

It took Melanie a while longer to get Dean used to the idea that he had a partner with a healthy sexual appetite and distinctive sexual tastes. She developed an almost insatiable appetite for oral sex, and now she took the opportunity to suck his penis whenever she felt like it. She would kneel in front of him in the shower, licking and sucking him; or wake him up early in the morning. In return, she expected oral sex, too, and would climb astride his face when he was lying in bed, open up her vaginal lips with her fingers, and sit on his mouth.

Dean said, "She was like a sex fantasy come true. I never knew that a woman could really want sex so much. Most of the time she makes me feel like I can't keep up with her. But she's wonderful. I used to think our sex life was pretty dull before that day, but the only reason it was dull was because *I* was dull. Melanie changed me, overnight; and totally changed our marriage, too. Do you know how satisfying it is to go to work every day and your cock's been sucked so sore you can hardly walk, and you can think to yourself, 'my wife did that.' You can't wait to get home, believe me."

We'll be discussing oral sex later, because almost every man finds it one of the most stimulating of erotic fantasies, and I have rarely come across a husband who has left a wife who is enthusiastic about fellatio. Again, oral sex has a strongly visual appeal: a man can look down and see his erect cock sliding in and out of his partner's lips. In fact the visual stimulus is very much more intense than the physical stimulus: many men find it impossible to reach a climax from oral stimulation alone, and usually some brisk hand rubbing is required to bring them off.

We'll talk about dressing and undressing. We'll be talking about dream sex, in which you and your partner play different roles. We'll be talking about do-it-yourself erotica, and ways to make your evenings more sexually exciting. We'll be talking about sex aids and sex toys, and several incredible new ways in which you stimulate your partner so that he'll be convinced that you've been trained in a Thai massage parlor!

Most of all, though, we'll be talking about *talking*. How to explain to your partner that your sex life is lacking, without upsetting him. How to tell him what you want; and how to ask him what he wants. How to suggest that you try some new and exciting ways of making love ... and how to keep your sex life fresh and stimulating every single day.

It isn't at easy to start talking about sex, especially if neither of you is really used to it. Almost every sex guide talks glibly about the importance of "communication," as if telling your partner what you want in bed is as easy as ordering thin-crust pizza with extra pepperoni.

Let's not make any bones about it: it's extremely difficult to put your sexual feelings into words, especially if you feel your relationship has been lacking in some way (he hasn't been arousing you enough ... he's always too tired ... he never waits for you to reach a climax).

But this book will tell you how you can initiate conversations about your lovemaking without upsetting your partner ... and what you can say to encourage him and to put him at ease, even if you're trying to tell him that he hasn't quite met your expectations. It will show you how to be sexually positive in everything you say, and even how to use a kind of erotic "show and tell" so that your partner will understand exactly what you want. Sometimes a silent demonstration is better than a thousand embarrassed words.

Once you've explained to your partner what you want from your sex life, and once you've encouraged him to tell you what turns him on, the battle is two-thirds won.

But before you go rushing off, eager to tell him how you feel, you have to make sure that you're ready.

You have to understand that everyone's sexual preferences are different, and that every man and woman has his or her own sexual fantasies—some of which you may find profoundly alarming when you first hear about them.

That's why this book explains some of the more extreme sexual acts that men fantasize about ... and how you can tell whether he really wants to do them, or whether he's going to be satisfied just by talking about them—as many men are.

Every man has different sexual tastes, and even some very ordinary, unpretentious men secretly harbor some wild and unusual desires. When you discover the secret fantasies that turn *your* partner on, it's likely that some of them will shock you. At first, some of them may even disgust you. But before you reject them out of hand, try to understand that all of the things he fantasizes about are intended to give you sexual pleasure, and that even the most extreme sexual acts are ways in which two people try to get closer together. In fact, the more extreme they are, the closer the couple become, physically as well as emotionally. They are powered by the greatest urge of all, which is the urge of two people who love each other to become one.

To begin with, many women find their partner's fantasies threatening. But if they realize that every act of love is an act of *love*, then they will not only open their minds and their bodies to a wider variety of sexual pleasures, they will become much better lovers, too.

Like Helen, a 49-year-old schoolteacher from Oakland, California, you may soon find that a sexual act you once thought would be totally abhorrent will turn out to arouse you more than anything you've ever done before.

"I was looking in my husband's toolbox for a small screwdriver for my glasses when I found a big vibrator. It was shaped just like a man's penis, and it was enormous. I didn't know what to think about it, and I went around worrying all weekend. I wondered if he was gay, or what. In the end I had to say something, so I did. I just came right out and told Gary what I'd discovered.

"At first he was very embarrassed and he refused to tell me. Then he said that it had been given to him by the guys in the office as a joke, and he hadn't known what to do with it. I still didn't believe him, but I was prepared to let it go. In the end, however, he told me that when he was working alone in the garage sometimes, he looked through sexy magazines and masturbated. Now and then, he used the vibrator, running it up and down his penis, or holding it between his legs, or smothering it with K-Y and pushing it up his ass.

"As you can imagine, I was dumbfounded. I felt as if I was married to some kind of pervert. Gary kept insisting that there was nothing wrong with our sex life ... he masturbated because he enjoyed it, that's all. But I couldn't get over the idea of him standing in that garage with a huge vibrator up him, jerking himself off over photographs of young girls. I felt totally confused; and hurt, too. I mean, it just couldn't be normal, could it?"

Helen wrote to me asking for advice. She was surprised to learn what surprises many woman—that a large percentage of men continue to masturbate long past their adolescent years and well into middle age, and beyond—whether they are married or not. They don't necessarily masturbate because they are frustrated or dissatisfied with their partners. They do it because they enjoy it—a few minutes of erotic fantasy coupled with a pleasurable release of physical tension. Fewer than three percent of those surveyed see it as a substitute for sexual intercourse with their partners, and almost all of them regard it as "harmless."

As one young man said, "You work out every other part of your body? Why not here?"

While your partner's masturbation may be completely harmless, it is actually very important, because almost every man masturbates with a very potent sexual image in his mind—something he's seen, something he's done, something he'd like to do. If you can discover what that image is, you can use it to tremendous advantage in your love life. It's the key, in fact, to discovering his sexual fantasies.

No one expects you to look like the centerfold in *Hustler* (unless, of course, that's the way you look all the time). But it takes very little effort to appear in a fresh and erotic light, so that instead of turning back to his *Playboy* he'll turn to you.

Not all men feel the need to masturbate, but a very large percentage do, especially those who have to spend long periods away from home. Here's Jim, 32, who sells air-conditioning nationwide: "When I'm away from home, I buy two or three really strong pornographic magazines, and I use them to jerk off in my hotel room. I'd say that every single guy who spends time away from home does the same thing. Why do hotels put those soft-porn movies on cable? Because there's such a demand. You don't jerk off because your wife doesn't satisfy you. Jerking off and real sex are two different things. You jerk off because it relaxes you, because you like doing it; and because you can't wait to get back home and get your wife into bed."

I used to edit *Penthouse* and *Penthouse Forum* magazines, as well as being the editorial director of a hardcore Swedish sex magazine *Private*. If all the men who denied buying copies of those magazines were telling the truth, our circulation would have been minimal, and we would have gone out of business. But men *do* buy sex magazines and sex toys, in very large quantities, and they *do* use them to masturbate, and the only harm that can possibly come out of it is if their partners fail to understand that neither looking at pictures of naked women nor masturbation causes infidelity.

One senior salesman told me, "Going on a business trip combines stress and loneliness in equal measures. I know scores of sales personnel who resort to prostitutes, and I can't blame them for that. But I would prefer to buy a dirty magazine and whack myself off. I mean, who does it hurt? And there's no risk of AIDS or any other complication."

There should be no guilt or secrecy attached to masturbation. Instead, you and your partner should be able to find ways to help it bring you closer together. Another salesman told me, "My wife Darlene is the most enlightened woman in the world, as far as I'm concerned. When I go traveling, she always includes a really sexy letter in my baggage, as well as a G-string that she's been wearing, and some new Polaroids that she's taken of herself ... what can I say? in the kind of poses that men like."

Other wives and girlfriends give their partners cassette tapes of themselves masturbating ... complete with gasps and moans and juicy noises. One wife said, "I push the microphone right up inside my vagina, so that he can hear every single squish."

All of these women have gone a long way toward making their partners' wildest dreams come true. They have treated sex as fun; as a shared delight; as a way of getting closer to their partners, even when they're temporarily separated.

If you can succeed in developing a sexual relationship with your partner in which neither of you has any secrets, you will both reap the rewards in far greater intimacy, far more exciting and interesting sexual pleasures—and, most of all, far more trust.

I can never overemphasize the importance of trust in a sexual relationship. If you trust your lover, you can try all kinds of new and varied sexual acts with far more confidence. I have been approached by many women who are cautious about trying bondage or other sadomasochistic acts with their partners—"not because they don't turn me on, but because I'm not 100 percent sure that I can trust him."

You can help to develop that trust by being open-minded, enthusiastic, and never scorning or ridiculing anything that turns your partner on. If he's aroused by a picture of a sexy woman, why don't you say, "Yes, she is sexy, isn't she?" instead of wrinkling your nose? And if he likes sexy magazines, why not encourage him to look through them when you're in bed together, so that you can masturbate him, instead of him having to do it alone? After all, the women in *Hustler* are only paper and ink, and they can hardly jump out of the page and take your man away from you—whereas your refusal to discover what turns him on might very well have the effect of driving him into the arms of another, real woman one day.

Remember that a considerable number of women masturbate, too—out of loneliness, or frustration, or simply, like many men, for erotic pleasure. One of the biggest-selling sex aids is a "weekend-kit" for women, which includes a vibrator with a variety of attachments for vaginal, clitoral, and anal stimulation, and the company which sells it says that more than 70 percent of their orders come from women.

Janie, a 27-year-old homemaker from Wheaton, Maryland, said, "Burt leaves the house at eight o'clock in the morning and he doesn't get back till way after six. I love him, but I do get sexual feelings during the day, and I don't think that there's any harm in masturbating. It's not like I've gone to bed with another man, is it? Usually, when I'm feeling horny, I take off all of my clothes and lie on the couch in the living room and slowly play with myself. We have a big Dalmatian called Henry and sometimes he sniffs around when I'm masturbating. I think he likes the smell of it because his cock goes stiff.

"Sometimes I use a cucumber or a soda bottle to masturbate, but most of the time I prefer my fingers. I don't think men understand that you only need a really light touch . . . so light that you can scarcely feel it. I flick my clitoris like a butterfly's wings, and when I come it feels like heaven lighting up. But it doesn't compare to Burt. I like masturbating, but I love Burt."

That was what Helen should have realized about Gary. He liked masturbating, but he loved her. He simply didn't feel that he could ask her to give him oral sex, in the way that the women in his magazines did, or to stimulate him anally, in the way that he could do with his vibrator.

I advised Helen to accept the fact that Gary enjoyed pornographic magazines, and to look at those magazines herself to see what his particular sexual preferences were. There was no question that he liked the idea of having his penis sucked, which Helen had never done for him, and that he also liked the idea of a woman penetrating him anally with a vibrator.

Few women seem to realize that a man's anal area is crammed with erotic nerve endings (just as yours is) and that men are just as aroused by anal stimulation as women are.

I pointed out to Helen that if she could indulge Gary's sexual predilections, instead of feeling as if they were some kind of betrayal, she would almost certainly reap all of the benefits herself: a happier relationship, with far more honesty, far more closeness, and far more exciting sex.

All she had to do was accept (a) that Gary's behavior was perfectly normal, and that (b) it didn't threaten their relationship in any way. In fact, if she could persuade him to *include* his interest in pornography and anal stimulation into their love life, she would be well on the way to making his wildest dreams come true.

Until you've done it yourself—until you've made up your mind that you're not going to be sexually inhibited in any way—you have no idea how liberated it can make you feel. Other sex counselors talk about "open marriage" as a marriage in which partners feel free to have affairs with other people. But *my* idea of an "open marriage" is a relationship in which partners feel free to do anything and say anything, not with other people, but each other.

So many sexual relationships are hampered by embarrassments and inhibitions—and, more than anything else, by the way in which partners misread each other's feelings.

At my suggestion, Helen encouraged Gary to bring his pornographic magazines into their sex life, rather than keep them as a separate self-indulgence. At first she thought that she would find pornography shocking and distasteful, but she quickly discovered that she "quite liked it" and that it "quite aroused me."

"My first impression was a whole lot of naked flesh, like a meat market. But when I looked at it more closely, I saw pretty girls and good-looking young men, and I began to understand what the point of it was. It's vicarious sex, yes. But it's no more sinful than looking at a color picture of a Thanksgiving turkey in a magazine, and salivating. It's no more sinful than looking at a beautiful home in *Architectural Digest* and wishing it was yours.

"I saw girls doing things I that I never did . . . girls licking men's penises, and sitting on top of them . . . girls taking penises up their bottoms . . . girls allowing men to masturbate on their faces. I was shocked for the first few minutes, but then I realized that they all looked as if they were enjoying themselves . . . and I thought, why shouldn't they? What are they doing, except giving each other pleasure, and giving other people pleasure by allowing them to look at them, while they make love? If anything should be banned, it's violence, people hurting each other. The people in these magazines certainly weren't hurting each other."

Helen persuaded Gary to show her the pictures that turned him on the most, and she learned more about his sexual tastes in 20 minutes than she had in the previous 20 years. "I found out that he loves bottoms, and anal sex. In all the time we've been together, he's never tried to make love to me in anything other than the good old-fashioned way. Maybe he thought that I wouldn't want to do anything different—that I'd be offended, or something like that. But I've never had any inhibitions about sex. As far as I'm concerned, if it's exciting, I'll do it."

Helen arranged an evening when she and Gary spread all of his magazines across the bed and picked out the pictures that turned them on the most. "Then I said, 'let's act them out ... let's do them for real ... we can't let people in magazines have all the fun.' I lay naked on my back, and took a dollop of cold cream from the nightstand, and smeared it all around my asshole. Then I turned on my side. Gary came up behind me, and I could feel his hard-on bobbing against my thighs. First of all he kissed the cheeks of my bottom ... then he slid a single finger into the crack, until he found my asshole. It was all slippery with cold cream, and he slid his finger right up inside it, as far as it would go.

"I had never felt anything like that before, a finger up my ass, and I absolutely loved it. He waggled it around, and then he drew it out, but I wanted more. Then next thing I knew, he had slipped another finger in, from the other hand, and he was stretching my asshole open.

"All the time he was kissing my hair and my neck and my shoulders, and telling me how much he loved me. He was so passionate, he was just like the time we first dated, and that was more than 30 years ago.

"His cock was so hard it could have been carved out of bone. He pressed it up against my asshole and my first instinct was to twist away, so that he couldn't hurt me, that he couldn't penetrate me. But after what you wrote to me, I decided not to fight it, I decided to enjoy myself ... even though I never would have thought that I could have enjoyed myself, doing this.

"I relaxed, and felt his kisses on my shoulders, and then I felt his cock forcing its way into my asshole. My first instinct was to grip in tight, but in all of your books you say to push against it, so I did. It slid in so easily, and it felt so thick and good. He went so far into my ass that I could feel his hair tickling against the cheeks of my bottom. All the time I remembered to open myself out, to keep pushing my muscles out instead of pulling them in, and Gary made love to my ass just as gently and beautifully as he always made love to my cunt.

"He was very excited. He fucked me quicker and quicker, and then he climaxed, right up inside my ass. I had never actually felt him come before, but this time I did. It was warm and wet; and when he drew his cock out, I could feel sperm running out of my asshole."

Helen didn't leave her indulgence of Gary's sexual fantasies at that. Later, she produced his vibrator, liberally smothered with K-Y, and began to give him the anal stimulation of his life.

"He was lying facedown on the bed, naked, half-dozing after making love. I kissed his back, and ran my fingers down his spine. Then I gently opened the cheeks of his ass, until I could see his asshole. I kissed it, and licked it, and then I pushed the vibrator up against it. He said, 'What—?' but I shushed him, and told him not to fight it.

"I screwed the vibrator slowly into his asshole. It was bigger than a real cock, but the K-Y made it so slippery that it slid in quite easily. His asshole was stretched wide open, but I kept on screwing the vibrator deeper and deeper, until nothing but the end of it was showing. Then I switched it on, and moved it around and around, really churning it up inside his ass.

"He turned onto his back. His cock wasn't totally stiff, but sperm was running out of it and dripping over his balls. I took hold of his cock and rubbed it, and then I took the bull by the horns and put it into my mouth. It was slippery and it tasted like sugar and salt, but I kept on licking and sucking it until it went stiff, and filled up my whole mouth.

"I worked that vibrator around and around; and after a time he started thumping the bed and telling me to stop, it was hurting him. I started to pull it out, but when I did, he climaxed. No warning. His cock just stiffened and bulged, and out it came, two huge blobs of sperm. They landed on the back of my hand, and I licked them off, and swallowed them. Again, this was nothing that I'd ever done before, or ever dreamed of doing before. But I realized afterward, when Gary was sleeping, that both us had managed to cross a huge barrier between us."

Like so many other couples, Helen and Gary had started to take sex for granted—never exploring its numerous possibilities, never quite summoning up the courage to fulfill their wildest dreams. If Helen hadn't discovered Gary's vibrator, they could have gone on forever, locked in the same underdeveloped sexual relationship, making love but never exploring that extraordinary sexual opportunity that a long-term partnership can give you—the opportunity to try out anything and everything—the opportunity to expose yourself to your partner, body and soul, so that there is literally nothing that you won't do together, to give yourselves pleasure.

"We feel released, free," said Helen. "After all these years of marriage, we're having sex like two kids. We make love in the afternoons, on the couch. We make love in the morning. We walk around naked in front of each other, which we haven't done for years. Last week, we spent over a half-hour in bed, while Gary slowly fucked me in the ass—very, very slowly—and caressed my breasts at the same time. I had an orgasm that almost made me black out. I had a sore ass the following day, but I was proud of it.

"I feel like a new woman. I feel younger, I feel more attractive. I feel as if Gary and I really belong together."

This feeling of "belonging" is one of the most fulfilling and exciting results of making your partner's sexual dreams come true. It's that feeling you had when you first dated, when you were always kissing and touching and holding hands—when he breathed out and you breathed in.

When you first went out together, the sexual feelings you had were natural and urgent, and it didn't really matter if your lovemaking was clumsy or not. But as time passed, there was far less urgency, and clumsiness lost its charm. You wanted a partner who knew how to arouse you ... someone who knew how to stimulate you ... someone who could take you further into the reaches of sexual experience.

It is almost certain that your partner has fantasized about sexual acts that—if he tried them out—would give your love life all the variety that you've been looking for. But it is almost equally certain that he doesn't know how to tell you what he's been daydreaming about, because he's afraid of sounding shocking or disgusting. For instance, how do you think Helen would have reacted if Gary had come straight out and said, "I want to have anal intercourse with you—now!"?

Or how do you think you would react if your partner said that he wanted to tie you up, or dress you in rubber, or urinate all over your breasts?

Men and women have very different ideas about sexual excitement and sexual fulfillment. But they can learn to understand and accommodate each other's urges, so that they both get the very best out of their relationship.

Davina, a 23-year-old editoral assistant for a large New York publisher, said that six months ago her boyfriend Ned had bought her a short, skintight, black-rubber dress.

"When I took it out of the box, I didn't know what to say. I knew that some people were into rubber, but I never was, and I never knew that Ned was, either. I mean, we'd been living together for over 18 months and he always seemed so normal! He seemed kind of embarrassed about giving it to me, and I had the impression that it had taken him a whole lot of nerve to buy it. So even though my first reaction was to say, 'What the hell's this? You don't expect me to walk around dressed in rubber, do you?' I managed to bite my tongue.

"He said, 'You don't like it, do you? I'll take it back.' But the more he said that he'd take it back, the more I realized that this wasn't just about giving me a gift, this was a sexual confession he was making, without actually saying it out loud. I guess it was the same as men who give their wives G-strings and crotchless panties for Christmas. They're trying to suggest to their wives that they should dress up in something sexy once in a while, and the trouble is that instead of wearing them once in a while, and turning their husbands on, they take the crotchless panties back to the store and exchange them for thick woolly passion-killers.

"Anyhow, I insisted trying the dress on. I have very big breasts, but it was so tight that I couldn't wear anything underneath it. I had to dust my skin with talcum power first, and then slide into it naked.

"It was very different from what I'd imagined. It

was very tight, and it clung to every single curve like a second skin. It was a good thing I'd been working out: I might just as well have been naked and covered in black paint. You could not only see the outline of my nipples through it, you could see my navel as well, and every curve of my bottom.

"I gave Ned a little fashion show and I could tell that he loved it. It really turned him on. The funny thing was, it turned me on, too—partly because *he* was turned on, and partly because it was a very sexy thing to wear, especially since I had no panties on, and the hemline was so short. Not only that, rubber *is* very sexy to wear. It's the way it grips you all the time, and the whispery kind of noise it makes. I never thought in a million years that you'd ever catch me wearing a rubber dress, and liking it.

"As soon as he realized that I liked it, Ned took hold of me and gave me the kind of kiss that goes all the way down to the soles of your feet. He was really excited. In fact I don't think I'd ever seen him so excited before. But his excitement was infectious, you know, and I started to get real excited, too, until the both of us were on the couch and we were kissing and struggling like we'd only just met each other.

"I tugged open Ned's belt and dragged down his pants and his shorts. His cock seemed to be bigger than I'd ever seen it before, and the end of it was all slippery with juice. I lay back on the couch and opened my legs up wide. Ned opened up the lips of my pussy with his fingers and pushed the head of his cock into me, only the head. I was dying to have all of it, I needed it all the way up. But he said, 'You turn me on so much, I'm going to have to take this real slow, otherwise I'll come right here and now.'

"We did it so slow. He waited for a few moments,

and then he slid his cock right up inside me, so far that it touched my womb and made me jump. Then he slid it out again, and waited, with just the head of it inside me. He said, 'Look at that,' and I looked down, and there was my pussy wide apart, with the lips just managing to cling to the head of his cock . . . then white thighs and stretchy black rubber.

"It seemed like we were fucking for hours, and every thrust was so beautiful. Then he started to pant, and I reached down and felt his balls tighten, and I knew that he had to be very close. I stroked my clitoris, quicker and quicker, so that we could come pretty much together. I felt hot and sweaty and slippery inside of that dress, and it smelled of rubber, but that really aroused me. I climaxed before he did, and I shouted out loud. Then he climaxed, and he *shook*, I mean he really shook.

"Afterward we sat on the couch and shared a glass of wine and talked. I'd really learned something . . . not so much that Ned was into rubber, but that he liked to *look* when we were having sex . . . he liked to see it happening. I must say that I liked it, too. But what I really enjoyed was the exhibitionism of it. I think all women are sexual exhibitionists, but most of them don't allow themselves to do it because they think it's crude or vulgar. I sat on the couch in that black rubber dress with my legs apart, and I could see myself in the mirror on the other side of the room. My pussy was still gaping open because Ned had been fucking me, and sperm was pouring out of it and running down the crack of my bottom. I guess I looked like a scene from a porno flick, but so what? It was exciting and *very* satisfying . . . and it gave us both a kind of mental image to think about at any time in the future . . . anytime we felt like turning ourselves on."

Davina's inspirational understanding of male sexual response ensured that what could have been an embarrassing and possibly disastrous moment in their relationship became the moment when she and Ned came closer than they had ever been before ... not just physically, but emotionally, too. She saw that no harm would come to her from wearing a garment that aroused him so much, and she was sufficiently open-minded to try to discover what it was about rubber that he found so appealing.

Moreover, she saw that it was *looking* at her dressed in rubber that made his satisfaction complete, especially since she adopted such a provocative and uninhibited pose. It was a pose that said: look, I'm wearing this dress to turn you on, and here's your semen running out of me, to prove that you've made love to me. Very potent stuff, and (as she intelligently guessed) an image that would stay with both of them for a long time to come, giving color and excitement to their relationship.

For Ned, Davina's acceptance of his minor fetish was "a huge relief." Once his taste for latex had been brought out into the open, he could introduce her to other variations on the theme, such as rubber thigh boots, rubber basques, and rubber panties. She particularly enjoyed the pair of rubber dildo panties that he bought her—tight black panties with a solid rubber dildo inside them for all-day stimulation.

"I can sit in the office talking about a travel book on Chile, and every time I cross and recross my legs this dildo slides up and down inside me. By the end of the day I need Ned so badly that I can't wait to get home."

Didn't she think that rubberwear was perverted or "dirty" or vulgar in any way?

"Our sex life was good before we got into rubber together. Now it's terrific. We don't do it all the time, only now and then, but when we do, we always spend hours and hours making love, until we're absolutely exhausted. You can't tell me there's anything perverted or 'dirty' about two people loving each other so much, no matter how they do it."

You are about to take part in a sexual experience that will give you the same open-mindedness and the same sense of sheer enjoyment that Davina found with Ned, and that many other couples have found by using the same technique. Remember, you may come across things that shock you. But if you've been brave enough to pick up this book in the first place, you've already taken the first step toward making not only *his* wildest dreams come true, but yours, too.

Questionnaire: What Does Your Lover Secretly Want?

In order to build up a profile of your lover's secret sexual desires, you will have to prepare a Sex Orientation Chart. This is not only easy but a great deal of fun, particularly when you get to the practical tests. All you need to do is draw a vertical line down the page of a ruled notebook to divide it in half. Head the left-hand side "Dominant" and the right-hand side "Submissive."

This doesn't mean that you're going to find out whether your partner is into sexual domination or not—it's simply a way of showing which sexual acts he would like to do to you and which sexual acts he would like you to do to him.

Head the next page, "Visual Stimuli"—because this

is where you're going to record the sexual sights that always catch your partner's attention.

Head the third page "Physical Stimuli"—because this is where you're going to list all of those touches and caresses and nips and scratches that turn your partner on.

Head the fourth page "Fantasies"—but divide this page in half, too. Give the left-hand side the subheading "Yes" and the right-hand side the subheading "No." This is just a way of separating the fantasies he would like to act out for real with the fantasies he would rather remain fantasies. For instance, a 34-year-old airline pilot from Fort Worth told me that when he was masturbating he would have strong fantasies about being chained naked to the floor of a dungeon while a dominatrix in spiked heels lashed his erect penis with a thin whip. "But there is no way in the world that I would ever want that to happen ... I wouldn't even care to be paddled, thanks." On the other hand, a 28-year-old realtor told me that he would love his young wife to tie his wrists and blindfold him and "do whatever she felt like doing."

To start your profile, ask your partner these 44 questions. You can tell him exactly what they're for—because the more truthful he is, and the more cooperative he is, the more he's going to benefit. However, if you don't think that he would be willing to participate, or if you think that his reaction might be strongly negative, don't give him the whole list of questions, but see if you can ask them one at a time over a period of days, so that you won't arouse any suspicion that you're "prying" into his sexual fantasies. Even though a man may have very extreme sexual desires, that doesn't necessarily mean that he's comfortable with them, or that he's willing to open up and tell you all about them.

Some men are afraid of shocking their partners. Others feel it's perverted to have thoughts about extreme sex, and are ashamed to confess that they do. This is a time when you will have to judge your partner for yourself and use a little sensitivity.

1. I like it when a woman makes it clear that she wants sex (YES: S/ NO: D)
2. I prefer it if women dress discreetly (YES: S/ NO: D)
3. If I like a woman, I will try to make love to her, even on a first date (YES: D/ NO: S)
4. I like it when a woman undresses me (YES: S/ NO: D)
5. It's a woman's responsibility to use contraception (YES: S/ NO: D)
6. I like women to be naked under their outer clothes (YES: D/ NO: S)
7. I like it when women put up a show of resistance (YES: D/ NO: S)
8. I always enjoy it when women talk dirty (YES: S/ NO: D)
9. I expect women to show that they're really enjoying sex by making a lot of noise (YES: S/ NO: D)
10. I like women who shave off their pubic hair (YES: S/ NO: D)
11. I expect women to give me oral sex (YES: D/ NO: S)
12. When a woman gives me oral sex, I expect her to swallow my semen (YES: D/ NO: S)
13. A woman should expect to have her anus pene-

trated with a finger as part of sex (YES: D/ NO: S)

14. A woman should expect full anal intercourse as part of sex (YES: D/ NO: S)

15. I like it when women sit on top of me during intercourse (YES: S/ NO: D)

16. Women need orgasms (YES: S/ NO: D)

17. I wouldn't try anything "different" unless I was sure that my partner wouldn't object? (YES: S/ NO: D)

18. I would have sex with my partner whether she showed any sign of wanting it or not (YES: D/ NO: S)

19. If a woman really loves a man, she should be prepared to do anything he wants (YES: D/ NO: S)

20. Women know more about sex than men (YES: S/ NO: D)

21. I like making love in risky locations (e.g., in an elevator or public park) (YES: D/ NO: S)

22. I like the idea of making love in front of other people (YES: D/ NO: S)

23. I would like to make love to more than one woman at the same time (YES: D/ NO: S)

24. I would like to have a threesome in bed with one woman and another man (YES: D/ NO: S)

25. The idea of being tied up by a woman arouses me (YES: S/ NO: D)

26. I would like a woman to penetrate me anally (i.e., with finger or sexual prosthetic) (YES: S/ NO: D)

27. I like women to wear stockings and garter belts and other erotic underwear (YES: S/ NO: D)

28. I would like to dress in women's underwear during lovemaking (YES: S/ NO: D)

29. I find it difficult to talk about sex with my partner (YES: D/ NO: S)
30. I would never tell my partner my secret sexual fantasies (YES: D/ NO: S)
31. I like watching porno videos and looking at porno magazines (YES: S/ NO: D)
32. I would like to make videos of myself and my partner making love (YES: D/ NO: S)
33. I suspect that my partner sometimes fakes orgasms (YES: S/ NO: D)
34. I would like to tie up my partner so that I could do anything I wanted with her (YES: S/ NO: D)
35. I am cautious about trying certain sexual acts on my partner (YES: S/ NO: D)
36. It would arouse me if my partner had a tattoo, or nipple rings, or vaginal studs (YES: S/ NO: D)
37. It would excite me to watch my partner on the toilet (YES: S/ NO: D)
38. It would excite me to urinate openly in front of my partner (YES: D/ NO: S)
39. I think that I am the one who usually initiates sex in our relationship (YES: D/ NO: S)
40. I think that I am physically more attractive to the opposite sex than my partner (YES: D/ NO: S)
41. I wish my partner were more aggressive in bed (YES: S/ NO: D)
42. I wish I had been my partner's first lover (YES: D/ NO: S)
43. I would like to try more adventurous sex but I don't think my partner would like it (YES: S/ NO: D)
44. There are some sexual acts which I would never do (YES: D/ NO: S)

Once your partner has answered all of these questions, add up how many "D's" he scored and how many "S's" he scored. If he has more than 30 "D's," then he is a dominant sexual type who believes that sexual relationships should be initiated by men and that a woman's place is on the bed with her legs wide apart and her mouth open just waiting to accommodate that rearing male member in whichever orifice he wishes to push it. He isn't all macho, though. He subscribes very strongly to the idea of his partner sharing his sexual pleasures, such as his porno videos and his raunchy magazines, and he is not altogether an inconsiderate lover. He will make sure for the sake of his own sexual pride that you reach an orgasm (unlike some of those sweet, considerate men who will smile at you dreamily after they've ejaculated, and then fall asleep instantly). He is keen on frequent, powerful sex, but he is worried about anything that might be regarded as "kinky" or "perverted." In other words, real men don't wear garter belts.

He can be selfish and impatient when it comes to bedtime, but if you can show him how to make love the way you like it, he may eventually give you the sexual time of your life.

There are risks with a man like this. He doesn't like to be told that he's doing anything wrong—whether it's adjusting the fuel injection of his Mustang or twiddling with your clitoris. He's a man who needs space, but whose appetites are strong, and if you're prepared to tolerate a certain amount of male posturing, he'll give you an active, and very satisfying love life.

If your partner scored just about equal "D's" and "S's," then he's an eager and well-balanced lover but he is lacking a certain amount of sexual confidence.

He knows that you find him sexy but he can't quite believe how sexy he's capable of being, and because of that he sometimes shies away from creative or adventurous sex because he's not sure how you're going to react. In the back of his mind, he's a little concerned about being rejected or ridiculed.

Because of this, he expects you either to make the first move or at least to give him some clear indication that you like what he's doing to you and that you want more of it. This is the kind of man who responds positively to unequivocal visual turn-ons such as nudity or part-nudity, erotic underwear, T-shirts worn with no bra underneath, skirts with no panties underneath.

On the other hand, this lover *does* give you an equal chance to enjoy the kind of lovemaking that you prefer. Kerry, a 21-year-old singer from Cincinnati, told me, "I love to sit on top of my man when I'm making love. That's my favorite position. His cock goes so deep inside me that I feel like it's going to come out of my mouth, and I can change the angle so that his cock stimulates me the way I really need. I can go fast or slow ... I can sit up so that it's almost out of me, and wait while he's panting to put it inside me. Then I can slide down on it until you can't tell whose pubic hair belongs to who."

Kerry's previous lover was "a real jerk" who was good-looking and fit and supremely sexually confident. The only trouble was, he didn't like her sitting on top of him because he felt that it wasn't a macho thing for a man to do—lie on his back while his lover controlled the pitch and pace of their lovemaking. "He let me do it once or twice, but halfway through he always rolled over and climbed on top of me.

"Fortunately, my new man loves it. What really turns him is that he can touch and suck my breasts while I'm sitting on top of him ... besides that, I think it makes him feel that I really love him, which I do."

Of course, the previous 44 questions are not a mathematically-correct portrait of your lover's sexual personality. But they should paint a very illuminating portrait of how he feels about sex. I found it interesting, for example, that the men who said that they were unafraid to try new sexual practices with their partners were largely the same men who claimed that they found it difficult to talk about sex. They were prepared to act, but not to discuss. Although this type of lover might give you some pretty exciting lovemaking, he may not be too interested in finding out what *you* want from your love life.

It's also interesting that the men who admitted to having a taste for pornographic videos were also the least likely to want to make their own home videos of themselves making love. Most of them were afraid that the video would show up their lack of sexual skill or any physical imperfections.

If your partner scored mostly S's, then he is definitely the kind of lover who needs all of the encouragement and all of the confidence you can give him. Tell him very openly what you want from your love life—or, if you can't find the words to tell him, then *show* him. "I wanted to try anal intercourse for years," said Wanda, 36, a supermarket supervisor from Omaha, Nebraska. "My friend kept telling me what a turn-on it was, and how you could carry on making love while you were having your period. But the trouble is, I couldn't find the words to tell Bradley what

I wanted him to do. He's a wonderful man, and a very considerate lover, but he doesn't do anything in bed that you might call 'different.' One evening, however, I got slightly drunk at a dinner party, and when I went to bed afterward I took some K-Y jelly with me and lubricated my bottom with my finger. Then, when Bradley came to bed, and snuggled up behind me, I reached around and took hold of his cock and rubbed it until it was totally hard. Then I positioned it right up against my anus, and pushed myself down onto it. Bradley was so surprised and turned-on that he almost came then and there! I was surprised, too, because his cock seemed so big that he brought tears to my eyes. But we took it slowly, and after a while I started to relax, and in the end there was no feeling better than lying in Bradley's arms, with his hand holding my breasts, and his cock right up inside my bottom. We stayed like that and didn't move, except every now and then I'd give Bradley a squeeze with my muscles, and he'd give me this little flexing feeling in return.

"He reached down between my legs and started to stroke my clitoris, and of course he could slip his fingers into my pussy and feel his own cock inside my bottom. He stroked me and fingered me very, very slowly, and after a while I had one of the most devastating climaxes of my whole life. It seemed to go on and on and never stop. We have anal sex quite regularly now, and of course it's much easier now. But, no, Bradley never would have tried it if I hadn't showed him that I wanted it. I wouldn't have known how to suggest it, and even if I had, I'm not at all sure how he would have taken it. Some of these things you have to introduce into your sex life in the heat of the moment, don't you? They sound too dirty when you come out and say them cold."

Wanda's experience was not unusual, especially among women who have submissively oriented partners. When I talked to Bradley, he admitted that he had occasionally felt like trying anal sex with Wanda, but simply "hadn't had the nerve" to suggest it or attempt it. A considerable number of men fall into the Bradley category, and that is why it is so important for you to discover what their sexual fantasies are, and then to see what you can do to fulfill them.

Many women are amazed when they discover what their partners have secretly wanted to do to them— sometimes for years and years, without ever having the nerve to try it.

Jane, 33, a systems analyst from Pasadena, California: "When you told me that my boyfriend had always wanted to tie me up to the bed before making love to me—even have me blindfolded and gagged—I couldn't believe it. To tell you the truth I don't mind the idea of it at all. It quite turns me on. But I wouldn't do it with anyone I didn't trust."

Bobby, 23, a law student from Boston: "I'd read about men who like to spank women ... but Philip? He never once mentioned it to me. In the end I let him try it, provided he promised not to hurt me. He put me over his knee, lifted up my skirt, and pulled down my panties. I felt very exposed and vulnerable, but it was exciting, too, in a very strange way, like an erotic dream. He spanked me two or three times with a hairbrush—not hard. In fact, not hard enough. In the end I was telling him to spank me harder and harder. My bottom was flaming red by the time he'd finished. We climbed onto the bed and made love like tigers."

Sue-Anne, 27, a realtor from San Francisco: "When you told me that David's strongest fantasy was for me to shave off all of my body hair and smother myself in baby oil, I had to admit that I laughed. I thought he must have said it as a joke. But when he said that it was true, and that the idea of it really turned him on, I was angry. I would have done it for him anytime he wanted. We had a bit of an argument about it, but one evening about two weeks later I went home early and made sure that I was lying on the bed for him when he arrived ... completely naked, completely hairless, and shining all over with baby oil. We had the slipperiest, sexiest two hours of lovemaking ever. I'm amazed that men keep their fantasies to themselves. Do they really think that their partners are going to give them a hard time for having a few sexy thoughts?"

Similarly, of course, many women have sexual fantasies that they are too shy to tell their lovers about, and so *their* wildest dreams never get fulfilled. Later on, we'll see how you can make sure that you get to play out your favorite fantasies, too.

Now that your partner has answered the first part of his sexual profile, you can complete page 1. Write down all of his D answers in the left-hand column and all his S answers in the right-hand column (you can abbreviate the answers, such as "women don't need orgasms" or "likes bondage" or "fancies threesome"). Now you can see whether you're dealing with a mainly dominant lover or a mainly submissive lover.

Remember, just because your partner has a taste for a particular sexual act, that doesn't mean that you are in any way obliged to go along with it. In our next questionnaire, we'll be dealing with Visual Stimuli— what sexy sights turn him on. Provided his answers are reasonably honest, you will then be starting to get a clear idea of what your lover wants from his sex life and how to trigger him into achieving it. In other words, how to make his wildest dreams come true.

TWO

Who Told You to Stop Flirting?

Can you remember how you behaved when you met your partner for the first time? You flirted, right? You smiled at him, you licked your lips, you laughed, you threw back your head, you touched and you pouted.

Flirting is much more than a frivolous bit of fun. Some experimental psychologists have come to believe that it explains the whole nature of human sexual relationships. In the past, social studies tended to conclude that men control the preliminaries of courtship, by approaching a woman and "opening negotiations" by asking her to dance, or if she's interested in a date, or by trying out one of a thousand well-worn pick-up lines.

"Did it hurt?" he'll ask her.

"Did what hurt?" she'll reply.

"When you fell from heaven."

But new studies have shown that most of the time it is the woman who selects the man, and that she then sends out literally hundreds of signals encouraging him to approach her. Psychologists call it "nonverbal solicitation behavior," but we can call it flirting.

You may not even be conscious of how you react when you see a good-looking man across a crowded room. But Monica Moore, a professor at Webster University, Missouri, has undertaken exhaustive studies of the way in which women try to attract the men they like, and she has listed 52 basic come-hither moves that a typical woman will use, sometimes as frequently as 70 or 80 times an hour.

And there's no doubt that flirting works. When she studied women in a singles bar, Professor Moore discovered that the big flirters attracted four times as many approaches from men as the ones who were "low-signalers."

The flirt begins with the smile, followed by the pout, the eyebrow flash, and the eye contact. The first darting glance lasts only about three seconds, with the woman's head rotating between 25 and 45 degrees. (Can you see how scientific all of this is?) The opening moves are followed by the sensual caressing of objects (wineglass, cigarette lighter, pepper mill); then the skirt hike, the hair patting, and the unnecessary primping and smoothing of clothing.

One of the most potent moves is the head toss, frequently done at the same time as pushing her fingers through her hair. Then there's the lip lick, wetting either the upper or the lower lip, or occasionally running the tongue around the entire lip area, while gazing for at least 15 seconds at the man who attracts her. Sound familiar? Then so will "the parade"—that way of walking across a room exaggerating the swaying of your hips, while holding in your stomach and arching your back so that your breasts are pushed out.

Another effective flirting technique is the solitary dance. Seated or standing, a woman will move her body in time to the music ... an immediate male response is to ask her to dance.

In crowded rooms, women flirt by coming in close—bumping into the men they like, tapping the backs of their hands to emphasize what they're saying, caressing their hair, patting their backsides, whispering in their ears, making knee-to-knee and foot-to-foot contact. Professor Moore also observed deliberate breast touching. "The upper torso was moved so that the breast made contact with the man's body, usually with his arm. Most often the contact was brief (less than five seconds), but sometimes women maintained this position for several minutes."

Much of this flirting behavior is unconscious, but "low-signalers" can learn to flirt more obviously, and the effects are always positive. One of the best ways of flirting is simply to listen, maintaining constant eye contact, so that it looks as if—as far as she's concerned—nobody else in the room exists.

What particularly interested me about female flirtation is that it shows clearly just how much a woman is in control of a man's sexual responses—right from the moment they meet. Even very young girls are capable of the most outrageous flirting, so obviously it's natural for women to do it, and it's just as natural for men to react to it.

Flirting is a familiar part of new sexual relations. Even when she catches her man, a woman will continue to perform for him to engage his interest ... smiling and pouting and looking deep into his eyes, pressing her breasts against him not only to show that he and she are now physically intimate, but to warn off any other women who might be interested in him.

Recognizing the importance of flirting, I began to wonder if and when women *stopped* flirting in their sexual relationships, and whether this could be an important key to reviving a man's erotic interest. I talked with more than 60 women from different backgrounds, and I found that well over two-thirds of them "no longer saw the need" to flirt with the men in their lives ... and none of them had been married or involved in a long-term sexual relationship for longer than two years.

"I'm confident that Peter's faithful," said 26-year-old Rosemary, from White Plains, New York. "I don't think it's necessary for me to keep on winking and batting my eyelashes and waggling my tushy at him. He'd begin to think I needed a shrink."

"Flirting is what you do when you first meet a man," said Josie, 28, from San Antonio. "I still flirt with strangers but I don't flirt all that much with Clyde. He knows that when he wants me he can have me."

"I flirt with John when he's depressed or moody or when he has too much work to do," said 25-year-old Geraldine, from Van Nuys, California. "I tease him and touch him and try to make him feel sexy. It works most of the time, because most of the time we wind up in bed making love, and I think that's the best cure in the world for feeling depressed or moody."

Of course, you don't need to do the same kind of flirting within a marriage or a long-term relationship as you need to do when you're looking for a lover in a crowded singles bar. Your flirting can also be a great deal more provocative, involving seminudity and nudity. But the goals are the same: to make your lover notice you; to make him feel confident and important;

to make him feel sexually aroused; to make him want to make love to you as soon as possible.

If you take time to flirt with your lover long after your first passionate months together, you'll find that your actions have a very stimulating effect on his sexuality and his general self-confidence. All of us want to be noticed and desired, and there is no harm whatsoever in reminding your lover every now and again that he still excites you.

Here are 10 flirtatious things you could do for him anytime, anyplace:

1. Hold his gaze and smile, and then flick out the tip of your tongue to touch your upper lip.
2. Place the tip of your middle finger against your lips and gently pout, as if you wish it weren't your middle finger at all, but his erect penis.
3. Cross and uncross your legs, hiking your skirt up higher each time (the wearing of panties is recommended for formal gatherings; otherwise go without).
4. Sit on the edge of your chair with your legs crossed, rhythmically squeezing your thighs together as if you have the "hots" for him. Flutter your eyelashes and part your lips slightly to reinforce the impression.
5. Cup your hand lightly over one breast and give him a smoldering sideways look, licking your lips at the same time.
6. Stand very close to him with your breast touching his arm, and run your fingers through the back of his hair—only briefly, but enough to give him a pleasant sensation in the back of his scalp.
7. Deliberately leave the top button at the back

of your dress undone, and ask him to do it up for you. Don't be impatient if he's clumsy and it takes him a little time. When he's finished, turn around immediately into his arms and give him a kiss, as if he's done the cleverest, most helpful thing in the world. (Hint: it's amazing how seldom men touch or handle women's clothing, and they can be a very strong erotic stimulus.) You can use this same kind of flirtation when you're dressing or undressing. I know you don't really need his help, but think about asking him to fasten your bra or take off your sweater for you—you can't do it yourself because you have lotion on your hands. Ask him to unclasp your bracelet, or your necklace—but again, don't be impatient if he fumbles.

8. If you're feeling daring, go to your next party wearing a short skirt and no panties (although you can wear pantyhose if it's nippy, or the summer sun hasn't yet tanned your legs.) When you know that only he can see you, flip up your skirt at the back so that he can see your bare (or barely-clad) bottom.

9. If you're feeling even more daring, go to that barbecue party or weekend cookout and accidentally-on-purpose forget to zip up your jeans. Position yourself where only he can see you, slide your hand into your open fly, and make it quite clear to him that you're feeling yourself inside your panties. At the same time, give him one of those smoldering looks that only you can do so well. Later—and in the full sight of everyone—ask him if he likes the smell of your new perfume, and trail your fingers right under his nose.

10. When you're with others, lean over and whisper in his ear that you want him to fuck you as soon as you get home ... then, whenever you get the opportunity, elaborate on what you want him to do to you, in the dirtiest language you can think of. Oh—and when you get home, do it. He should be raring to go.

All of these flirtation techniques were described to me by the women I talked to when I was preparing this book ... so they're all tried and tested, and carry the Good Lovemaking seal of approval. You can see that all of them are intended (a) to catch and hold your lover's attention; (b) to increase the intimacy between you and your partner; and (c) to give him the clear impression not only that he turns you on but that you need him, too. For a man, there are few more potent aphrodisiacs than the feeling of being protective—hence all of those incidents in romance comics when a woman pretends to slip as she reaches the edge of a cliff, so that her Romeo can take her into his arms to "save" her.

Acting as if you need your lover's help and protection is the single most effective flirting technique of all time. Think about it: how would *you* feel if that cute little blond divorcée next door came into your kitchen with a cute little smudge on her cute little retroussé nose, wearing skintight jeans and her blouse knotted underneath her breasts, and asked your lover in a cute little voice if he could spare a minute to help her because her sink was blocked? You'd give her the number of Acme Plumbers and give her the cute little bum's rush, wouldn't you? But *you* can have the same effect on your husband by occasionally being less efficient and confident and managerial as you usually are. Ask his advice more often, even when you already know what to do. Listen to what he has to say. When a couple has been living together for more than two or three years, they tend to ignore what the other person is saying. Remember—it's flattering to be listened to, and it's an excellent flirtation technique if you do it well.

Top of the list of "vulnerable-little-me" flirtations is, of course, the pickle jar. Never, ever, be strong enough to open any pickle jar. Always tighten it as much as you can when you close it, and always ask him to open it for you. A 26-year-old aerobics instructor told me that she was capable of unscrewing the nuts on automobile wheels with her bare hands, but she *always* gave her lover the pickle jar to open. She said, "It doesn't cost anything. I know I could do it, but it makes him feel just that tiny bit more protective."

It's with flirting that you can start to create your new Sexual Character. The point of having a Sexual Character is that it can help you to overcome any shyness or inhibitions that you have about sex. It's rather like the man who puts on a funny voice whenever he tells jokes ... his real personality is too inhibited to stand up in front of people and try to make them laugh. But by using a funny voice, he temporarily becomes "somebody else."

For the same reason, people find it difficult to socialize at parties until they've had a few drinks. Alcohol quickly impairs your brain's higher reasoning, and to an extent you become a different person—uninhibited, uncritical, and flirtatious. How many times have you talked to a hungover friend about what they did at that party last night, and they say, incredulously, "Did *I* do that?"

As a matter of fact, they didn't. It was "somebody else"— a version of themselves without any of their usual inhibitions.

In creating your Sexual Character, you'll be inventing another version of yourself—a sexy, uninhibited you who isn't afraid to say anything, do anything, or try anything. If you're not already sure that you're the sexiest woman he knows, then make sure that your Sexual Character *is*.

Maybe you think you can't compete with his hip-swinging secretary or the women you see in men's magazines or even that blond divorcée next door with the blocked-up sink. But your Sexual Character can and will ... because she is the kind of woman who knows how to attract his attention, how to make his temperature rise, and how to give him sexual pleasures that, until now, he could only dream about.

Your Sexual Character will not be concerned about her own sexual satisfaction, because she will know that the best way for a woman to improve her sex life is to give her lover the skills and the knowledge he needs to excite her, and to arouse her so much that he always repays the compliment.

As I've said, the first characteristic of your new sexual personality will be flirtatiousness. Not just the flirting that we've been talking about so far, but almost daily acts of sexual provocation that will keep him interested. He won't be able to wait to get home at night, because he'll never know how you're going to flirt with him next.

And remember—although this flirting is sexually explicit, it's still flirting. Just because you've been sleeping together for a long time, don't let him immediately take you to bed (or onto the couch, or onto the kitchen table) just because you're teasing him. The more you flirt, the longer you tease, the higher his sexual tension will rise. And—more important—the more ready *you* will be for adventurous lovemaking.

As Libby, a 31-year-old schoolteacher from Baltimore, told me: "I knew all about extreme sex, like bondage and things like that, and sometimes I used to fantasize about them. But the trouble was that my lovemaking with Hank never got that far. Sometimes we'd have a kiss and a cuddle on the couch, but that never led to anything. I'd want him to get his hand into my panties and he'd get up and pour himself another drink. For him, sex was intercourse, and that was all. He used to climb on top of me without warning, penetrate me, and come. I realize now that he didn't understand sex at all. He never knew that it takes time for a woman to be fully aroused ... but that when she is, she'll do almost anything. Once he tried to push his penis into my mouth but I wouldn't let him do it. Of course, he called me frigid. He couldn't get it through his head that I *would* have done it, if only he'd aroused me. He couldn't get it through his head that I was eager to do it, and a whole lot more besides.

"We split up, not just because of sex, but sex was a large part of it. That was when I met Allen, another schoolteacher. I was determined that I wasn't going to go through the whole Hank thing again, so I made a point of showing him that I was interested in him, that he turned me on, but not making it too easy for him. I flirted with him atrociously. I used to let him go nearly the whole way and then I'd say no. But we had some incredible times together, kissing and fondling and sucking, it made me feel like a teenager again.

You know, all hot and excited. When we first made love, it was like making love for the first time to anyone. We spent almost the whole day in bed. Allen sat on the end of the bed, and I sat on his lap, with my back to him, so that we could both see ourselves in his closet mirror.

"He opened up my vagina with his fingers, and pushed his cock up inside me. I watched it in absolute fascination. I'd never seen myself making love like that before. I opened my legs wider, and I held open the lips of my vagina with my fingers, stretching them wide apart so that I could see everything. I could see his hard hairy balls, and his thick dark cock, and the way my lips seemed to want to cling to it as it went in and out. I could see my clitoris, all hard and pointy. Allen reached around and stroked all around my vagina while I stroked his balls. Then he gently started to flick my clitoris ... so gently that I could hardly feel it. With his other hand he was rhythmically squeezing my left breast ... that was an amazing sensation, because he went on and on until my breast felt strange and warm. I'm sure that he could have given me a climax just by doing that alone, if he'd done it for long enough.

"I was getting very wet now, and the lips of my vagina were flushed and swollen. Love juice was running all over Allen's balls and between our thighs. I was starting to pant, and I knew that I was going to reach a climax soon. But I wanted it to be slow and I wanted to see it happen.

"His fingers kept on flicking my clitoris so lightly ... I wanted him to rub it harder and I tried to press his hand against me, but he wouldn't. He reached down and felt all around the place where we joined, where his cock went into my vagina, and the feeling of his fingers made me shiver. His fingers were all covered with love juice, and he reached up again and massaged my nipples with it, twisting them and tugging them until they stood out hard.

"That was all it took. I felt as if I was crunching up, and then I was climaxing, right there on Allen's lap, with his hard cock right up inside me. I felt as if I was pinned on it, as if I would never be able to get off it. But then Allen climaxed, too. He actually shouted. I reached down and gripped his balls and I could feel him squirting his sperm up inside me.

"He lay back on the bed, and I climbed off his lap. I knelt astride him, and leaned forward to kiss him, and nuzzle him. You don't know how much I loved him at that moment. I felt that I'd started a whole new life, right from the very beginning again.

"Allen said, 'Hey . . . you're dripping!' and I looked between my legs and saw that a mixture of sperm and love juice was dripping out of my vagina onto his stomach. I kissed him again and I crawled up the bed a bit further, until I was kneeling astride his face. I held open my vagina with my fingers and let the sperm drop onto his lips and his cheeks and his chin. In the end, he took hold of my hips and pulled me down on him, and thrust his tongue right up inside my vagina, so that he could drink his own sperm right out of me.

"We kissed like two people never kissed before, and we shared the taste of both of our juices, all mixed up. We kissed and licked until there were none of them left. Then we lay back together and looked into each other's eyes and that was when I knew that I could do anything in bed, *anything*, so long as I was doing with a man who could really turn me on."

Thinking back to her relationship with Hank, Libby

admitted that she had partly been to blame for the peremptory nature of their lovemaking. She had never really tried to flirt with him, and she had never made any coherent effort to tell him what was wrong. One possible reason for this, of course, is that she may not have loved him as much as she thought she ought to. In common with many women who are involved in a long-term relationship with a man whom they don't really love, Libby didn't try to make their sex life any better, so that she would always be able to blame him for being an incompetent lover.

Once she did find somebody she could love, however, she virtually "reinvented" herself, sexually. Her Sexual Character was that of a chronic flirt—a teasing, provocative woman who was hot for sex but who wouldn't give in too easily. During the early part of her courtship with Allen, she says that she did everything to make him feel as if he were 10 feet tall, with a 10-inch penis. But she wasn't going to take that penis inside her until she was sure that he was going to be able to arouse her properly.

To be a successful flirt, you not only have to encourage your lover, you also have to keep him at bay. You can let him know that he's going to get what he wants in the end, but you shouldn't give in too easily or too quickly, and you should demand plenty of arousing foreplay before you do.

Libby said that she and Allen dated for more than two months before they finally had intercourse, but that during that time they had plenty of arousing petting sessions. "My favorite was in a beautiful wood . . . it was a glorious summer's day. We couldn't take off any of our clothes or anything, because there were too many people around, but we lay on a blanket close to each other and I started to stroke and squeeze Allen's cock outside of his pants. You could see that he was totally hard. He said, 'I don't care who sees us . . . let's just do it.' But I said no. Instead, I reached inside his pants pocket, took hold of his cock, and slowly rubbed him. He lay back on that blanket and closed his eyes and I rubbed him faster and faster until he climaxed in his pants. I was so excited that I wanted him to do the same to me, but I was wearing a skirt and it would have looked too obvious, a man with his hand up a woman's skirt."

The Libby of before would never have attempted anything like this. But a great deal of her ability to act as this flirtatious, prick-teasing Sexual Character was that she told herself that *she* was in charge of her own body, and that she was going to make love only when *she* decided, and not before.

In a reasonably happy, ongoing relationship, two months of slapped hands and "not tonights" would obviously be out of the question. But you could still try teasing him now and again—kissing him and fondling him and making him feel good, and then leaving him in sexual suspense.

Once she and Allen had made love, there was one thing that Libby did really well—and that was to make sure that she left him with as many vivid erotic images as she could. Don't forget—men are strongly stimulated by sexually-explicit sights, and Allen was no exception. He would be unlikely to forget the mirror image of he and Libby making love in front of the closet, or the way in which she knelt astride him and dripped his own semen into his mouth. Visual, different, and memorable.

Let's take a look at the way in which four women

in varying relationships improved their sex lives by taking on a Sexual Character of their choice and used that character as a way of flirting.

Jenny, 24, is a petite blonde from Seattle. A dress designer, she met Ryan, 33, when she was still attending college, and "he bowled me over with his charm and his sophistication and the way he took charge of everything." Ryan, for his part, was charmed by Jenny's youth and innocence. She was only 19 when they first slept together, and she says herself that "I only looked about 14, tops."

Jenny moved in with Ryan shortly after her twentieth birthday, and for the first 18 months their relationship was "idyllic, I have to admit ... parties, sailing, lots of fun, lots of lovemaking." But as Jenny grew older and wiser, their relationship subtly began to change. She began to question some of Ryan's opinions and decisions, and to criticize some of his views of the world. This caused any number of arguments. But the greatest problem was sex. Although Ryan could be passionate, his lovemaking was very straightforward, and Jenny began to think "is this all there is to it?" However, she was reluctant to suggest anything different because she was afraid that Ryan would be offended or hurt, and because she didn't think that she could find the words to tell him what she wanted. "He always treated me like a little, innocent child."

There were other, more mundane problems, too. At the same time as their initial ardor was beginning to cool off, Jenny was preparing a fashion collection for her college finals, and Ryan said "every time I wanted to make love it seemed like she was crouching over her sewing machine with her glasses on."

Jenny realized that their relationship was slowly falling apart from lack of care and attention, and that was why—when she wrote to me—I suggested that she try to develop a Sexual Character for herself, and see how this Sexual Character could improve her love life.

I asked her to prepare a quick profile of Ryan's sexual behavior, and to tell me what *she* thought his sexual fantasies might be.

Her answer was: "He likes to be in charge of everything and everyone around him, including me. When it comes to sex, he's always the one who makes the first move. He kisses me, he runs his hands through my hair, he starts to unbutton my dress and feel my breasts. It used to turn me on when he first did, but now it's the same every single time. I know what he's going to do next and there's no tingle, no surprise.

"I knew when I first dated him that he was nine years older than me, but now that we're living together those nine years might just as well be 90. He's gorgeous. He's kind and considerate and witty. He knows so much about art and music, and he takes me to some wonderful restaurants. But he won't do anything really spontaneous, especially when it comes to making love. Sometimes I feel like he's studied a book on lovemaking and he's trying to remember it a line at a time, even when he's actually on top of me.

"There's something else, too. I think he's lacking in sexual confidence for some reason. He's always attracted to girls who are very young and naive—like I was, when he first met me. The trouble is, I'm worried that he's going to find somebody younger and even more naive than I am, and that's going to be the end of our relationship."

Ryan admitted to preferring women who were

"fresh and innocent." He said that they helped to keep him young. "I've seen so many guys of my age turn into fossils. You know, they get locked in an era. But going out with somebody like Jenny, you have constant access to whatever's new."

What about sex? "It's quite exciting to teach a young girl how to make love. There's no sexual experience in the world like sliding your cock into a virgin for the very first time."

But what happens when the virgin grows more experienced, and wants more sexual variety? "What are we talking about, whips and chains? Girls just like tender loving, that's all."

What was interesting about Ryan and Jenny's case was that *he* had started off teaching her about sex, but now the relationship had reached the stage where *she* needed to teach him. Because his sexual relationships had been confined to five or six very young women, his sexual performance had never matured or developed. He had once dated a woman his own age, but it was obvious that he had found her too assertive and demanding.

Although it seemed at first that Ryan was repressive and domineering, his lack of sexual adventurousness was caused solely by lack of sexual and emotional self-confidence. It was hard to say exactly where that lack of self-confidence stemmed from, but photographs of Ryan as a teenager and a young student show a skinny, awkward-looking boy with glasses who wouldn't have been an obvious choice for King of the Prom.

He had taught himself many of the social graces, which gave him an air of sophistication, but he had never developed the skills of an experienced lover.

Jenny said, "I decided that the best Sexual Charac-

ter I could adopt would be kind of a Wild Child ...
somebody very young and free, but very sexually liberated, too. Actually I think it suited me more than the
kind of character that Ryan had turned me into. I was
like a very demure schoolgirl, you know. He kept buying me these Italian blouses and these expensive hand-knit cardigans, when I really felt like wearing short
skirts and boots and skintight tops with feathers on
them. He liked me to wear my hair very straight, in
a bob, but I liked it raggedy and all messed up.

"Anyhow, I stopped working around lunchtime and
then I ran myself a huge deep bath. I washed my hair,
and then I sat on the edge of the bath and soaped my
cunt and shaved off all of my pubic hair with Ryan's
razor. I wanted to look really young and virginal, but
sexy, too. Actually, I'd always wanted to shave it off
but I'd never had the nerve to do it before. I think it
looks beautiful, a grown woman's cunt without any
hair on it. You can see everything, your clitoris, your
lips, even up inside your cunthole, if you sit with your
legs open.

"My nipples are quite wide, but I have really tiny
breasts, and very narrow hips, so when I looked at
myself in the bathroom mirror I looked like a young
child. But when I got dressed I didn't. I'd bought myself a ridiculously short tight black skirt, with black
socks that came right up over my knees, and a huge
loose Japanese shirt made of black silk, which I knotted around my waist and left unbuttoned most of the
way down. No bra, of course. My breasts are so small
that I hardly ever wear one. I gelled my hair so that
it looked all young and punky, and that was it. That
was the look. Except that it was more than just a look.
It was me being as sexy as I knew how—not caring
what anybody else thought, not even Ryan, really, be-

cause he needed to find out what it was to be sexy, just as much as I did.

"I genuinely felt different. I couldn't believe how turned on I was. I kept putting my hand down and fingering myself between my legs because I felt so excited. I loved the feel of my cunt now that it was all smooth, and I'd never been so juicy before. I went to the mirror and watched myself while I slipped my fingers up myself, and then took them out from under my skirt and licked them. That really put me in a wicked mood! In the end I got so turned on that I had to put on some artiste-previously-known-as-Prince music and dance around, just to get rid of some of my adrenaline.

"By the time Ryan came home I was completely into my wild-child character. He'd had a pretty difficult day and he didn't know what hit him! The first thing he noticed was my hair all sticking up. He said, 'Have you just washed it?' and I said 'Sure, and I can't do a thing with it.' Then I kissed him, and said, 'By the way, I washed my cunt too, but I think I know what to do with that.'

I took off his coat for him and pulled him by his necktie into the living room. I said, 'You sit down on the couch, I'll go get you a beer.' He said, 'Why are you all dressed up like that? Are we going to a fancy-dress party or something? That skirt's so short it isn't even legal!' I came back with his beer and smiled at him. I mean I really gave my flirtiest, sexiest smile. I said, 'My stars said I should stop pretending to be somebody else and start being me.'

"I sat astride his lap and opened his beer for him. My blouse was gaping open and I could see him looking at my bare breasts. I gave him his beer and he sat back and gave me this funny look—like, he was enjoying all of this, but he didn't know what to make of it. Usually, he wanted to be in control of what happened, especially when it came to sex, but this time *I* was. I was doing all the flirting, I was doing all the coming-on. I didn't want him to feel threatened, so I was very playful, you know, and I didn't allow things to move too fast, either. I didn't want this all to be over in three minutes flat.

"He gave me a kiss, and then another kiss, much deeper. I bit his tongue—hard enough to hurt, not so hard that it put him off. He stuck his tongue into my mouth again, and I bit him again. I could taste the blood. He slipped his hand into my blouse and touched my nipple: it stiffened up immediately. When I bit his tongue a third time he twisted my nipple, really tweaked it, and for a long moment there I was gripping his tongue between my teeth and he was pulling my nipple until it hurt so much that both of us had to let go.

"I had never bitten him like that before. I don't think I would have dared. But in *this* Sexual Character, I could. In fact I felt like I could do anything at all.

"He kissed me some more, and stroked and tickled my nipples, gently this time. My cunt was pressed against his pants and I could feel that he was growing hard. I started to rotate my hips on his lap, and I could feel his cock growing harder still, until his pants could hardly hold it in. I started nuzzling his ears, too, and whispering into them, 'Tonight I want you to fuck me all night. I'm not going to let you sleep. I want you to force your cock into my mouth. I want you to force your cock into my cunt. Then I'm going to lick your cock and I'm going to suck your ball bags until you scream.' I mean, all this kind of stuff, but said very, very quietly so that he could hardly hear it, and very girlishly, too, so that it sounded like sweet nothings.

"It was then that he slid his hand up my thigh, and up underneath that little short skirt, and discovered that I wasn't wearing panties. Not even a G-string, like I usually did. And of course it was then that he discovered that my cunt was totally bald, too ... not only bald, but very, very juicy. I think he nearly climaxed on the spot. He said, 'You've shaved!' and I said, 'Sure ... plenty of women do. Don't you like it?' He couldn't think of anything to say. He just kind of blew out his cheeks and said, 'Wow.'

"He tried to touch my cunt, but I cupped my hand over it, so that he couldn't. He tried again, he even tried to twist my hand away by force, but I wouldn't let him. I knew what would happen if I did ... he'd be right on top of me and that would be the end of it, and that wasn't the way I wanted it. So I said, 'You can look if you promise not to touch.' He said, 'How can I stop myself from touching?' I kissed him again and said, 'Self-control, Ryan. That's what it's all about.'

" 'Okay, then,' he said, because I was really turning him on. You don't have any idea. So I knelt up straight, and pulled up my skirt so that it was over my hips. Then I started to stroke myself very, very gently between my legs, right the way down the line of my cunt, and when I got down to my cunthole I slipped just the very tip of my finger into it. I did this five or six times, real slow. Ryan was staring at me and shaking his head. He just couldn't believe it. We'd been together all of this time, and made love so many times, but he'd never experienced anything like this before. Well, neither had I. Until I decided that I was going to play the part of this wanton young girl, I never would have had the nerve. I *never* would have let Ryan look at my cunt that way.

"I flicked at my clitoris with one finger, and I used other fingers to open up my cunt as wide as I could. I wanted Ryan to see right up inside me. He tried again to touch me but I cupped my hand between my legs again, and I wouldn't let him. I leaned forward and kissed him and kept on saying, 'What would you like me to do to you? Hm? What's the dirtiest things you can think of?'

"I kept on flirting with him and teasing him and in the space of a half-hour our whole sexual relationship was changed. I'd shown him that I was sexy in my own right—that I could take the initiative, when it came to lovemaking—and he'd realized that he liked it. Well, he didn't just like it, he *loved* it.

"I kind of half-slid off his lap, so that I was kneeling in front of him on the floor. He kept running his hands into my hair and kissing me and touching my nipples. But I wasn't going to let him make love to me just then—even though I did feel like it! I pulled open the zipper of his pants, reached inside, and took out his cock, which was thick and red and so hard it felt like it was carved out of wood. Ryan was never circumcized, and I love his foreskin. But now I had a chance to play with it, the way my wild-child character would. I rolled it up and down over the head of his cock a few times. Then I dragged it downward as hard as I could, so that the head of his cock bulged out totally bare. I slowly raised it up again, and then I bent forward and nipped and nibbled it with my teeth. I bit it—not too hard—and stretched it upward as far as it would go. Then I ran my tongue tip all around, in between his foreskin and the head of his cock.

"I took his cock in my hand and smeared it from side to side across my lips, like a huge fat lipstick, while I stared right into his eyes with the most daring, challenging look I could manage. Let me tell you, he was in seventh heaven, or even eighth heaven, judging by the look on his face.

"I licked his cock all around, and then I took it into my mouth, as deep as I could, turning my head sideways so that he could see how it made my cheek bulge out. I rubbed it up and down, gently digging my nails into it at the same time, so he had a little pain with his pleasure. He was actually groaning! He said, 'I have to fuck you . . . let me fuck you.' I said, 'Later.' But he said, 'The way I'm going, there isn't going to be any later.'

"He pushed off his slipper and started to caress me between the legs with his bare foot. I was even juicier than ever, so it wasn't difficult. He slipped his big toe into my open cunt, and masturbated me with it. Nobody had ever done that to me before, and it felt amazing. I felt like sitting right down on it, so that his whole foot went up inside me.

"I took his cock out of my mouth and massaged my face with it, licking and biting it. He climaxed without any warning at all—this huge warm jet of sperm suddenly jumped out of the end of his cock, all over my forehead and into my eyelashes. Then another, and another, until my whole face was smothered with it. One of my nostrils was clogged with sperm, and there was even a long string of it connecting my nose to the end of Ryan's cock.

"My own sexual character would have rushed for a towel and wiped it all off. But this is when I had the real revelation . . . when I really understood that two people in love with each other can do *anything,* and it's beautiful. I sat up on Ryan's lap, and I kissed him, sticking my tongue right into his mouth. I wiped my cheeks with my hands, and I massaged his sperm all over his face, too, and around our mouths, and then I licked his face all over. By the time I'd finished, his cock was coming up again, and he was ready for some more.

"Before I tried out this Sexual Character idea, I didn't really think it would work. I mean, a leopard can't change its spots, right? But you *can* change yourself, if you want to. It may be play-acting, to start with. It was with me. But ever since that first evening, our sex life has just gotten better and better ... because I realized I had a right to good sex, and Ryan realized that I wanted it. As a matter of fact, we've *both* grown up."

Flirting is a positive sexual act, and as we have seen, women are far better at it than men. The only trouble is—once they've captured the man they want—they often forget to flirt, which is one of the reasons that other flirtatious women may catch their partner's eye. One of the great advantages of adopting a Sexual Character is that *you* can be one of those other women, just as flirtatious, just as eager to please, and much better in bed. Why? Because this "new you" will not only be totally uninhibited, and sexy as anything on two legs, but you'll already know how to please him more than any other woman can.

Here's Frances, 31, an agricultural economist from Cedar Rapids, Iowa. From the first photograph that she sent me, I saw that Frances is a tall blue-eyed brunette, with short-cropped hair, a well-sculptured face, and large breasts. If she hadn't been totally dedicated to her career, she could have been a *Playboy* centerfold. Frances married her husband Paul when they were both 27. Paul is a research chemist for a large agricultural corporation, but according to Frances "he also has his cultural side." They both enjoy concerts, art exhibitions, and craft fairs, as well as "dumb things like hamburgers and TV."

When they first went out together, their relationship was "The Fourth of July, every day." They made love with an intensity that Frances had never experienced before. But soon after they were married, she was disappointed to find that their sex life rapidly became "repetitive, and humdrum."

"The first few times we slept together, he used to go down on me ... I wasn't used to that, none of my men friends had ever done it before ... well, certainly not like *that*. It sent shivers down my spine, the way he licked me, and after I'd climaxed, he'd spread my legs wide apart and plunge his face right into my cunt, so that he could suck up every last ounce of juice. It was terrific when he first did it. It made me feel that he loved me so much that he wanted to eat me alive. Which I think was true, to start with. But when he did it every single time it began to feel like a routine, you know? It never varied. He went down on me, until I climaxed. Then he climbed on top of me and fucked me. Then he kissed me, and rolled off me. Then he lay there twitching for a while. Then he said, 'How about some hot milk with chocolate sprinkles?'"

"It was *so* romantic the first time. It was *so* boring the twenty-third time."

Paul was perfectly capable of being a terrific lover. He had all the right ideas ... such as making sure that Frances reached a climax before he did, and making her feel that he loved her so much that he could almost eat her. But his lovemaking bore all the hallmarks of a man who thinks that sex can be learned out of books, or the *Playboy Adviser,* or *Penthouse Forum.*

The plain fact is that you can't learn to make love from any book or magazine. When I prepare a book like this one, I'm not trying to tell you how to whip up a good sex life in five minutes, like Fannie Farmer. I'm simply trying to give you the facts you need to know about your sexual responses, and then show you how other people managed to improve their sex lives by using sensible, sensitive, and creative techniques.

You can effect an overnight change in your sex life. But that change has to come from you. That is why I developed the Sexual Character idea ... to make it easier for you to become what you want to be, to focus your sexuality, to have, if you like, an Out-of-Inhibition Experience, when you can do and say absolutely anything you like. Do you want your partner to massage your breasts with his erect penis? Tell him ... or put him in a position where he hardly has the choice. Do you want your partner to take you from behind? Turn over, and make your passions plain.

Don't believe a single sex book that tells you that if you use the X position or the Y position you'll be making love like Don and Mrs. Juan within two weeks. Have you ever met anybody who actually uses the positions in the *Kama Sutra?* I mean, seriously, without spending the next two weeks in traction?

Don't believe a single sex book that tells you there's a secret spot in your body that can instantly trigger ecstasy such as you've never known. Don't believe a single sex book that tells you there's a special exercise your lover can do to make him stay hard all night. Exciting sex doesn't happen by magic. Diet can help, exercise can help, meditation can help. Looking at

Buttman videos can help. But the greatest, most satisfying sex comes simply from opening yourselves up to each other, so that you have no unfulfilled frustrations, and no fantasies that you are too inhibited to try out for real (except for that deepest, darkest fantasy, which you only think about when you're *really* turned on, and which everyone is entitled to keep private).

The only hitch is that—human nature being what it is—one partner usually has to initiate this opening-up, because the other won't (too shy, too inhibited, doesn't think it's necessary, never even *thought* about it). And because women have always had a positive role in sexual relationships, whatever men may imagine, that one partner will probably have to be *you*. In Frances's case, it certainly had to be her.

Her husband Paul simply didn't realize that the same sexual routine can become monotonous, no matter how ecstatic it seemed to be the first time he tried it. However much you may love pâté de foie gras, you still wouldn't want to eat it every single day, any more than you would want to make love in exactly the same way, every single day. Frances loved Paul, but she was becoming increasingly concerned that their sex life was becoming predictable. "I was still enjoying sex, but I was enjoying it less and less. I was yearning for something really exciting. You know, something *dangerous*."

The kind of Sexual Character that Frances wanted to adopt was that of a daring, highly sophisticated women who was prepared to take unusual risks to enhance her sex life. "In the very early days of our relationship, Paul and I made love in the woods, just after it had been raining. We were completely naked in the wet leaves. That was a terrific turn-on for me, and I know it was for him, too, because it was one of the few times that we ever talked about afterward."

Frances decided to use that memorable incident of al fresco sex as the idea for a flirtatious escapade which she hoped would show Paul that, when it came to lovemaking, she wanted more than the usual routine. They regularly went for weekend walks with two other couples from their local kennel club. This particular Saturday, Frances groomed herself "to perfection," polishing her finger- and toenails, putting up her hair, and plucking her eyebrows. "I know I looked far too chic for dog-walking, but that was the point. I wanted to create a very dominant, demanding kind of Sexual Character, the sort of woman who looks as if she eats men for breakfast. Of course I'm not usually like that, but I've always had fantasies about treating men like dirt—even down to whipping them, sometimes, when I'm really turned on.

"That Saturday morning I wore a long black raincoat and a scarf, but underneath I wore some underwear that I'd bought specially: black stockings and a black garter belt, and a black push-up bra, which supported my breasts but left them bare.

"Frightened? Yes, I guess you could say I was frightened. But it was so exciting, too. I was cold, I was aroused. My nipples were sticking out like bullets. I really felt like another personality. Much stronger, you know? Much more sophisticated, much more wanton. I could do anything I wanted, no matter what it was. I had no inhibitions, no shame at all. And why should you be ashamed of anything you do, with the person you love? Sex is a way of showing your affection, why should everybody think that it's so disgusting? You can show a movie with somebody cutting off somebody else's head, and that's fine. But you can't show a movie of two people making love . . . *whoa*, can't do that, it's pornographic.

"I'm a shy person, normally. I don't like drawing attention to myself, and I don't like a fuss. That's partly because of my parents. Well, my mother, in particular. She was very loud, very bombastic, always making a scene wherever she went. I used to cringe whenever she went into a crowded room, and started flirting and prancing and showing off. She always made me feel like hiding behind the couch, with a cushion over my head. And then there was my figure, too. My breasts started to develop when I was 14; and by the time I was 15 I was 38DD. I was called 'Tits' by all the boys in high school, and I couldn't go any-place at all without men staring at my breasts. I used to wear huge sweaters and loose-fitting shirts so that nobody would notice, but of course they did.

"Paul didn't notice that I was already wearing my coat when Danny and Marcia came around. We put the dogs in the back of the Chevy, and we drove off together to John and Erica's house. Then we all went to the woods together, like we always do, and let the dogs out. I stayed close to Paul; partly because I felt close to him, and partly because I felt vulnerable. I was almost completely naked under my raincoat, re-member. The lining was sliding against my nipples and I could feel the breeze blowing up between my legs.

"It's a fantastic sensation, being naked out of doors. I can understand why people want to be naturists. I felt like throwing off my raincoat and walking through the woods in nothing but my stockings and garter belt, or nothing at all. But what I really wanted was for Paul to notice me . . . and not just to notice me, to *want* me, too.

"We reached a long slope in the woods. The dogs ran on ahead, like they always do. Danny and Marcia were busy talking to John and Erica about real estate, and they went on ahead, too. Paul was bringing up the rear. He was kind of *whittling* this walking stick that he'd found, and he wasn't paying much attention to anything. That was when I stopped by an oak tree, pressing my back against it so that the others couldn't see me, and opened my coat.

"Paul stared at me with his mouth open. Then he said, 'For Christ's sake, close your coat!' I said, 'Why should I? I like it in the open air. And so do you.' He came up to me, and tried to button up my coat, but I wouldn't let him. In fact I let the coat fall to the ground, and stood there in front of him, wearing nothing but stockings and a garter belt and a bra that hid nothing at all.

"For one moment I thought he was going to be angry, but he wasn't, not really. Surprised, yes. Turned on, yes. Worried that our friends might see us, for sure. They were only a hundred feet away—laughing, and making jokes, and whistling for their dogs. He took me into his arms and kissed me, and touched my breasts, but he didn't really seem to know what to do next. Like, he wasn't capable of doing anything spontaneous, when it came to sex. He didn't know how to. He didn't realize that you don't have to follow a formula when you're making love. You can do whatever you like.

"I said, 'Get down on your knees!' and he said, 'What?' but I said, 'Get down on your knees and lick my pussy!'

"For a moment, I didn't think he was going to do it. He looked around the tree to make sure that all of our friends were well away from us, then he got down on his knees in the leaves, right in front of me. I leaned back against the trunk of the tree, and bent my legs ever so slightly, so that my thighs were wide apart. Then I reached down and opened up my pussy with my fingers, so that he could lick it.

"He stuck out his tongue, and I could look down and see him licking my clitoris and my pussy lips, and sticking his tongue right inside me. My flesh looked so pink and his tongue looked so pale. He sucked my lips into his mouth, pubic hairs and everything; and then he probed his tongue into my pee hole, it's very small, but he just managed to nudge the very tip of his tongue into it, and lick all around it, before he went further down, and licked all around my pussy.

"I wouldn't have thought it was possible, to have an orgasm, standing up against a tree, but I nearly did. In fact I think I would have done it if the others hadn't started whistling and calling, wondering where we were. Paul called, 'It's okay! Frances lost her earring! We're coming!' and if they'd given us two or three minutes more, those could have been the truest words he ever spoke.

"Paul said, 'Let's go.' But it was so chilly and I was so excited that I had to pee. He said, 'Catch up with me when you're through.' But I said, 'No. You're not going to leave me now.' I didn't ask him; I didn't cajole him. I *ordered* him, which I couldn't have done, not normally, but my Sexual Character could do it. I took hold of his right hand and held it between my legs, and I peed. He looked at me and he was totally astonished. He always locked the bathroom door when he went to the toilet, and to have me peeing openly right in front of him was almost more than he could take. But I felt like one of those French movie stars, like Edith Piaf or Jeanne Moreau, women who were real women and who were never embarrassed about it. I peed all over his wrist and into the palm of his hand, and before I'd finished he was fondling my clitoris and slipping his fingers into my pussy, with warm pee running through his fingers. It splattered all over my stockings and ran down my legs, but I didn't care. This was bliss, this was real sex, this was real lovemaking, without any embarrassment at all.

"When I was finished, Paul sucked his fingers, and then he knelt down in front of me again, and he licked my pussy. If the others hadn't been there, I think he would fucked me there and then, right up against the tree. But they were still calling us, so I had to button up my raincoat, and follow the rest of them up the hill."

Obviously, urinating into his open hand wasn't the kind of flirtation that a woman would do with a man she didn't know. But it was flirtation all the same. It was a way of breaking out of a sex life that was threatening to become repetitive and routine, and of showing the man she loved that she was adventurous and daring, and prepared to try anything that might spice up their sexual relationship.

All of us are naturally reserved about exposing ourselves, both physically and emotionally; and however illogical it may be, our society conditions us to be more censorious about explicit sex than we are about explicit violence. Why it should be considered pornographic for a loving wife to show her affection and her closeness to her husband by urinating over his fingers, while it is perfectly acceptable to show a man having his head blown off, or people being burned alive, I will never be able to figure out. I mean, can you? It makes no sense whatever.

And if you can bring that sense of logic to your own

relationship ... that belief that there can be nothing "wrong" or "dirty" or "immoral" in anything that two loving people do together, provided they both enjoy it, without duress, and provided it's safe ... then you, too, will have the kind of sex life that most people can only dream about.

To sum up, it's time you looked at yourself in the mirror, and rehearsed the flirtatious winks and pouts and come-hither looks. It's time you took stock of yourself and your sex life, and asked yourself what's missing. Then, it's time to say that you're going to change yourself into the kind of sexy, provocative woman that you've always kept hidden inside of yourself, because that woman can restore all of the sparkle that your sex life has been lacking.

You don't need a new man. Your man needs a new woman. A woman who's going to tempt him and tease him and bring out the best in him. Yes, I agree that it's unfair that you should have to be the one to revive your sex life. But you're the one who has the initiative, the understanding, and the power to do it.

Sometimes it may seem as if you're being submissive. But you're only going to be submissive when you want to be; and in a way that you happen to like it. For example, Ginnie, a 22-year-old law student from Brockton, Masschusetts, said that she was aroused by her boyfriend tying her hands and feet to the bed, blindfolding her, and inserting various assorted objects into her vagina and her anus, making her guess what they were. She said, "It was a game, that's all, it made sex fun ... but there was also this sense of being violated, which was exciting, without actually being hurt. Ned used to take Polaroids, and there's one shot of me with a huge cucumber up my vagina and a stick of celery up my bottom. You can't say there's anything wrong with it. It was sexy and it was funny. He even put a rolled-up newspaper up my vagina and an umbrella tip up my ass."

All of us have dreams. We'd all like to be wealthy, we'd all like to be happy In every other sphere of life, we consider it legitimate to make our dreams come true by whatever means we have at our disposal. Only in sex do we keep our dreams to ourselves—afraid of shame, afraid of embarrassment, afraid of *what*, exactly?

I got a letter from Maureen, a 53-year-old sales manager from Madison, Wisconsin, telling me that "sex, for me, has always been something 'not quite nice'—a duty which a woman had to perform to satisfy her husband's animal instincts. My mother never discussed sex with me when I was in my adolescent years. The only advice she gave me was that I should gasp very loudly after five minutes of what she called 'my wifely responsibility' so that my husband would assume that I had reached an orgasm, and climb off me.

"I was a virgin when I married my first husband Dennis at the age of 22. I was absolutely terrified on my wedding night. But Dennis was just as ignorant and embarrassed about sex as I was, and we managed a few minutes of fumbling before he ejaculated onto my leg and that was the end of it. Our sex life didn't improve very much after that. We never made love anywhere except in bed and it was always in the dark. I went through six-and-a-half years of marriage and I never saw him completely naked: not to *study*, anyhow. Not to really scrutinize, so that I knew what a man's genitals actually looked like.

"We were divorced because Dennis lost his job and then he took to drinking. I was alone for over three years before I met Charles at a Jaycee fund-raiser.

Charles was nine years older than me, much more worldly than Dennis, and I fell for him almost at once. When he took me to bed I really felt that my life had changed forever. He was gentle, considerate, and for the first time in my life I forgot to gasp after five minutes—although I did eventually gasp, after 10!

"From then on—whenever the subject of sex came up at any of my coffee klatches, which it often did, I always used to say that I had a perfect love life, and that Charles satisfied me completely. My favorite phrase was, 'I'll never need another man, as long as I live.'

"But after 11 years of living with Charles, I began to feel dissatisfied, for no reason that I could clearly understand. I began to get bouts of moodiness and depression, and I began to feel as if I simply wasn't attractive anymore. At first I put it down to the onset of the change of life, and that was probably a part of it. But the most important reason was that I wasn't enjoying sex any longer. It seemed to be the same every single time, and we seemed to make love less and less frequently.

"That was when I saw a copy of your book *How to Drive Your Man Even Wilder in Bed* in my friend's dressing room. I'm afraid to say that I put it into my pocketbook without asking her. I took it home with me and read it from cover to cover. I didn't know whether to laugh or cry. All these years I had been boasting about my fantastic love life, and all these years I hadn't known anything at all about sex. I hadn't known anything about my own body. I certainly hadn't known anything about Charles's body. I hadn't known anything about different sexual positions, or how to make sex last longer, or how to make sure I always had an orgasm. I had heard about oral sex, but

I had imagined that it was simply kissing one another on the genitals. I had heard about anal sex, too, because of all of the publicity about AIDS, but I hadn't realized that it was common for married couples to do it, and that a woman could do it to a man.

"I think the bitterest disappointment was to discover that so many other men and women had the same sort of sexual fantasies that *I* had been having for so many years—but whereas *I* had been keeping mine to myself, because I had been led to think that they were unnatural and disgusting, other men and women were actually doing them and enjoying them, and using them to enhance their sex lives.

"Still, it's no use crying over spilt milk. At least you've given me the knowledge and the courage to make my sex life more exciting. I've tried a few things already—*including* doing my weekend house chores completely naked. Charles didn't know what to say at first, but we ended up on the couch together, and I count that as a victory. Please keep up the good work: you're never afraid to discuss the things that really make me excited, and as far as I'm concerned, nobody should ever be afraid of anything so wonderful as sex."

You'll have noticed that the flirting techniques which Jenny, Frances, and Maureen used all included very powerful visual images. In Maureen's case, walking around the house completely naked. In Jenny's case, giving Ryan very demonstrative sex and encouraging him to ejaculate all over her face. In Frances's case, the opening up of her raincoat in the woods, to reveal that she was dressed in nothing more than stockings and a push-up bra—not to mention the highly visual aftermath of wet sex. We'll discuss wet sex a little later on: many women enjoy it because their sexual arousal is usually so deeply hidden, and wet sex gives them a rare opportunity to display their excitement openly.

Meanwhile, however, let's give your partner a few more questions to answer, to see what visual images arouse *him* the most.

Questionnaire
Sexy Sights: What Turns Your Man on Most?

There are no right or wrong answers to these questions, but they will give you an insight into your partner's sexual personality. He should try to answer them as truthfully as he can.

To begin with, ask him which physical characteristics first catch his eye. He should circle 1 2 3 or 4—1 = very attractive; 2 = very attractive; 3 = not especially attractive; 4 = not attractive at all.

1. Hair—long (1 2 3 4); shoulder length (1 2 3 4); bobbed (1 2 3 4); very short (1 2 3 4); blond (1 2 3 4); brunette (1 2 3 4); redhead (1 2 3 4); black (1 2 3 4); dyed any other color (1 2 3 4).
2. Eyes—blue (1 2 3 4); green (1 2 3 4); gray (1 2 3 4); brown (1 2 3 4)
3. Face—fair Caucasian (1 2 3 4); dark Caucasian (1 2 3 4); light Afro-American (1 2 3 4); dark Afro-American (1 2 3 4); Chinese or Japanese (1 2 3 4); other Asian (1 2 3 4); Native American (1 2 3 4); other (1 2 3 4)
4. Height—very tall (1 2 3 4); tall (1 2 3 4); medium (1 2 3 4); short (1 2 3 4); petite (1 2 3 4).
5. General physique—very thin (1 2 3 4); thin

(1 2 3 4); medium (1 2 3 4); plump (1 2 3 4);
very plump (1 2 3 4)
6. Dress—couture (1 2 3 4); very elegant (1 2 3
4); smart casual (1 2 3 4); casual (1 2 3 4);
scruffy (1 2 3 4)

What does he first look at when he sees a woman
he likes? Number in order of priority.
7. Her face( ); her eyes ( ); her hair ( ); her
breasts ( ); her bottom ( ); her legs ( )

What does he consider to be *your* most attractive feature?
8. Your face ( ); your eyes ( ); your hair( ); your
breasts ( ); your bottom ( ); your legs ( )

If he could look through a peephole and see a
restricted vision of an unidentified naked woman,
which of these parts of her body would he find the
most exciting? He should circle 1 2 3 4 (1 = intensely exciting; 2 = exciting; 3 = not particularly
exciting; 4 = not exciting at all).
9. Her face (1 2 3 4); her back (1 2 3 4); her
breasts (1 2 3 4); her stomach (1 2 3 4); her
bottom (1 2 3 4); her vulva (1 2 3 4); her thighs
(1 2 3 4); her legs (1 2 3 4); her feet (1 2 3 4)

How would he rate his sexual response to these
sights?

10. A woman in a very short skirt (1 2 3 4)
11. A woman in a very low-cut dress (1 2 3 4)
12. A big-breasted women in a sweater who was
obviously wearing no bra (1 2 3 4)
13. A woman in a pair of very tight jeans (1 2 3 4)
14. A woman in a slinky dress, stockings, and high
heels (1 2 3 4)

15. A woman in black leather pants (1 2 3 4)
16. A woman in a high-cut, one-piece swimsuit (1 2 3 4)
17. A woman in a tiny bikini (1 2 3 4)
18. A woman in lacy bra and panties (1 2 3 4)
19. A woman in stockings, garter belt, and nothing else (1 2 3 4)
20. A woman in jeans, but topless (1 2 3 4)
21. A woman in chains and leather straps (i.e., bondage gear) (1 2 3 4)
22. A woman dressed in rubber (1 2 3 4)
23. A woman wearing nothing but a G-string (1 2 3 4)
24. A woman wearing nothing but shoes or boots (1 2 3 4)
25. A completely naked woman (1 2 3 4)

If he had the opportunity to see them, how would he respond to these sexual acts?

26. A woman playing with her own breasts (1 2 3 4)
27. A woman masturbating with her fingers (1 2 3 4)
28. A woman masturbating with a dildo (1 2 3 4)
29. Two women masturbating each other (1 2 3 4)
30. Two women using dildos on each other (1 2 3 4)
31. A women masturbating a man with her hand (1 2 3 4)
32. A woman giving a man oral sex (1 2 3 4)
33. A woman penetrating a man anally with her fingers (1 2 3 4)
34. A woman penetrating a man anally with a dildo (1 2 3 4)
35. A man playing with a woman's breasts (1 2 3 4)
36. A man giving a woman oral sex (1 2 3 4)

36. A man and a woman having full sexual intercourse (1 2 3 4)
37. A man penetrating a woman anally with his fingers (1 2 3 4)
38. A man penetrating a woman anally with his penis (1 2 3 4)
39. Two men penetrating a woman simultaneously, one vaginally and one anally (1 2 3 4)
40. Two men penetrating a woman simultaneously, both vaginally (1 2 3 4)
41. A woman giving oral sex to two men at once (1 2 3 4)
42. A man giving oral sex to another man (1 2 3 4)
43. A man penetrating another man anally (1 2 3 4)
44. A naked woman blindfolded and tied to a bed (1 2 3 4)
45. A naked woman being spanked (1 2 3 4)
46. A naked man blindfolded and tied to a bed (1 2 3 4)
47. A naked man being whipped (1 2 3 4)
48. A woman openly swallowing a man's ejaculate (1 2 3 4)
49. A woman shaving off her pubic hair (1 2 3 4)
50. A naked woman being fondled by several fully-dressed men (1 2 3 4)
51. A sexual orgy involving several naked couples (1 2 3 4)

This list of sexual acts is not intended to be comprehensive, but I have carefully selected it to give you a very clear picture of your partner's sexual inclinations. Even if he has been only 80 percent truthful (and there will always be some sexual secrets that he wants to keep to himself), you will easily be able to see whether he prefers dominant acts or submissive acts

. . . and whether he is interested in sexual games that you haven't yet tried.

Incidentally, if he expresses an interest in witnessing any male homosexual acts, that doesn't mean for a moment that he has any homosexual inclinations himself—any more than *you* could be considered a lesbian if you find yourself being aroused by watching videos of two women making love. We are all curious about unusual sexual behavior, and the idea of it can stimulate us without us necessarily wanting to try it for ourselves.

Perhaps the most common example of a sexual fantasy that many women have but which few wish to have fulfilled in real life is that of being raped by one or more men. Another popular fantasy is that of being the victim of a cruel and sadistic lover, such as "O" in *The Story of O* or *Bijou* in Anais Nin's story of erotic domination. In *The Basque and Bijou,* for example, the domineering Basque delights in exposing the beautiful Bijou to his friends, in various highly-inventive ways. "Once he asked one of the painters for his warm pipe. The man handed it to him. He slipped the pipe up Bijou's skirt and laid it against her sex. 'It's warm,' he said. 'Warm and smooth.' Bijou moved away from the pipe because she did not want them to know that all of the Basque's fondlings had wetted her. But the pipe came out revealing this, as if it had been dipped in peach juice."

Not many women would want to be subjected to this kind of treatment, but the *fantasy* of it is very erotic, and it is a mistake not to share your fantasies with your partner even if you want them to remain imaginary.

It's important to stimulate each other verbally as well as physically. In other words, talk dirty during love play, and tell your partner the secret sexy things that run through your mind when you're feeling really aroused. Encourage him to tell you his, too. You can use his responses to the last set of questions in this questionnaire as a guide to finding out what excites him. For instance, if he says that he finds the idea of watching two women making love to be "intensely exciting," ask him a few more questions about his fantasy. Would one of those women be you? If not, who would they be and what would they look like? Where would he imagine their lovemaking to take place? Here, at home, with both of you watching and/or participating, or in some totally imaginary locale?

What would he find most exciting about watching these women make love? Just to see two women kissing, or to see them fondling each other's breasts? What about oral sex—would he like to watch them licking each other's vulvas? Would he be aroused by seeing them use dildos or other sex toys?

Once your partner has completed this questionnaire, try answering it yourself to see how *your* sexual inclinations compare with his. Is there anything that excites him but *definitely* doesn't excite you? Is there anything he doesn't like that which really turns you on? For example, more than 60 percent of the women with whom I talked and corresponded during the preparation of this book said they were "excited" by the idea of seeing men performing homosexual acts, particularly oral sex.

On the whole, most women's magazines that have attempted to show naked men have not met with great commercial success. Part of the reason for this—as we have seen—is that women do not respond to visual stimulation in the same way that men do. But another reason is that magazines that are openly available on the newsstand are prohibited from showing erect penises. If a man's penis is flaccid, he is showing no outward sign of sexual arousal, and therefore women are not particularly excited by looking at them.

This is Esther, 23, a tour guide from Los Angeles. "I saw a picture of a great-looking guy, perfect teeth, perfect tan, six-pack stomach muscles—but there was this floppy little thing lying on his thigh, and all I could do was laugh."

When Esther saw photographs of naked men caressing each other and taking each other's erect penises into their mouths, she was "very aroused ... I never saw anything like that before. Look at this young guy's cock ... it's huge, he's practically choking the other guy with it. And look at practically every other page . . . huge stiff cocks, they're fantastic." She said that the models' homosexuality didn't offend her. "Given a choice, I would prefer to look at pornography with gay guys in it rather than heterosexual pornography, because I'm not turned on by naked women."

Once you have a picture of what sexual sights and what sexual acts really turn your partner on, you can go include some of them into your love life. Karen, 32, an insurance broker from Cleveland, said, "I never knew that Paul was at all excited by erotic underwear. I've always worn plain briefs and plain bras, and he never complained. But when he answered your questionnaire and said that he was 'intensely excited' by stockings and garter belts, I could hardly believe it. It was then that he told me that he loved all that kind of underwear—G-strings, split-crotch panties, bras with holes for the nipples to poke through, one-piece playsuits with open crotches, everything.

"I think he was embarrassed about it. It was almost

like he was a teenager and I'd found a pile of dirty magazines under his mattress. But I was so pleased that he'd actually found a way to tell me. I don't think he ever would have done if I hadn't asked him to answer the questionnaire. I talked to a friend of mine and she has a catalog of all that sort of sexy underwear. I bought a black lace catsuit that's open between the legs; three different G-strings; two garter belts, one red and one black; and some red and black stockings. I also bought two bras, one with holes for the nipples, and another which didn't cover my nipples at all.

"I wear it for him . . . especially in bed, at weekends, but sometimes I wear it under my clothes when we go out to dinner or a party. He likes that a whole lot, and I always know that he's going to make love to me when we get home. I don't think it's demeaning at all. It really turns him on to see me wearing it, and even though I wouldn't always wear underwear like that by choice, I'm doing it to please and excite the man I love.

"I've already bought two more pairs of sexy panties . . . they're so small they're practically nonexistent. I will probably buy something new every two or three weeks. Then I can put on a bit of a sexy fashion show for him. There's no question about it. Men like to look. But so long as Paul's looking at *me,* and not somebody else, then I'm happy to wear anything that pleases him."

Karen was right: there is nothing demeaning in dressing up in erotic clothing to excite your partner. Later, we'll see how many women like to see their men in sexy underwear, too—so it's obvious that a visual response to sexual stimuli isn't completely one-sided!

Now, however, let's take a look at how you can turn yourself into just the kind of Sexual Character who can release all of your sexual inhibitions and give him the kind of lover that he dreams about.

THREE

You Sexy Thing, You!

"I love sex, but I've never thought of myself as sexy. I mean, the girls in *Playboy* are what I call sexy. The girls on *Baywatch* are sexy. I quite like my looks, and I think I dress pretty good. But I don't think I can compete with any real lookers."

This was Fay, a 25-year-old assistant for a quality used-car dealership in Houston. Her thoughts about herself echo the thoughts that literally millions of other women have, too. They have confidence in themselves as people—as lovers and wives and friends and career people. You then find it difficult to believe that they're really sexy.

Fay is five feet three, with straight dark hair, green eyes, and a full-breasted figure. She thinks she's a little plumper than she ought to be.

"When I was in high school I used to think I was quite sexy looking, because I was skinny in those days and I had long hair. I didn't often lack for a boyfriend. I was still skinny when I met Frank, although my hair was shorter by then.

"I don't know when I stopped feeling as if I was not attractive. It was gradual. I guess it was a combination of marriage and work and having a child. One day I just looked in the mirror and thought, you're not sexy any longer. Not *sexy* sexy. Not the kind of sexy that has men turning around and staring at you in the street.

"Frank still says that I'm sexy. But it doesn't matter how much you love your husband, or how much you respect him, sometimes you need to hear that you're sexy from some other man, or have him flirt with you. When you're in a marriage, you kind of forget how you got men to do that."

The way to regain your lost sense of sexuality is to *be* sexy. This may sound simplistic, but in actual fact it's going to involve you in a whole program of developing your own Sexual Character and using that character to restore your self-confidence and bring back all of the excitement that your sex life used to have, plus a whole lot more.

What is the most important factor in revitalizing your sex life? The answer, believe it or not, is *time*. You already devote a certain amount of time to eating, washing, cooking, cleaning, working, exercising, relaxing, improving your mind, and socializing. You know that you couldn't get any of these things done unless you allocated a certain number of hours to them in each week. Let's take your job, for example. Fay wouldn't have dreamed of buying or selling a used automobile until she had checked its origin, its condition, and its mileage, and made sure that she could stake her dealership's reputation on it. That kind of preparation takes time.

Or let's take cooking. Fay wouldn't think of starting a meal unless she had read the recipe and bought all the ingredients. Again, that kind of preparation takes time.

You want to turn yourself into the sort of woman who is capable of making your partner's sexual dreams come true. You want to be confident that you can make love in any way that your partner might want, in any locale, in any position. You want to be knowledgeable about straightforward sex, and also about adventurous sex, so that you can initiate the kind of lovemaking that will have you *both* wondering what hit you.

That's what you *want*. What you *need* is a few private minutes each day to prepare yourself. Developing your Sexual Character will take thought and care. You will have to be able to understand your sexuality more than you have ever done before. You can't become the sexiest woman your partner is ever likely to meet in between answering the telephone, making lasagne, and changing a tire on your station wagon.

Only you can determine how you're going to fit your sexual development into your busy schedule. But you shouldn't need more than 10 to 15 minutes every day ... with an occasional hour-long session so that you can really groom and pamper yourself, and spend some uninterrupted time on sexual exercises, including full self-stimulation.

If you have children, don't feel guilty about farming them out for a half-hour or so while you concentrate on yourself. You deserve a little time off, and if your relationship with your partner improves as a result of how you spend that time, then the children will benefit, too.

Your Sexual Character is the kind of sexy woman that *you* want to be. Maybe she's a famous woman whose style and sexuality you happen to admire—a singer, maybe; or an actress. This imaging is a very positive way of developing your Sexual Character, since you must potentially share some strong and positive qualities with your sexual role model in order for you to feel so much empathy for her—even if you haven't yet realized them.

Maybe, like Fay, your character will be based on how you remember yourself when you were younger, and you had far more time and freedom. Then again, your Sexual Character could be inspired by a fictitious woman in a book or a movie. An heiress in a Judith Krantz novel, maybe, lifting her elegant silk gown so that her chauffeur can forcibly take her from behind? A lust-hungry Kim Basinger, from *9½ Weeks*, making love in the rain, up against a grimy city wall? Sharon Stone, cool and erotic, suggestively crossing her legs in *Basic Instinct*?

Here's Marcia, 26, a journalist from Seattle: "You won't believe this, but I've always fantasized about being Jane, in *Tarzan*. You know, a kind of wild nature girl. You wouldn't think it to look at me, would you? I mean, the business suit and the glasses and the sensible shoes. But the idea of roaming through the jungle half-naked is really erotic. Usually I fantasize that some muscleman like Tarzan is making love to me in our tree house. He's not like any of the men I've ever been out with; and he's nothing at all like Wayne, who's my current partner. He's just big and muscular and sweaty and silent. But he has this long braided hair and he'd incredibly handsome, and he has a huge penis, a real fantasy penis that looks like a brown boa constrictor when it's soft and like a big gnarled branch when it's hard. He has no body hair at all. I read in one of your books about a woman who shaved off all of her lover's pubic hair, and how much she liked to see a completely naked penis, and ever since then I've fantasized about doing it to Wayne. So far, though, I haven't had the nerve!

"Anyhow this Tarzan character is so strong that he can lift me up, right where I'm standing, and open my legs, and make love to me in midair. I open up my vagina for him, and he places the head of his penis right between my lips. His penis looks like a fat red rosebud with petals clinging around it, and the petals are the lips of my vagina. I kiss him. He still doesn't say anything, but I ease myself right down. I can see his penis sliding into me inch by inch by inch. It's so thick and it seems to go so far up that I'm worried that it's going to kill me. My vagina is stretched open as far as it can possibly go, and he's right up inside me, nudging my womb. He lifts me up a little way, so that I can look down between my legs and see his bare penis and his bare balls, halfway inside me, all shining with love juice. Then he lets me go, and my own weight takes me down again, so that his penis drives right up inside of me, pushing the whole of my insides, my stomach, my lungs, everything. I want him to flood me with sperm. I want sperm to come pouring out of my mouth. I want him to take me, completely. He makes love to me harder and harder. His huge penis thrusts in and out of me, and I can feel every vein, every curve, and his bare slippery balls bouncing against the cheeks of my bottom.

"When he comes, he comes in a great thick gush— because this is only a fantasy, after all. He lifts me up, and sperm comes sliding down my thighs, and down my calves, and drips off my toes. I feel *taken*, do you know what I mean? I feel completely possessed. I'm a strong woman; I'm independent and I feel like I'm totally in control of my own destiny. But when it comes to sex, there are times when I want to let that independence go, and just be *fucked,* if you'll excuse my French. I want to be picked up like a doll and have a huge penis pushed up inside of me, so big that I can barely take it. I want to be *dominated,* yes, and I don't mind admitting it."

Marcia's fantasies even extended to being captured by African tribes and gang-raped. "I'm tied to this wooden frame, and these warriors are lining up to take me ... 20, 30, maybe more. They're all naked, except for headdresses and bangles and nipple rings. Their penises are long and thin, like black walking sticks. They poke them right in me, and there's nothing I can do. Sometimes I fantasize that three or four of them are all massaging their penises against my breasts. One of them comes, and so they can massage me with sperm. Then they all try to force their penises into my mouth, three or four black penises, all at once, and all I want to do is suck them and swallow them and eat them."

It took me several hours to persuade Marcia to tell me these few fragments of sexual fantasy. I didn't force her. If at any time she hadn't wished to continue—or if she had felt afterward that she hadn't wanted her fantasies disclosed, then I would have honored her wishes and destroyed them. But she was adamant in wanting to share them. "So many women have strong sexual fantasies, but most of the time each woman thinks that she's the only one, and that there's something wrong with her for thinking such thoughts, that she's perverted or abnormal. I think it's time that women understood that there's nothing wrong about having sexual fantasies, no matter how crude or filthy they might seem to be. It's human nature; it's normal; it's healthy. I love fantasizing about Tarzan and his huge oversized penis. I love fantasizing that I'm being gang-raped by two dozen Zulus. What harm can it do? It's only imagination."

Some advisors say that it's important for people to try to play out all of their erotic fantasies in real life. Personally, I strongly disagree. Your brain creates fantasies in order to heighten your sexual arousal—and the more aroused you become, the more extreme your fantasies become. Gemma, a 19-year-old student nurse from Los Angeles, said, "I never had any really graphic fantasies ... just nice feelings that a man was holding me, or making love to me ... or that maybe two men were making love to me, both at the same time. Even then, the fantasies were very blurred, very warm. What was exciting about them was the feeling that somebody wanted to make love to me so much ... they were desperate to get inside of me. Sometimes I fantasized about three men, or even more. They were all stroking me and caressing me ... I could feel their cocks bobbing against me. Cocks with wet, slippery tips, all aching to get inside of me."

In reality, Gemma said that group sex with more than one man was the last thing she wanted to try: she was totally satisfied with her boyfriend Ken. "I wouldn't have minded if every one of those other men had been Ken ... but I don't really want to take part in an orgy. It's just a fantasy. It happens in your mind, that's all."

Kate, 24, an advertising copywriter from Chicago, said, "For a long time I had a very erotic fantasy that I was a dancer in a circus. I suppose it came from the fact that I always wanted to join a circus, when I was younger. I had a costume that consisted of nothing more than a white plumed headdress and some silver-spangled straps that left me virtually naked. I had to come into the ring riding a huge white stallion, bareback. There was a huge audience, and they were all watching me avidly. I climbed off the horse, and walked around it brushing it and grooming it. It was a beautiful horse, all sleek and muscular and in my fantasy imagined it smelled like white chocolate, for some reason. Anyhow, I knelt down beneath it and started to massage it in both hands. It had an erection almost at once, and this huge glistening red cock came sliding out. The audience was totally spellbound, watching me rubbing it harder and harder. Then I licked all around the end of it, and forced as much of it into my mouth as I could. I sucked it—and of course, being a horse, I could suck it much harder than a man's cock. It tasted like salt and warm rubber. Then I turned around, and crouched underneath it, and guided that huge swaying cock between my legs. I reached behind me to pull my vagina open as wide as I could, and the stallion's cock pushed its way into me ... well, part of it, anyhow. It was too bag for me to take it all in. I looked down between my legs and saw this immense red shaft stretching my vagina to the utmost. I ran my hands up and down it, and then the stallion climaxed, and sperm came squirting out everywhere, even though my vagina was so tightly filled, and ran down my thighs. I stood up, and the audience cheered, and then I went riding around the ring again."

Kate said that she had no desire whatsoever to have sexual contact with a real stallion. "As a matter of fact, I'm very nervous about horses." However, her fantasy clearly revealed several key factors in her sexual personality—factors that she could use to transform herself into an exciting and alluring Sexual Character. *One,* she has a sexually exhibitionistic side to her which she doesn't normally allow to come to the surface. She likes the idea of being the center of attention (hence, the circus scenario) and she is aroused by the thought of wearing erotic underwear. *Two*, she is stimulated by the idea of doing something sexually forbidden—in this case, having sex with a stallion. But notice that in spite of the stallion's size and strength, she is in charge of everything that happens. If she is going to do anything adventurous, *she* wants to be in control of it. Nevertheless, *three*, she is excited by the idea of being sexually penetrated "to the utmost," which is an erotic fantasy that many women have told me about. Kate tried to explain it by saying that "it's the thought of being totally filled up, violated, stretched ... of taking such an enormous thing inside you ... possessing it. It's a very feminine thing."

Like Marcia, Kate was very reluctant at first to talk about her fantasy because she thought it was "dirty," and she was embarrassed. But it was obvious that she had no real intention of having intercourse with a stallion; and by describing her fantasy openly and honestly, she was able to show me what sexual feelings she was repressing. When you can admit to those repressed feelings ... when you can look at your own needs and desires in the light of day ... then you can start to satisfy them, and use them to satisfy the man you love.

I suggested a Sexual Character for Kate, based on what she had told me; we will see later how her new erotic personality changed her love life. First, however, let's go back to Marcia and her Tarzan fantasy. Again, there was a high degree of sexual exhibitionism in the idea of walking half naked through the jungle. There was also a similarity with Kate's fantasy in that the man to whom she was making love (Tarzan) was little more than a beautiful but inarticulate animal. He, too, had an immense penis, which gave Marcia a similar sensation of being "totally filled up with penis."

There was a coda to Marcia's fantasy, which was the idea of being abducted and raped by "tribesmen." There are some masochistic and fetishistic elements in this part of the fantasy, which (if they were interpreted harmlessly) could add a considerable amount of extra excitement to Marcia's lovemaking.

Marcia spent a half-hour alone every day for two weeks, relaxing, meditating, and trying to decide what kind of Sexual Character she wanted to adopt. "I didn't have a jungle, or a treehouse, or a pet chimp, so I couldn't actually play out my fantasy to the full. But I decided that I wanted to be a kind of 'nature girl' ... completely free and uninhibited, and that I wanted to get my toes tanned!"

She did away with her braids and treated herself to a new, carefree hairstyle. She stopped wearing all but a minimum amount of makeup ("and it was amazing how many men said I was looking good!"). She wore looser, prettier, more casual clothes. She didn't go on a strict diet, but she stopped eating cakes and pastries ("I'm afraid I've always been a sucker for raspberry danishes!") and began drinking mineral water instead of coffee or soft drinks or wine.

Meditation is a very important part of finding your Sexual Character. The best way is to find a quiet corner somewhere, to take off all your clothes, and to sit cross-legged in front of a full-length mirror. If you like, set a lighted candle on either side of the mirror, it has a calming effect, especially if the candles are scented. Look at your whole self in the mirror and say to your image, "Your whole self is beautiful. You are a beautiful woman, inside and out."

Breathe in through your nose and out through your mouth—slow, even breaths. Close your eyes for at least 30 breaths, and try to visualize in your mind's eye what you looked like in the mirror. Think of what you liked and think of what you *didn't* like. If you were your partner, would you be aroused by what you saw? Try to imagine that you're him, and that you've just walked into the room to find you naked. What would excite you? What would turn you off? Don't make the mistake of judging your body from *your* point of view: once I asked a sample of over 50 large-breasted women what they considered to be their worst physical feature. More than 40 of them were dissatisfied with their breasts ("far too big" "not firm enough") but their *partners* told a completely different story. All 50 of them thought that their breasts were "beautiful," "very sexy," "round, full, fine!"

If anything turns men off, it appears to be careless grooming (unwashed hair, blotchy mascara, chipped nail polish). Men do appreciate a woman who is well groomed, far more than they care about their weight or their bust size. They feel that their partner has made an effort to look attractive especially for them (even if they don't always say so). That's one reason I've always recommended pubic trimming or complete shaving. It gives you a very well-groomed look, and apart from that it will give your partner the feeling that you've exposed your genitals especially for him to look at. A bare-shaved vulva counts as one of the most striking of visual stimuli—as Janie, a 28-year-old accountant from Minneapolis told me, "The second Mark saw it, he couldn't wait to get his mouth around it ... I never had so much cunt licking in my life!"

You're still meditating. Open your eyes and look at your face. Look at your eyes. They're beautiful, and you should tell yourself so. "You have beautiful eyes." Look at your hair, your nose, your lips, your neck. You're a beautiful woman, so why have you forgotten? Too much routine, too much rushing, always too much to do. You've gotten yourself stuck in a rut, no matter how comfortable that rut may be. Now it's time for you to reinvent yourself.

Close your eyes again. Cross your arms over your breasts and touch your nipples. Gently fondly and stroke them with your fingertips. You have beautiful breasts and they feel beautiful. Take your breasts in your hands, massage them and squeeze them. At the same time, arch your back, so that your spine is very straight, and allow all the tension in your shoulder muscles to flow slowly down your spine like mercury sliding down a thermometer. When you've felt it all flow out of you, sit quietly with your-hands in your lap and your eyes still closed for another 30 breaths. Think about your lover. Think about the way he makes love to you. Think about all of those sexual things that you would like him to do to you, but he doesn't; and then think about the things that you would like to do to him, if only you dared.

Tell yourself: you're beautiful, and from now on you're sexually empowered to do anything you want, and to act in any way that pleases you (and which also pleases him).

Sex is the physical expression of love, and if both partners enjoy it and it does no physical harm, nothing that two people do together sexually is either "dirty" or "wrong." A young woman from San Diego wrote to me, shocked, because her husband of only 10 months had pushed a peeled banana into her vagina and then tried to eat it out of her. From the tone of her letter, you would have thought that her husband was the most perverted beast who ever walked the planet. "Should I divorce him?" she asked. I wrote back suggesting that she buy him another bunch of bananas, lie back, and enjoy his midnight feasts as much as he obviously did.

As you meditate, think in particular about those sexual variations that you try to avoid. Do you do whatever you can *not* to give your partner oral sex? If you do give him oral sex, do you always make sure that he doesn't ejaculate in your mouth? Do you dismiss erotic underwear as sleazy and whoreish? Do you refuse to watch sex videos, or look at pornographic magazines? How about sex toys? Would you consider using a vibrator, or Siamese love beads? Do you resist any attempts he makes to insert his finger or his penis into your anus? Do you brush off his attempts to make love in unusual places (kitchen, backyard, hottub, woods)? Have you ever refused to dress up in special clothing while you have sex—or do you suspect that he might like you to, but hasn't had the nerve to ask? Have you ever refused to let him tie you up, or handcuff you, or blindfold you? Have you ever suspected that he might like you to tie him up, but doesn't think that you'll agree?

Think about *why* you feel reluctant to try some more adventurous sexual variations. Do they frighten you? If so, why? Is there any logical reason why you couldn't try using two or even three vibrators, for example, and both have a really exciting time? Try to forget all of the conditioning that you have had from childhood that sex is "forbidden" and "rude." It's satisfying and it's fun and quite apart from that, it's good for you.

Now, open your eyes again, and sit in front of your mirror with your legs apart. If they haven't opened already, spread the outer lips of your vulva (your *labia majora,*) and then your inner lips (your *labia minora*). At the top of your inner lips, where they meet, is your clitoris. Gently stroke it in the way that arouses you the most. Tell yourself that you're going to show your partner how to do this, just as openly as you're doing it now—nothing hidden, with the lights on. Not only will you be showing him how to arouse you more readily, you'll be giving him one of those all-important visual stimuli. Your vulva, open wide, with his finger stroking your clitoris.

Below your clitoris is the small opening of your *urethra,* from which you urinate. Some women like to have their partner to stroke or touch their urethra during intercourse, or to insert his tongue tip into it during oral sex (*cunnilingus,* when a man performs it on a woman). I have heard of women inserting objects into their urethra while masturbating, such as Q-Tips or cocktail stirrers, but this is a very risky practice that can lead to serious infection.

Below your urethra is your vagina. Open it with your fingers and look inside. Far from being a hole, it is a complex and responsive organ that actually changes shape during intercourse, and is capable of remarkable feats of elasticity. When I was working in Stockholm, Sweden, I was discussing a woman's vaginal capacity with a 24-year-old live sex model named Carine, who performed nightly at Ulrich Geismar's Pussy Cat Club.

Carine told me that she had dated twins when she was 18 years old, and that she had slept with both of them simultaneously. "They were terrific in bed. They had such empathy. They were very lean and very fit and they both had so much staying power. They could fuck all night! And if one was tired, then the other one would take over. I remember one night in winter when we went to their house in Uppsala. We went to bed at half past two in the afternoon because it was already dark, and we didn't get up until eleven o'clock the next morning. In this time, they must have fucked me 15 or 16 times. I lost count! All I know is that I always seemed to have a cock up my cunt or a cock in my mouth, sometimes both at the same time. But the time that I remember the most was when I was lying on my back between the two of them. Both of their cocks were very hard. Birger reached underneath my thigh and opened up my cunt with his fingers. Then Ingemar did the same from the other side. They pressed their cocks together, and Birger held them both in his hand, like two fat asparagus, and then they pushed both of them into my cunt at once. Right inside, right up to their balls! I had to open my legs as wide as I possibly could, to get them both in. At first I could feel them jostling and rubbing against each other, but then they both found the same rhythm, and two cocks were fucking me at one and the same time. They took turns playing with my clitoris, and I had an orgasm, a tremendous orgasm, but still they didn't stop. They kept on fucking me until I thought I was going to die. Then one of them slid his finger up my ass; and the other one did, too, so that they both felt their two cocks inside me. I was so full of fingers and cocks that I had another orgasm, and then another. I couldn't stop. In the end they both climaxed, and I had to get them out of me. There was sperm everywhere, all over our thighs, all over the bed. Birger smeared his hands in it and massaged my breasts with it, and then Ingemar did the same. I had two men massaging my breasts with their own sperm. I felt that I was going to have another orgasm but I couldn't. In the end the two of them knelt beside me and let me suck their soft cocks, one after the other, and that was all I needed."

Carine was only one of several women who had been able to accommodate two penises in her vagina at the same time. In her autobiography, *Deep Throat* star Linda Lovelace claimed that she trained herself not only to take two penises in her vagina simultaneously, but two in her anus as well. Not only that, she said, but "one fun thing" she learned after developing vaginal muscle control was to have "one of my many girlfriends put her hand inside me; first a couple of fingers, then three, then four, and so on, until her fist was inside me to the wrist. Then she would open her fingers and give those muscles a crazy workout. The big thrill would come when she would yank her hand out full fist."

During sexual arousal, your vagina can expand between 1½ to 2 times its usual size, but you should be cautious about trying to accommodate anything too large. However, even small women can accommodate the biggest commercial vibrator, the King Kong Dong, which is 1 foot long—"just an enormous faithful replica of a super hard cock." And sexologists Phyllis and Eberhard Kronhausen reported the case of a notorious Victorian philanderer named Walter who inserted as many coins as possible into a woman's vagina. He produced five English pounds, all in shillings (£ = 20 shillings in those days). "Shilling after shilling I put up her, until forty were embedded in that elastic gully." She accommodated 70, and then "triumphantly she walked up and down the room, none falling out of her vagina." In the end she managed to retain 84 shillings, and said, "I wish somebody would do this every day."

Although the Kronhausens believed this story to be true, it's only an excerpt from one man's ribald memoirs, and I wouldn't expect you to think about filling yourself with quarters. It does illustrate, however, the extraordinary capabilities of the female vagina. Just because it's internal, just because it's never seen, both men and women fail to realize it has shape, form, strength, and extraordinary sensitivity. It lubricates itself when you're sexually excited, it enlarges itself to take in your partner's erect penis, and to make sure that he ejaculates his semen in the most advantageous place. It can take in the thickest of dildos, and yet it can cling to the slimmest of pencils.

Until she had meditated and examined herself in the mirror, Marcia had no clear idea of what her vagina looked like and what it was capable of doing. "I mean, you don't usually sit down in front of a mirror and explore your cunt, do you? But it was worth it. It was interesting. And, yes, it was beautiful."

For the last stage of sexual meditation, close your eyes and breathe deeply, and start to think about your anus. You can touch it and stroke it with the tip of your finger if it helps to focus you. It's remarkably sensitive, in a very different way from your vagina. It's richly supplied with nerve endings, so that stroking it can give you some pleasant sensations, but its muscles work in exactly the opposite way. Whereas your vaginal muscles are designed to draw your partner's erect penis into you, your anal muscles are designed to keep him out. Therefore it usually takes time and self-training for women to be able to enjoy anal intercourse without pain or discomfort.

The best way to start is by lubricating your anus

with K-Y or any proprietary lubricant, and gently inserting your finger. If you have very long fingernails, use a very slender vibrator instead, or a specially-made anal stimulator: most sex-toy catalogs have plenty to choose from, such as the Ass Master, a slender finger with a wide flange at the base to prevent anal "swallowing." A word of caution here: anal stimulation can be very exciting and very intense, but never forget that your anal tract was not naturally formed to take in a man's erect penis or any other object, so treat it with great respect. Anal tissues are very delicate and easily torn (hence the wildfire spread of AIDS) and foreign objects can easily be "lost" inside your rectum, necessitating embarrassing removal at your local emergency room, possibly even surgery.

My medical adviser tells me that he has had to remove from women's bottoms an incredible variety of objects, including ballpoint pens, lipsticks, glue bottles, bars of soap, strings of pearls, cucumbers, and relish jars. "I never judge," he told me. "Everybody tries anal stimulation now and again. It's very erotic. All I can say is: think before you start pushing any kind of foreign object into your anus. If you lose it, how are you going to get it out again?"

Despite this warning, anal stimulation, sensibly undertaken, can add a whole new perspective to your sex life. There are few pleasures greater than having your partner's erect penis inside your vagina while his fingers slide into your anus and massage your slippery anal tract. There are few sensations that will bring you closer than having your partner's penis buried deep in your ass, right up to his testes, while both you and he titillate and play with your clitoris.

As Xaviera Hollander, *The Happy Hooker,* once said to me, "To allow a man to fuck you in the normal way, that's closeness. But to allow a man to fuck you in the rear, that's surrender. But—may I add—a very delicious surrender. And one that he will have to beg you for, every time he wants it. There's nothing like making your partner beg now and again to keep your relationship hot."

As a way to end your meditation, lie back on your cushions with your eyes still closed, your arms by your sides, utterly relaxed. Try to imagine your sexuality as a tightly-closed flower inside your head, with layer upon layer of desires and fantasies, instead of petals. It's time for you to let the flower open out. If you don't think that you're the sexiest woman he knows, then you're about to be. You're going to blossom and develop—not only to make his wildest dreams come true, but to give him experiences that he hasn't even dreamed about.

If you feel like it, masturbate yourself slowly with your fingers. Don't try to conjure up your own erotic fantasies, however. Try to think of *his*, and ways in which you could talk, act, and dress in order to excite him. You may not be too anxious to dress up in black stockings and garter belt. You may be dubious about shaving your pubic hair. But try to imagine what the effect will be on him. Not only will you be giving him a stunning visual stimulus ... an erotic mental "pin-up" of you which he will still have imprinted on his mind even when he's at work ... he'll have an open invitation to make love to you, then and there.

The frequency with which many couples have sex often dwindles because they stop giving out those signals that mean "I want to make love to you ... and I want to make love to you *now*." You wouldn't believe the number of men who are astonished to discover that their wives or lovers are dissatisfied. "I didn't know she wanted sex so often! Why didn't she say so?" To which, of course, their partner usually retorts, "Why should you have to be *told?*"

But, for better or for worse, many men *do* have to be told, and that's where your flirting techniques come into the equation. As we saw in the previous chapter, it's a fallacy to think that men initiate sexual acts. Woman invites—man approaches—woman has a chance to make up her mind—man cajoles—woman says yes—man believes that he has made a conquest. Even partners in long-term sexual relationships go through a form of the same ritual every time they make love. Your initial invitation may not amount to much more than a sexy look or a lingering kiss; or a not-quite-accidental nudge with your bottom under the sheets. But almost every man needs some kind of signal that you will be less than averse to some loving. His boilers may be fired up, his tender may be full of coal, but if he doesn't see a green signal, he could stay in the siding for days.

A man who complains that his wife doesn't seem to be interested in sex anymore is a man who needs her to give him clear, unmistakable messages every time she feels like making love. Many people think of "sexual communication" as a deep dialogue on desires and fantasies, and explaining to your partner the best way to give you an orgasm. Of course, these are all part of it. But none of this deep dialogue will ever take place unless you use the primary function of sexual communication, which is simply to make it obvious to your partner that you feel like sex.

There will be times when you *don't* feel like it, and he'll have to talk you into it, and you'll be glad afterward that he did. But that's something that he has to learn to do . . . and which he can if he consults *How to Drive Your Woman Wild in Bed* or any of my other manuals for men.

Taking on a Sexual Character is one of the most dramatic ways of telling your lover that you're interested in sex—not just now, tonight, but every night. After all, how could you have transformed yourself into this irresistible fantasy woman unless you'd been turning it over in your mind for quite some time?

Let's see how Marcia became a "nature girl," and what effect it had on her relationship with her boyfriend Wayne.

"Relaxing the way that I dressed did a whole lot to help me relax myself altogether. I found the meditation was incredibly helpful. I used to meditate before, when I was in college, and it used to relieve all of my stress, but I'd never thought of meditating on sex before. It made me realize how confused and defensive I was about sex. I had this great idyllic fantasy, for sure, me and this Tarzan character in the tree house. But when I was meditating I began to see that my fantasy wasn't just a way of turning myself on, it was a way of hiding from the fact that my love life with Wayne was so unadventurous. I loved him, for sure, but our sex life just didn't seem to be going anyplace.

"After I meditated, I found the courage to talk to a whole lot of my friends about sex, and I was surprised how many of them felt the same way. They all loved the men in their lives and wouldn't even think about separation. But they all felt that what they were getting wasn't enough. They'd read all the articles in *Cosmopolitan* that promised them a wonderful sex life, but what was the point when their partners hadn't read it, and there was no way of persuading them to read it, either?"

This was where Marcia's Sexual Character came

into its own. If Wayne was unimaginative, if their sex life wasn't developing and improving in the way Marcia expected it to, then her "nature girl" would have to take over. When you create a Sexual Character, you don't just give yourself the means to express your sexuality openly—you create a whole sexual environment, an erotic world of your own imagination. Whether your partner wishes to join you in this world or not is ultimately up to him ... but none of the men on whom we tested the validity of the Sexual Character showed any signs of refusing. Quite the opposite, in fact.

"I stayed home, the day that I was going to play at being 'nature girl' for the first time. I had a breakfast of peach juice and the sunflower muesli that my health store makes up for me specially. I guess they never had designer muesli in the jungle, but I wasn't going to eat bananas and monkey meat, or whatever it is that Tarzan used to have for breakfast.

"I felt very excited. I really want to explain this feeling of excitement, so that when you put it in your book, other women will understand it. I felt almost like I was going to be reborn. I felt close to myself, to what I was. I felt like I was in touch with my sexuality. I wasn't worried anymore that Wayne was going to treat me like a sex object, or any other guy for that matter. My breasts are mine, my cunt is mine, my asshole is mine. I wanted to share them, openly, you know, without any inhibition at all, but only on my own terms. And—you know—only with the exception that my sex life was going to get a hundred times better.

"After breakfast I showered and washed my hair, and I rough-dried it so that it looked really wild. Then I sat down naked on the deck, with a long mirror in front of me, and meditated about sex, very gently touching my nipples, and then stroking my clitoris. The morning was beautifully warm and I felt so much at peace. Not a shred of guilt, that I wasn't working. Not a shred of guilt, that I was sitting here cross-legged in the sun, quietly masturbating myself, and watching myself masturbate in the mirror. It was the peace of knowing that it wasn't wrong, and that there was nothing bad about it, and that at last I was taking control of my own sex life ... which, after all, is one of the most important parts of anybody's life, isn't it?

"I really played with myself. I pinched my clitoris between my finger and my thumb. I've always liked the feeling of that, but this was the first time that I'd ever done it openly, in a mirror, outdoors, so that I could see myself doing it. Then I stretched my cunt lips open, and pushed my pinkie and my ring finger right inside my cunt. It was only eleven o'clock in the morning and I wanted a cock already! I pushed my fingers in and out of my cunt faster and faster, and soon they were covered in juice. I lay back on the deck and propped my feet on the rail, and opened my legs even wider. I dipped three fingers into my cunt, then four, then I got all of them in. Not very far ... I couldn't bend my wrist around that much. But my cunt had never been so wet in my whole life. I was making this sucking, sloshing noise and I loved it. It sounded so wet and dirty, like two people fucking. I just didn't care, even when a quail came and perched on the rail and watched me.

"I didn't have a climax. I think I was too excited. But I lay back and closed my eyes and stroked and massaged my wet cunt, until the sun and the breeze began to dry it for me. I wondered what Wayne would think, if he could see me. Shocked? Excited? I really didn't know, and I was beginning to wonder if this was a good idea. I mean, supposing he didn't like it at all? Supposing he thought I was kinky, or weird? Supposing he took it as some kind of reflection on his manhood? After all, what was I trying to tell him, except that he didn't excite me as much anymore?

"I went inside and finished dressing. Well, 'dressing' wasn't quite the word for it. What do they wear in the jungle? I put on this Navajo bead necklace that Wayne had brought me from Phoenix, and which I only wore once before. It's beautiful, in its own right, but it doesn't go with anything that you can wear to the office. With bare breasts, however, it looked fantastic. I put a gold chain around my waist, and a gold chain around each of my ankles, and that was it. I was ready. I wondered if I ought to shave my cunt but I always clip it so short that there's scarcely any hair there anyway, so I left it. I don't suppose Jane would have had a Gillette Sensor for Women, in any case. She probably shaved her pubes with a sharpened mussel shell.

"Wayne leaves early in the morning and generally gets back around three. After lunch I went out into the yard and started watering the shrubs. We're lucky, because we're right at the end of a dead-end street, and our yard isn't overlooked by anybody. It's small—there's just enough room for a bean-shaped pool and a rock garden and a patch of grass that you can squeeze a couple of lounge chairs onto, but it isn't overlooked, which meant that I could go out there practically naked to water the grass and nobody could see me. That's when I began to feel like a real 'nature child,' hosing the grass and the flowerbeds, on that beautiful warm afternoon, completely nude except for a necklace and a couple of chains. It's the way the breeze blows on your body, it's the feeling of freedom. Even if you don't have a place where you can walk around out of doors without being overlooked, I'd recommend that you spend a whole day naked, without any clothes on, whether you do it on your own or with somebody else. You could always walk around your apartment with all the windows open, if it's summer. The main thing is feeling free. Nakedness gets you in touch with yourself, with your body and your sexuality. Now I know why naturists do it. Whatever they say, it's *sexy* to feel the breeze between your legs; it's sexy to sit on chairs with no panties on; it's sexy to see yourself in the mirror.

"When I'd finished watering, I went for a swim. I lay on my back and closed my eyes and made out that I was in a jungle river someplace, and that this was the way I was going to live forever, just me and my mate. I was still daydreaming when I heard footsteps coming down the steps. I opened my eyes and it was Wayne. He came up to the side of the pool and he said, 'What the hell are you doing? You're not wearing any clothes!' Not exactly the most romantic greeting I've ever had in my life.

"I said, 'I'm the queen of the jungle, who are you?' He said, 'A man who's kind of surprised to find his girlfriend swimming around with nothing on but necklaces.'

"Now, normally, I never used to make the first move with Wayne. It always seemed to make him irritable if I came on to him when he wasn't interested—when he was watching TV or reading a book or something—and that always put me off. But this time I was wild and I lived in the jungle and I had an appetite just like all the other animals in the jungle had appetites. I held out my hand, making out that I wanted Wayne to help me climb out of the water, but instead I pulled him in with me.

"He yelled at first, but I wrapped my legs around him and kissed him and started to unbutton his shirt. He kept on saying, 'What the hell are you doing?' But he didn't struggle too much and I kept on kissing him and kissing him until he had to shut up.

" 'I told you,' I said. 'I'm the queen of the jungle, and you're my mate, and I want you to fuck me.'

"He was totally amazed. He'd never seen me like this before. *I'd* never seen me like this before. I twisted open his pants, and his cock was already hardening up. By the time I'd managed to tug his pants and his shorts halfway down, he was fully erect.

"He said, 'We can't do it here. Supposing—?' But I said, 'Supposing what? Somebody sees us? They'll just think how lucky we are.'

"He tried to talk again, but I said, 'I'm the queen of the jungle and you're my mate and you can only speak in grunts.'

"I pushed him gently backward until he was sitting on the pool steps, and then I dragged off all the rest of his clothes. I'd never seen his cock so big. I bent over him and kissed him, and then I knelt in the water between his legs and took his cock into my mouth. I sucked it very slowly up and down, and ran my tongue around and around it. Wayne was staring at me like he was hypnotized or something. I took his balls, one in each hand, and gently rolled and squeezed them. Then I bent my head down and took the whole of one his balls into my mouth, and bared my teeth, as if I were going to bite it off. But all I did was suck it and roll it around my tongue, and then very slowly let it plop out from between my lips.

"I climbed out of the water and lay back on the

grass, with my legs apart. I guess I would have been more comfortable on a towel or a lounge chair, but I wanted to feel the grass on my bare back, I wanted it all to be wild and natural. I guess a lawn in L.A. isn't exactly the forest floor in Africa, but I still had the wind and the sun on my naked body, and that was beautiful. For the first time in a long time, I *felt* beautiful. I felt that Wayne really wanted me.

"And he did. He came out of the water holding his cock in his hand, and the head of it looked like some dark red fruit. He climbed on top of me, and tried to push his cock into me right away, but I held my hand between my legs and wouldn't let him. He said, 'Come on, Marcia, you've gotten me all excited, you can't stop now.' But I said, 'I'm queen of the jungle and you have to massage my breasts with your cock first.' There was a bottle of sunscreen lotion on one of the chairs, and I said, 'Use that. And don't talk. Remember you don't know how to talk.'

"You don't have any idea how *powerful* I felt. I was living out my own fantasy, and at the same time Wayne was living it out with me, too, and he was loving every minute of it. He poured lotion on my breasts. It had been lying in the sun, and it was almost red hot. Then he sat astride me, and massaged my breasts with his cock and his balls, then squeezed my breasts together with his hands so that he could slowly fuck my cleavage. I looked down and I could see the head of his cock appearing and disappearing between my breasts.

"Usually, when we made love, Wayne hardly bothered to touch my breasts, which always used to disappoint me, because I have very, very sensitive nipples and if he plays with them enough, he can give me an amazing tingling feeling in my breasts that almost makes me come. But of course he loved massaging my breasts with his cock and his balls because it turned *him* on so much, too. He stretched open the hole at the end of his cock and managed to poke my stiff nipple right into it. It's amazing that a nipple can fit into that hole. Then he ran my nipple all the way down the underside of his cock and between his legs.

"I made him massage my stomach and my thighs with his cock. Boy, if they could give a cock massage at some of these fitness clubs! But I still kept my hand between my legs. Wayne was getting desperate! But what I wanted him do to was to fight for it, to pull my hand away, and then to stick himself into me like he was forcing me. I wanted it to be rough, and violent, and animal. I wanted it to have some anger—you know, some *danger*.

"That's what happened. He pried my fingers away from my cunt, and then he took hold of my wrists and pinned me down while he jabbed his cock into me. It was all slippery with sun lotion ... and in any case I was wet again, from all that breast massage—and his cock went right up inside me, right up to the balls. I felt his cock head touch the neck of my womb and I couldn't help jumping and crying out. That's one of those sensations that you either love or you hate, but sometimes you can love it and hate it at the same time, like having your nipples bitten or a finger pushed up your ass.

"He started fucking me like the wild beast that I wanted him to be. Once he'd pushed himself inside me, he let go of my wrists, so I could reach around and stroke and scratch his back. I scratched his back until it bled, but that only made him fuck me harder. His cock felt huge, and it was slamming in and out of me so hard that I could feel his balls swinging against my bottom, two soft heavy weights. He grunted, just the way I wanted him to. His stomach muscles were all hard and his thighs were hard and he was glistening with sweat. I dug my fingernails into the cheeks of his ass and his ass was hard, too, like tight sculptured rocks.

"I was totally into my fantasy by then. I was Jane, he was Tarzan. I opened my legs up wide, and lifted my hips, so that my feet were right up over my shoulders. He knelt in front of me, and I could see his big red cock plunging in and out of my cunt. One second he was almost all the way out of me, and I could see the head of his cock between my cunt lips. Then he was right down inside of me, buried, and all I could see was pubic hair.

"I rolled over on the grass, and then I got up on all fours, so that he could kneel behind me and fuck me animal fashion. At the same time, he reached around me and gripped my breasts, so that my nipples bulged out from between his fingers. He was fucking me harder and harder, and I knew that he was close to climaxing, but this was my fantasy, and I wanted it to go on longer. That was where I took control of the situation yet again, although I'd never tried to do it before. I mean, how many women tell their lovers to slow down, when they're right in the middle of making it, even though they *know* that their lover's going to climax too quick, and that they're going to wind up frustrated and disappointed, like they always do?

"But you told me that my Sexual Character was in charge; and even if *I'd* always been afraid to do it, the queen of the jungle sure wasn't. I enjoyed being fucked on all fours for a few minutes ... but then I rolled over again, and lay on my back, and took hold of Wayne's cock in my hand. It was so big that I could hardly close my fingers around it. I rubbed it a few times, and licked the end of it. Wayne said, 'Marcia . . .' but I put my finger to my lips to remind him that he was still in *my* fantasy, at least he was if he knew what was good for him, and that *I* did the talking.

"I picked up the bottle of sun lotion, opened my legs up very wide, and smeared a whole warm handful of it all around my asshole. Then I rolled over again, like an animal, and I presented my ass to him, holding my cheeks apart with my fingers.

"He was too eager. He forced his cock up my ass so hard that it really hurt. But it was a good hurt, and I wanted more of it. I thought: *I want you to hurt me, hurt me, hurt me, so that I can be angry with you and want to fuck you even harder.* He was so wild by now. He pushed my head down to the grass, so that my ass was lifted, and he was fucking my asshole as hard and as strong as if it was my cunt. I remember reaching around with my left hand and feeling my asshole, with his huge greasy cock sliding in and out of it. My asshole was all stretched and swollen, but I never had a feeling like that before. All I did to make it easier was to dip my fingers into my cunt and lubricate his cock with cunt juice, just as he drew it out.

"I thought: *I'm a female animal. I'm nothing, I'm just a receptacle for cock. But I'm much more than that, because I want to be nothing, I want to be a receptacle for cock. I want to be filled up with cock, and I'm doing it by choice, on my own terms, only when I want to, but whenever I want to.*"

Marcia said that she experienced "a very, very powerful feeling, very liberating. It changed my attitude toward sex completely."

Acting out her Sexual Character, she began to understand that—sexually—women potentially have total control of their relationships. Women are sexually excited by dominant men: that's just natural history. Many women enjoy having their lovers treat them forcefully. But Marcia learned that she had the power to say when and how and just how far she was prepared to go—although, once she'd found her Sexual Character, she was prepared to go pretty far.

Sexually, women have the upper hand, if only they could remember to remember it. If they weren't so afraid of jeopardizing their domestic security, they would probably exercise their love muscle much more often. I've been criticized for saying this, but 20 years of practical experience have shown me time and time again that the sexual tone in any relationship is set by the woman. Even if she's sexually inexperienced, it's set by her willingness (or lack of it); by the explicitness of her sexual signals (or by the fact that she rarely sends out any sexual signals at all); and by her lack of inhibition.

Taking on a Sexual Character is simply a means to an end: a role-playing device that will help you to express your real sexual personality, and to introduce this personality with the minimum of embarrassment to the man you love. The man you want to love you more . . . *much* more.

Marcia said, "It came to a moment when I was crouching head-down on the grass, and Wayne was standing astride me, pushing his cock in and out of my ass. I don't know how he managed to keep going that long . . . usually he climaxed much quicker. But then he suddenly drove his cock deep inside me, and clutched hold of me like he was afraid that there was no gravity, you know, and he was falling off the planet. He climaxed up my ass, very slow. I couldn't feel it deep inside me, but I could feel his cock bulging every time he out shot some sperm.

"He took his cock out of me so carefully. He said, 'Look at your ass, it's so sore.' But I didn't mind. If he'd tried to do it to me when I didn't feel like it, I would have been angry. I might even have left him. But this was a soreness I adored. It proved that I had allowed my lover to put his cock where no other man ever could, not unless I said so."

Marcia had successfully drawn Wayne into her fantasy and elicited a positive sexual response. At this moment, however, it was important for her to stay in character, and to make it clear that she expected adventurous sex to become the rule rather than the exception. After they had made love, Wayne was immediately anxious to leave Marcia's fantasy and return to "normality"—that is, a domestic situation in which he was the controlling influence. In postcoital moments, men almost always become introspective and reserved, and try to reestablish the status quo—even when their partners have made a conspicuous effort, as Marcia did, to show them that the status quo just wasn't sufficient for their day-to-day sexual appetites.

But I had forewarned Marcia that Wayne might behave in a negative or at least a disinterested way in the immediate aftermath to their lovemaking. Because of that, she refused to allow Wayne to leave the jungle, metaphorically speaking. She kept up the fantasy, making it clear to Wayne that she was still queen of the jungle, and that he was still expected to act the part of her strong, silent lover.

"Wayne picked up his clothes and we went back into the house. When we were back in the kitchen he started to dress, but I said, 'No ... I want you stay like that.' He started to protest about it, but I kissed him and fondled his cock, and it didn't take long before he stopped protesting and his cock started to get stiff again. I knelt down on the kitchen floor in front of him and I kissed and sucked his cock until it was fully hard. He had never gotten a second erection so quickly before, and he knew it.

"I led him through to the bathroom and we climbed into the shower. I have this marvelous aloe vera shower gel; it's really soothing, and I told Wayne to rub it on my back where I'd been lying on the grass, and on my breasts, and between my legs. All the time he was washing me, I kept hold of his cock, but I resisted the temptation to rub it. I wanted him to feel that his cock was mine, that he belonged to me. He slid one of his fingers up my ass when he was washing me, and I dug my fingernails into his cock and gripped it real tight, just so that he wouldn't make any mistake about who was boss.

"I was really amazed that he was so willing to do everything I wanted him to do. In everything else, he's so assertive, you know? He's the kind of man who knows what he wants and goes out to get it. But with sex he was completely different. He didn't seem to be able to believe that I *wanted* to do all of those things like sucking his cock and fucking in the yard outside. He didn't seem able to believe that I wanted to be sexy and dirty and try out anything that two people can possibly do together.

"I squeezed out a whole lot of gel and massaged it into his pubic hair. I said, 'I want you to shave this all off.' He said, 'No way . . . what the hell for?' I said, 'Because I'm your mistress and that's what I'm telling you to do.'

"At the same time I gave his cock a few long, slow rubs and I think that persuaded him. I took the razor

off the shelf, and I started to shave him. I think he
was afraid that I was going to nick him at first, because
his cock went soft, but when I shaved practically all
of his hair off, he started to stiffen up again, and by
the time I was kneeling in the shower and shaving his
balls, he was enormous. I kissed his cock and tried to
suck it but it was so big that I could hardly get it into
my mouth.

"We went into the bedroom, still wet, and lay on
the floor. By now we were both so turned on that we
could hardly speak. I pushed Wayne onto his back,
and then I took hold of that big, stiff magnificent cock
and rubbed it. It was completely bare, with no hair at
all, and it looked so much bigger than usual. I licked
it like a Popsicle all the way down to the root. I could
lick all around it, and of course there was no hair to
choke on, just smooth bare skin.

"I climbed on top of him, and fitted his cock into
my cunt. Then I slowly sat down ... and I can't tell
you how good that felt, sitting on top of that hard,
bare cock, right down as far as I could possibly go ...
and then a little wriggle of my hips so that I could fit
an extra inch into me. Wayne reached up and fondled
my breasts while I sat there, and all you could hear
was our breathing and the jingling of my Navajo necklace as he played with my nipples.

"At first I didn't move, but then I slowly lifted myself up, and sat slowly back down again. Each time I
swear I could feel every vein of his cock sliding inside
of me. I didn't go any faster—just *up*—and then
down—*up*—and then down, so that our lovemaking
would last as long as I could possibly draw it out.

"Wayne had never made love to me really slowly,
not as slowly as this. His muscles were all tense and
I could feel that he wanted to do it faster. But because

I was on top I wouldn't let him. I could do it just as slow and easy as I wanted. I was in control, you know? If I leaned forward his cock didn't go in so far. But if I leaned back a little it penetrated really deep.

"I started to squeeze my cunt muscles, and before I knew what was happening I was coming. I'd never had an orgasm like it: I felt like I was a window breaking, millions of pieces flying away. Wayne hadn't climaxed, but I climbed off him, and lay on my back, and said, 'Stand up. I want to see you do it yourself.' He stood astride me, and he masturbated, while I stroked his legs and his ankles. He had never masturbated in front of me before, and it was incredible to see how quickly he did it, his hand gripping his cock really hard, and his fingers literally flying. His balls clenched up into this little tight pouch, and then he suddenly said, 'Ah!' and drops of sperm came showering all over me, all over my breasts, all over my stomach.

"We lay side by side for a long while, holding each other but not talking. But then Wayne said, 'I never knew you were like this.' I said, 'Like what?' He said, 'I never knew you could be so sexy.'

"I told him that I was like this all the time . . . this was the real me, except that he'd never discovered it before."

Marcia's role-playing was extremely successful. It enabled her to show Wayne that she was very much more interested in exciting and adventurous sex than he had imagined, thus overcoming both her sexual shyness and his failure to take the initiative in bed (or in the pool, or wherever). So many husbands and lovers are simply afraid to suggest unusual sex to their partners, in case their suggestion is met with revulsion. Sometimes, of course, it is. Too many women still regard anything other than completely straight sex to be degrading and perverted, the kind of thing that only prostitutes indulge in.

You can't really blame them for feeling this way. Even straight sex has been openly discussed only in the past few years, and with a few notable exceptions, adventurous sex has been depicted and described only in the sleaziest of magazines and videos. It doesn't help that much of the attraction of some sexual acts is the very fact that they *are* sleazy, particularly those connected with sadomasochism. Linda, a 34-year-old teacher from Van Nuys, California, wrote to tell me that she had a "shocking" sexual fantasy about being stripped naked in a filthy men's restroom, handcuffed to the urinals, and repeatedly raped by six or seven different men. "My fantasy is about everything which I abhor. But every time I think about it, I become sexually aroused."

I pointed out to Linda that *thinking* about extreme sex was totally different from *doing* it, and that her fantasy was not only harmless but completely normal. She said that she abhorred everything in her fantasy—the filth, the humiliation, the forced sex—yet it was precisely these ingredients that made her fantasy so stimulating. Exciting sex is all about breaking your own taboos, about confronting your sexual needs and your deepest fantasies—about relishing them instead of feeling ashamed of them—and about using them as a source of inspiration for your love life.

Of course I didn't expect Linda to try to find a way of making her particular fantasy come true. But I did suggest that she try a little mild bondage with her husband, Terry, using handcuffs or cords. When women have strong rape/humiliation fantasies, the most common cause is a feeling that they are dominating their partners, both sexually and emotionally, and sometimes in every other aspect of their relationship, too. They are aroused by the idea of being in a sexual situation in which they are no longer in control in any way—in which they are unwillingly subjected, as Linda describes it, to everything they fear and hate the most.

Linda admitted that she was a strong personality, and that she controlled Terry in the same way that she controlled her students in college. "If you're not in control of everything around you, you can never be a good teacher." But the trouble was, Terry was beginning to feel increasingly inadequate, because he was unable to make his mark on their sexual relationship—and she, in turn, was beginning to resent his inadequacy, and to fantasize about men who could impose their will on her and subject her to whatever disgusting indignities they felt like.

At first, Terry was extremely reluctant to try a bondage session, particularly since Linda had initiated the idea. But once he had blindfolded her, gagged her, and handcuffed her naked to the bed, the balance between them changed dramatically. For the first time since they had met, Terry was able to do whatever he wanted, and Linda was unable to stop him.

"He was gentle at first, stroking and touching. But then he began to grow more aroused, and explored me with his tongue and his fingers. He didn't say a word. That made it more frightening and more exciting. All I could hear was this harsh panting. He pulled my nipples with his teeth. He licked me, all down my stomach and around my hips. He pushed the tip of his tongue into my asshole. I couldn't see anything, and I couldn't say anything. I started to think of those filthy men in the restroom, raping me, one after the other. He pushed a finger into my vagina, and then more fingers, three or maybe four, and I grew so panicky and excited that I tried to break free. It was like claustrophobia, when you have to get out because you'll go crazy if you don't. I wanted him to make love to me, and yet I was frightened of him because I couldn't see him and I couldn't get free. In the end he climbed on top of me and opened my legs and pushed himself into me. He didn't feel like Terry. His penis felt so hard, as if it were carved out of polished wood. He felt like a man who wanted to show me that he could do anything he liked with me, that he was going to take me and possess me and there was nothing I could do about it, which of course I couldn't. He thrust into me harder and harder. He gripped my breasts and twisted my nipples. When he climaxed, he shouted out; and I shouted out, too, because I had an orgasm almost immediately afterward. I was shaking and jumping but I was handcuffed to the bed, and being restricted like that seemed to make my orgasm even more intense. I thought it was never going to stop. When I was finished, he unfastened my gag. I was so relieved to be able to breathe properly. But almost immediately he placed his soft, spermy penis into my mouth, and told me to suck it dry for him. I did, of course. I loved it. I adore sucking a man's penis when it's soft. The trouble is, it always tends to go hard so quickly! But that bondage worked for us. We wouldn't do it too often. These days, we don't need to. Terry has learned to be a lot more dominant, even without handcuffs and gags."

So you can see that you don't necessarily have to take on a Sexual Character for very long. For Linda, one night of handcuffs was almost enough, although she and Terry did try it on several subsequent occasions, not for the therapeutic effect, but just for the fun of it. It was the same with Marcia. She didn't have to go on being the queen of the jungle forever. Her Sexual Character had served her purpose. It had given her the confidence to show her lover that she wanted a wilder, more exciting sex life; and it had given him a fantasy context in which he could freely experiment with some of the sexual variations that he had always been interested in without fear of rejection.

As Marcia said, "The funny thing was, as myself, as Marcia, the way I was, I think I *would* have reacted in a very negative way to oral sex and especially to anal intercourse. But I wasn't Marcia, I was the queen of the jungle, and that empowered me to demand and to have the kind of sex that I'd always dreamed about. It was a way of breaking down a barrier inside of my own mind. It was a way of setting myself free."

One of the most important lessons about sex which both Marcia and Linda learned was that sex, by its very nature, involves the penetration of a woman by a man, and that all of our sexual behavior is driven by the man's need to penetrate and a woman's desire to be penetrated. In order to satisfy these urges, we all have natural feelings of domination and submission. But the physical and instinctual way in which the sex act works does not demean or degrade either partner—meaning that a woman can encourage her lover to penetrate her orally, vaginally, and anally, and enjoy the forcefulness with which he does it, without losing any of her self-respect or her integrity. Despite the nature of the sexual acts that Wayne and Marcia performed, you could hardly describe her role in them as submissive. In fact, I showed Marcia and Linda that women have a much greater influence over their sexual relationships than they realize—if only they had the confidence to exercise it.

Let's look at four different women, and see how they took on a Sexual Character in order to bolster their confidence—and in one case, to save a relationship.

FOUR

Acts of Love

"I always saw myself as a very sophisticated, high-class whore," admitted 27-year-old Jolene, a librarian from Austin, Texas. "I'm afraid to say that I have quite an appetite for those sex-and-shopping novels, you know, the ones in which the heroine gets to wear beautiful expensive clothes and seduced by every man in sight. I think it's very erotic to dress perfectly but to act like a slut."

Not that Jolene *is* a slut. She's a pretty, small-boned brunette with a face her husband Tom describes as "Annette Funicello in her beach-party period." She dresses well, but not like any of the characters you might find in a Jackie Collins novel. She's a staunch member of her local church community, and in her own words her life is "spectacularly average." She and her husband have two children aged 4 and 19 months. They were high school sweethearts and Jolene said that she had never been tempted to have sex with any other man.

So why is a woman like this—apparently content

with her life—having fantasies of behaving like a wealthy courtesan?

The answer is simple. There are millions of women all over the United States who feel exactly the same way as Jolene. They have secure homes, secure relationships, and every material asset they could possibly need. And yet when it comes to their sex lives, they feel both dissatisfied and unfulfilled, as if all they can look forward to is year after year of the same bedtime routine.

As I said at the very beginning of this book, sexual familiarity can be a wonderful asset in a long-term relationship. Once you know your partner's body, and how he or she responds, you can always make sure that your lovemaking is skillful and highly stimulating. You know which positions are most effective . . . you know which touches produce the most arousing tingles. You know what words to say and what images to conjure up.

But familiarity has a downside, too. After a few years, sex with the same partner inevitably loses much of its surprise. After he's seen you naked every night and morning for five years, is he still going to turn his head around when you walk out of the bathroom and think *"wow"*? After he's made love to you, is he going to lie back and think "that was amazing . . . I just had sex with an angel"? Is he going to keep watching the clock in the last few hours of the afternoon so that he can hurry back to you and make love as soon as he walks in the door?

Other considerations arise that distract and worry you, and can diminish your partner's sex drive. Financial worries, career problems, bringing up children— any kind of stress can affect your love life. And it's not widely known that some of the common prescription drugs can seriously reduce your libido, too—causing loss of erection in men and vaginal dryness in women. We'll talk about those later.

Drug-induced problems, once identified, are comparatively easy to deal with. But how do you deal with a relationship that is failing for no other reason than overfamiliarity, and the feeling that you're never going to do anything more exciting than this?

This is where your Sexual Character comes into play. Think of the woman you'd really like to be—sexy, wild, uninhibited, and free—and bring her to life. If it helps you to overcome your nervousness and your inhibitions, you can even think about her in the third person, as if she really is someone else altogether—the kind of sexual personality you've always wanted to be, but have never had the courage to imitate.

Some of the women who tried developing a Sexual Character even called themselves by another name when they took on their Character's wild and winning behavior patterns. Janet, a 24-year-old secretary from St. Louis, called her flirtatious alter ego "Mitzi"; whereas Kerry, a 26-year-old computer programmer from Flint, Michigan, who was interested in leather and rubber and bondage, called herself "Ms. Kane."

Always remember that when you take on a Sexual Character, it should be *fun*. It has a serious purpose—to develop your sex life, and to enable both you and your partner to explore all of the joy and satisfactions that adventurous sex has to offer. But first and foremost, you're doing it for pleasure . . . which means that you don't have to be tense or deadly serious about it. If something goes slightly wrong . . . if your partner doesn't immediately react the way you wanted him to . . . then don't worry about it. Don't be embarrassed, and *never, never, never* say you're sorry. You're doing your partner a favor by introducing a completely new dimension to his sex life. You're trying to make his wildest dreams come true, and if he doesn't appreciate it now—well, he will later. Men can be just as embarrassed about sex as women, if not more so. They may tell bawdy jokes when it's all guys together, but present them with a real woman who knows what she wants in bed, and it's surprising how many of them are as shy and awkward as adolescents.

The first time you try out your Sexual Character, don't worry if your partner reacts in a negative way. Some men laugh, some get embarrassed, some even get angry. You're upsetting things, remember. You're challenging the status quo. You're saying that you want more out of your sex life . . . and it's not surprising that some men are going to take that as a criticism and a challenge, and react accordingly.

You could of course say "I'm quite bored in bed, and I'm not looking forward to another 20 years of boredom." But by taking on a Sexual Character, you're not being openly critical, you're not maligning his manhood. You're simply showing him what you need and what you're prepared to do in order to satisfy that need. It's like a lecture with slides, where the lecturer can sit in relative obscurity in the dark, while all of the bright and lurid things that he's interested in are shown up on the screen. You're the lecturer, telling your partner what you want. Your Sexual Character is the Technicolor screen on which your most colorful desires are openly portrayed.

If he reacts badly, stay calm, stay composed, and whatever you do, *stay in character*. Don't allow him to see that one negative response can put you off. This Sexual Character is you, it's what you want to be, it's what you are. You may have to use all of your feminine wiles to reassure him that this isn't a put-on, it's a sexy and amusing game. Not only that, it's a game in which *he* will be the winner, because from now on he'll be able to ask you to do anything he wants.

Having said that, none of the women who tried the Sexual Character technique reported anything but minor difficulties with their partners. One dressed up in scarlet stockings and garter belt and high heels to welcome her husband back from a six-day conference in Portland, Oregon. She shaved off all of her pubic hair, too—"I'd read about doing it in one of your books and I'd always wanted to try it, but hadn't dared." Her husband loved the underwear, and went wild about what one sex catalog describes as a "bald bippy." He carried her up to bed, opened her thighs, and began to give her enthusiastic oral sex, "sucking my cunt lips right into his mouth, which he'd never done before. It was ecstasy!" Unfortunately, her husband was so exhausted after his trip that he fell asleep in mid-cunnilingus. "I didn't mind .. there he was, deeply asleep, with his face between my legs. I finished myself off by masturbating, and pressing my cunt against his mouth when I came, even though he *was* asleep. I thought: that would definitely be the kind of thing that my Sexual Character would do."

Let's see what Jolene did to transform herself into the "high-class whore" of her fantasies. Having met her husband Tom, I was concerned that she not go too far with her fantasy. Tom appeared to be a steady, regular guy who was very reserved when it came to sex, and I felt that it would be a mistake to introduce him to Jolene's fantasies too abruptly.

Jolene didn't want to present him with any of the questionnaires in this book, because she thought he would be shocked or offended. She had never seen him read any sexy books or look at a men's magazine, and he had never discussed sex with her as a general topic. After I had talked with him, however, it became clear that he *did* have fantasies, but he had never told Jolene about them. He had been brought up to think of the woman you married as having to be "clean and pure, and above such things." He had daydreamed about unusual sex, but his parents and teachers and friends had given him very little useful knowledge about sex and sexual behavior, and he honestly believed that there was something "wrong" about making love to your wife in anything but the most straightforward way.

"There were always two kinds of women, as far as I was concerned. Decent women, who were suitable to be your bride, and good-time women. You didn't ask a decent woman to do anything degrading. If you wanted that kind of hanky-panky, you went to a whorehouse."

Had Jolene ever given him oral sex, for example? "No, sir. I don't suppose she's even heard of such a thing."

Had she ever dressed up for him in erotic underwear? "She's not a whore."

Had they ever made love out of doors, or in the kitchen, or on the backseat of an automobile? "We made love in the shower once; and another time, in a motel, on the couch."

Had he ever penetrated her anally—either with his finger or his penis? "No, sir, absolutely not. I wouldn't think of degrading her that way."

Had it never occurred to him that she might like the idea of oral sex, and that she might like to have him penetrate her anally? Had it never occurred to him that she might be aching for some much more adventurous sex, without being degraded, and without being unfaithful? He could have his own personal "good-time girl" without breaking his marriage vows. All he had to do was to recognize that his own wife was just as sexy as other women, and that she would be prepared to do whatever he wanted to do . . . and all within the bounds of a loyal, moral, and lasting relationship.

In loving sex between two caring and committed people, everything is pure. I have been saying for more than 20 years that no sexual act can possibly be perverted if it brings joy and satisfaction and excitement to the people who are doing it, if it helps to improve the relationship. If more men realized that their partners would love to do the things that they consider to be "whorish," then more relationships would be spicy, adventurous, and ongoing. It takes courage to break through the barriers of your own inhibitions (which is why I suggest that women try to adopt a Sexual Character) but it can be done . . . and very successfully.

I advised Jolene that Tom was aroused by the idea of going to a brothel, and having completely uninhibited sex. She could hardly believe it, because Tom had never indicated that he was dissatisfied with their sex life, and that he was interested in trying some new positions and some new techniques. "I would die for some new positions and some new techniques. Even a different time of day would be good. It's always five after nine on Saturday mornings, as if the Lord decreed it. He shifts himself across the bed and climbs on top of me, and before I know it, it's all over. I love it so much, but it's always all over. There's no tickling, no licking, no love play. By the time he's finished, I'm just about ready to get started."

In previous books (such as *How to Drive Your Man Even Wilder in Bed*) I've discussed the gap between the time it takes for a man to reach a climax, and the much longer time it takes for a woman even to become moderately aroused. Obviously there are compelling biological reasons why a man wants to ejaculate as soon as possible, but we are no longer living in the wild, our safety threatened at every second, and we are allowed to take our time when it comes to sex. In fact, we're entitled to all the hours that God gives us, because sex is a unique and wonderful gift, and if we're prudish or inhibited about it— if we call it "dirty" or "perverted" or "degenerate"— then all we're doing is turning our back on one of our finest instincts. Love comes first. Love always will. But sex is one of the most important expressions of love, and nothing you can do to excite and please each other is morally wrong. In fact, you'd be morally wrong not to try a few "perverted" tricks now and again, just to make sure that you and your partner aren't missing out on anything new.

Jolene didn't try anything too far-out on her first night. This was the night of their annual church ball, and she had decided that if she couldn't "out" her new Sexual Character on an occasion like this, then she never could. Most of the women wore brightly colored flouncy dresses. Jolene—who had made a point of exercising and dieting—arrived in a slinky black dress of "indecent shortness," as she herself put it. She wore an orchid corsage that Tom had given her, but that was about all. Underneath the slinky dress she wore a lacy black bra, a pair of black hold-up stockings, "and definitely no panties."

"Tom had argued with me when we were getting dressed. He said he liked the dress but it just wasn't suitable for a church event. I told him that was nonsense. It was a night for people to dress up; a night for people to let their hair down. If I was obliged to wear a dress that made me look like a character out of *Little Women,* then I didn't want to go at all.

"Tom gave in. He can be very stubborn sometimes, but I think he sensed that I really meant it this time—that it was make-or-break. Of course he didn't watch me dressing, so he didn't realize that I was naked under that dress, to all intents and purposes, otherwise I think he would have put his foot down and told me to change. Which would have been crazy, really, because he loved me, and he loved that dress. It was just that he couldn't imagine his own wife going to a ball dressed like one of those good-time women he was always talking about. It was like sex for him was in two separate compartments: the good, straight wholesome sex you had with your wife, and the lowdown dirty sex you had with other women. I just wanted to show him that I wanted some of that lowdown dirty sex, except that it wouldn't really be lowdown and dirty because he'd be having it with me.

"I walked into that church hall and I think I had quite a few long appraising looks, believe me ... just as much from the womenfolk as the menfolk. I mean it was like a shark swimming into a pool full of prize goldfish. But I made sure that I didn't flirt too much with anybody else's husband ... I was there to excite *my* husband, not theirs. I was all over him, all evening. I hadn't given him so much attention for a long time, and after a while he began to appreciate that not only did he have the sexiest woman at the ball, but that the sexiest woman only had eyes for him.

"Sure, I was playing a part. I was trying to be that slinky, seductive high-class hooker with the throaty voice. Not *too* much. I didn't want Tom to feel embarrassed. But I was surprised how much he began to enjoy it, especially after he'd had a couple of beers, and extra-especially after three or four of his friends had told him that he was a really lucky guy.

"I played the part, but I took care not to make myself look cheap, and the way I did that was by acting calm, and collected, and not laughing too loud, and—as I say—not making myself too obvious in front of other women's husbands. I couldn't spend the whole evening with Tom, but even when we were apart, I made eyes at him across the room, just to let him know that I was still thinking of him, and that I wasn't interested in anybody else.

"Toward the end of the evening they lowered the lights and began to play a few soft, smoochy songs. I accepted just one dance from another man—John, he's a very close friend, and I trusted him not to come on strong when we were dancing. I hate it when you dance with somebody's husband and suddenly they're pressing their stiff cock up against your stomach. After that I gave all the rest of the dances to Tom, and I danced so close to him that we practically melted right into each other. *His* cock was stiff, too ... I could feel it against my thigh. But I didn't mind that. In fact I made sure that I rubbed my thigh against it every time we took a step, and he kept closing his eyes and forgetting what he was saying. It's so great to have that effect on the man you really love ... and you *can* have it, if you try.

"The band had just started to play the very last dance when I whispered into Tom's ear, 'If I had met you for the very first time tonight, I'd go to bed with you.'

"Then I said, 'I didn't meet you for the very first time tonight, but I still want to go to bed with you.'

"He kissed me. His cock was so stiff that I thought it was going to burst out of his pants. I reached down and held it in my hand, through his pants, and nobody could see what I was doing because his tuxedo more or less covered us, and it was dark. Some friends of ours were dancing real close, smiling and finger waving to us, and none of them knew that I was gripping Tom's cock.

"I managed to jerk down his zipper. He tried to back away, this was too much for him, but I wouldn't let him. I was the hooker, I was in charge. I kissed him, and kept on holding him very close so that nobody could see. I said, 'You don't have to be afraid of me.' I distinctly remember saying that—even though I never would have said it in a million years if I hadn't been playing out a part. But it worked, you know. I knew he wanted it, even though he was afraid of it. He really wanted it, and I was the only person who could give it to him, and what made it all so special was that I was his wife.

"I reached my hand into his pants. I could feel his cock, and I could feel that his shorts had a wet and juicy patch on them. I pulled open his shorts, and took hold of his bare cock. He closed his eyes and let out this long, long sigh, and said, 'This is crazy ... you shouldn't. Somebody's going to see us.' But all I said was, 'Two things ... one is, I'm your lady and this is my job ... and second is, I'm not wearing any panties tonight.'

"He said, 'What? What are you talking about?' and I said, 'I'm not wearing any panties tonight. My pussy is completely bare.'

"He climaxed right then and there. I don't think he

meant to. But the next thing I knew he was gripping my shoulder, and warm spunk was pouring out of his cock and all down my fingers and running down my wrist. Loads of it—it was even dripping onto the floor. I managed to push his cock back into his shorts left-handed and zip up his pants. I had to be careful that spunk didn't drop onto his pants, because it would've shown up, white on black. He was shaking, he was so surprised. I don't think he could believe that this was his wife . . . his quiet, well-behaved woman-at-home. I think it was the greatest victory that I had ever achieved in our relationship. It broke the mold. And what broke the mold even more was when I lifted up my hand right in front of his face, and slowly licked all the spunk off my fingers, and licked it off my wrist. There was spunk on my charm bracelet, too, and I sucked that off right in front of him. Then I held him close and kissed him, a deep French kiss, so that he could taste his own spunk, and taste my tongue, and know that I loved him, and that I'd do anything for him, just so long as he'd do anything for me."

Although she introduced her Sexual Character reasonably quietly, in a nonconfrontational way, Jolene showed great skill and imagination in the way that she asserted herself, and displayed her sexual needs. By the end of the evening, Tom had no doubt that he had married a woman who was looking for more than regular, straightforward sex, and that the sexual possibilities in their relationship were limitless.

His reaction? "I have to admit that I was frightened at first. I have never taken Jolene for the kind of girl who wanted anything apart from a home, a family, and regular lovemaking. And by that I mean ordinary lovemaking. Straightforward. I was frightened because she'd caught me left-footed—made me feel as if I hadn't been doing my duty as a husband and lover. And, yes, you could say that I was just plain frightened. Suddenly my whole concept of what my marriage was all about had been turned upside-down."

He didn't respond to Jolene's Sexual Character immediately, because he simply wasn't sure how to. One incident of public petting wasn't enough to show him how far Jolene was prepared to go when it came to unusual and adventurous sex; thus it was important for Jolene to stay in character so that Tom could understand exactly what she wanted.

It is no good complaining that your partner doesn't give you the kind of loving you want if you never show him or tell him. Equally, it is no good complaining that he is trying to perform sexual acts which you really don't like if you don't show him or tell him *that,* either. The reason I say *showing* as well as *telling* is because one barely perceptible body movement can make it clear that you don't want him to touch you there, or that you *do* want him to touch you someplace else. Even when they're really enjoying their partner's caresses, it's extraordinary how many women simply lie still, giving almost no outward indication of their internal ecstasy. I fully understand that they don't feel the need to wriggle and writhe, and that any bodily movement would, to some extent, be play-acting. But a certain amount of play-acting is essential to satisfying sex: if you appear to be aroused, by panting and shifting your hips and pressing yourself more closely against your partner, then you'll arouse him in return. Men are *always* seeking reassurance that they are performing well in bed, and to give them that reassurance (when they deserve it, of course) is part of being an inspired and successful lover.

Back home that evening after the ball, Jolene went

to the bathroom while Tom undressed and reemerged a short time later in a new cream-colored satin robe. "I'd brushed my hair, freshened my lipstick, and sprayed myself with the most expensive perfume I was able to afford."

She was right to do that—it's better to wear no perfume at all, rather than cheap perfume. She wanted to exude an air of wanton class, and an $8.95 toilet spray from the drugstore would have spoiled the effect completely.

"Tom was standing on the opposite side of the bedroom, unfastening his cufflinks. I really sashayed over to him and said, 'Well . . . what are we going to do now?'

"He said, 'After what happened at the ball? Catch some sleep, I guess, and dream about it.' But I said, 'You're not even started yet, let alone finished.'

"I let the robe slip off my shoulders. Underneath I was wearing nothing but a black lacy teddy, which left my breasts bare, and black high-heeled shoes. Tom couldn't believe it. I don't know whether he wanted to make mad passionate love to me then and there, or run out of the house and put as many miles between him and Austin as he could.

"I kissed him, and he kissed me back, and then he asked me one thing, just one, which I thought was a wise and sensible question. He said to me, 'Jolene . . . is this really you?' I kissed him again and nodded and said, 'Yes, Tom, it's really me. I should have showed you what I was like a long time ago, but I guess we don't have the kind of relationship that makes it possible for us to talk together too easy, especially when it comes to making love. Better to let sleeping dogs lie, that's what most people seem to think.'

"He said, "If this is really you, then I sure do love

you, not that I always didn't. And I'm sure looking forward to making your better acquaintance.'

"I unbuttoned his shirt. I was really pleased that he'd taken it so well. But most of all, I was looking forward to the future, and feeling incredibly excited about it. I stripped off his T-shirt while he fondled my bare breasts. Then I loosened his belt, and let his pants fall. When he was naked, I pushed him back onto the bed. His cock was hard again now, and I rubbed it up and down a few times. Then I licked it. It still tasted of spunk. I reached into my nightstand and took out my jasmine-scented body oil. I poured a little onto his bare stomach, and let a few drops fall onto his balls. Then I massaged his stomach and his balls in this beautiful, slow, complicated massage of my own invention. It didn't matter that I was making it up as I went along, he lay back and literally went 'mmmmmm ...' and you can't get a better response to a massage than that, can you?

"He almost climaxed, but I wouldn't let him. I wanted to put his cock inside me at least once that night! I sat on top of him, and let his cock go right up me. Then I leaned forward and I spread his arms over his head and pinned down his wrists. That's when I started to fuck him hard. I had never fucked him so hard before and I don't think I've done it since. I was getting rid of all my pent-up frustrations, all those years of thinking that it wasn't proper for women to show how sexy they could be, and that they had strong sexual appetites that needed to be satisfied. Sex isn't everything; but then home isn't everything; and going to church isn't everything; and watching TV isn't everything. Women are allowed to satisfy any appetite they like, and to do it openly—except for the appetite for sex. I always believed that was wrong and when I stepped into my Sexual Character and did something about it, I *knew* it was wrong.

"Anyhow, there I was, sitting on top of Tom and giving him this hard, undulating fuck. By this time we were both gasping and sweating. There wasn't any play-acting. My breasts were swinging against his oily chest, and my thighs were making slippery, sucking noises on top of his thighs. I leaned forward even further and whispered in his ear, 'See what I can do for you, sir. See what pleasure I can give you. You never knew you could have pleasure like this, did you?'

"It was part dirty talk and part taunting. It was absolutely the kind of thing that my Sexual Character would . say ... she's expensive and high-class and there's a reason for that, because she can give men anything they want. In fact, she can give men things that they never even knew that they wanted.

"I don't know whether Tom's masculine pride was pricked, or what. But when I said that, he twisted around sideways so that his legs were on the floor. Then he put his arms around my waist, and sat himself up, still with his cock deep inside me, so that I was sitting on his lap. We kissed *very* passionately ... I thought my tongue was going to disappear down his throat forever. Then he braced his legs, and he actually picked me up, so that he was standing, and I was clinging onto him, my arms around his neck and my legs wrapped around his waist, and his cock plunged so deep inside me that I thought that I would never be able to get off it, ever again.

"He was showing off, of course. He was showing me how strong he was and how small I was. He was showing me that he could fuck me anywhere. But that was what I'd *wanted* him to feel. That was the whole point of taking on my Sexual Character. It brought out his own strength and his own sexual character—which was the character of a very virile young man.

"We were both close to having a climax, but then he had to lay me back down on the bed. He started to climb on top of me, but I wanted to do something really whorish, so I took hold of his cock in my left hand and started to masturbate him, very hard and quick; and masturbate myself, too. He went so tense it was unbelievable. You could see every muscle in his body bunched up. His cock was purple, and it was dripping out this clear, slippery stuff. I kept watching the hole in the end of his cock, waiting for the spunk to come shooting out. I didn't know how much he'd have left, after what I did at the ball. But I rubbed him even harder, and he suddenly grunted, and a long squirt of spunk came right out of him and hit me on the shoulder and my left breast. He squirted again, and the rest of it dropped down onto my pussy. I opened up my pussy as wide as I could so that the drops fell onto my clitoris and right down into my vagina. It felt like warm rain, it was beautiful. I took Tom's hand and guided it down between my legs so that he could carry on masturbating me, using his spunk as a lubricant. His hand went around and around, and I lay back on the bed and I felt like I was in heaven-on-earth. I closed my eyes and let him do whatever he wanted . . . play with my clitoris, slide his fingers up inside me. I was a high-class hooker and I was *his*. He knelt between my legs, and massaged his soft juicy cock against my clitoris, and that was when I came. It was too much. It was just too much. I felt like I was falling off a building."

Tom's last masturbatory technique—of using his softened penis as a way of stimulating Jolene's clitoris—is one that men who are suffering from any kind of temporary impotence should remember. Even a non-erect penis can be used to good effect, and even if it *still* doesn't show any signs of stiffening, no harm will have been done, and you might even regain just a fraction more confidence about your sexual ability.

Although the behavior of Jolene's Sexual Character was very forward and "whorish," she was careful to look elegant and well-groomed, so that what she was doing didn't seem vulgar or cheap. She knew that Tom valued her classiness and the sweet, well-mannered impression that she had given to his friends and his family and his business colleagues, and if she had played a street-strutting kind of whore (a role which, incidentally, a lot of men find highly exciting), there was a danger of him reacting in a very negative way.

If she had felt that Tom wasn't responding well to their intimate dancing, for instance, all she had to do was to act as if nothing had happened. She didn't have to admit to him that she was wearing no panties, and she didn't have to masturbate him on the dance floor. They would have had an enjoyable, routine evening with no hurt feelings and no burned bridges.

Encouraging your partner to show more interest in sex can be a slightly more delicate job than defusing a 1,000-pound bomb. To start with, you have to have nerve. Men can be *very* touchy if they feel that their sexual performance is being criticized. You'd be safer laughing at his golf swing, but there's no other way out of it. You have to be brave and say to yourself, 'I can do this . . . I really can. And I'm *going* to do it, because it's worth the risk.' You also have to have a clear idea of what you want and how you're going to achieve it. In this case, you're going to achieve it by allowing your true Sexual Character to step out of the closet or wherever you're been hiding her all these years.

You need to acquire some basic sexual expertise. You should at least know how your body works and how *his* body works ... and you can find some very comprehensive and detailed descriptions in several of my other books, including *More Ways to Drive Your Man Wild in Bed.* You should at least know the rudiments of oral sex, the possibility of anal sex, and most of the major acts of unusual or adventurous sex, such as threesomes and group sex, bondage and sadomasochism, cross-dressing, leather and rubber fetishes, and "water sports." You should also be aware that a tiny minority of men have some very unusual fetishes, such as a sexual interest in shoes or very tight clothing.

Many acts of adventurous sex seem shocking and even frightening—particularly acts in which more than two people are concerned. Most of the time, however, they seem threatening simply because few of us are used to showing ourselves sexually in front of strangers.

In *Burning Desires,* their fascinating study of American sexual behavior, Steve Chapple and David Talbot describe a "Jack and Jill-Off" party in a refurbished warehouse in San Francisco, where men and women go to parade themselves, to fondle each other, and to openly masturbate.

I was particularly interested in this party because it describes people putting on Sexual Characters in much the same way that you will be adopting a Sexual Character when you start to take control of your own love life. "It's hard not to stare," say the authors. "Many eyes are fixed on the young, lean blond with the bottle-brush haircut and the perfectly shaped salami dick ... Then there's the handsome, middle-aged woman encased in a black leather bodice, with port-holes for her jutting breasts, and black leather crotchless panties. Meanwhile a group of men is gathering around an elegant one-legged woman with a shimmering, diaphanous blouse and a beatific expression ... she is tumbled backward onto a sofa that is draped with a clean white sheet, and kissed and caressed by her retinue of admirers. Lips find her nipples, fingers taste her clitoris ... at the other end of the loft, a woman with hair like a mowed lawn is putting her young Chinese boyfriend on display. She has slid his Jockey shorts down to his ankles and is slathering his long, thin cock with baby oil. As his shiny, purple-knobbed affair jolts upwards, she boldly meets the stares of those who have gathered around them, as if to say, *Go ahead, take a good, hard look. See how excited I make him, see the power I have over him?*

While I wouldn't expect you to be as domineering as *that,* you should understand that you *do* have a power over your partner; you *can* make him excited; and if you use a combination of nerve, knowledge, and imagination, you should be able to do it without making him feel resentful or inadequate or angry. If you read erotic stories written by women, such as Pauline Reage or Anais Nin, women are usually helpless at the hands of sophisticated, dominant men. But in erotic stories written by men, it is almost always the woman who initiates sex—or is so obviously willing that it makes no difference. The men have to do almost nothing but enjoy the attentions of sex-hungry nymphomaniacs.

There is another element in erotica written by women that is noticeably absent from erotica written by men—and that is, intellect. For women, adventurous sex occurs just as much inside their heads as it does in their nerve endings, whereas male sexual response is much more external—and, again, visual.

For example, compare this excerpt from *Marianne* by Anais Nin with the following passage from the men's magazine *Men Only*. Marianne adores a young man who is aroused only by being gazed on and worshipped.

"She kneeled and prayed on this strange phallus which demanded only admiration. Again she licked it so neatly and vibrantly, enclosing it in her lips like some marvelous fruit, and again he trembled. Then, to her amazement, a tiny drop of milky-white, salty substance dissolved in her mouth, the precursor of desire, and she increased her pressure and the movement of her tongue. When she saw that he was dissolved with pleasure, she stopped, divining that perhaps if she deprived him now he might make a gesture toward fulfillment (i.e., have full intercourse with her—G.M.). At first he made no motion. His sex was quivering, and he was tormented with desire, then suddenly she was amazed to see his hand moving toward his sex as if he were going to satisfy himself.

"Marianne grew desperate. She pushed his hand away, took his sex into her mouth again, and with her two hands she encircled his sexual parts, caressed him and absorbed him until he came. He leaned over with gratitude, tenderness, and murmured, 'You are the first woman, the first woman, the first woman ...'"

Notice how much character and feeling and erotic tension have been created in just a few words. Women *think* their erotica. Men—as this example explicitly shows—need to "see" it visually. Although the following excerpt is alleged to have been written by a woman, it is quite obvious that a man was responsible.

"Declan laid me down on the sofa, raising my legs to ease off my dripping knickers, then he spread my thighs wide and drove his long tongue between my lips, making me squeal with delight. As Declan tongued me, Justin and Rob scooped my boobs from my bra and sucked and licked eagerly at my swollen nipples. But I knew John [her husband, who was secretly watching—G.M.] wanted to see me surrounded by stiff cock so I made them stand around me in a semi-circle. All were pretty well-hung but Rob was huge and I pictured my husband looking on with delight as I tried to cram that huge erection between my lips.

"I was conscious of the fact that he had to see everything so when Declan began rubbing his knob up against my pussy lips, I moved around so John would see every inch of Declan's fat prick as it squeezed into my pussy. He started to pump his hips back and forth and soon I was gasping in delight. And if that wasn't enough, Rob and Justin were rubbing their cocks against my face and occasionally slipping into my mouth and forcing me to suck the engorged head.

"I didn't stop orgasming till Rob threw his head back and hauled his cock from me as it started spurting thick creamy sperm all over my clit and pubes. 'She wants it all over her!' grunted Justin. I moaned happily and whorishly waggled my tongue, beckoning them to deliver their spunky loads. Declan's cream spurted on my cheek and lips, but Justin was happier gushing over my chest and rubbing it into my skin with the head of his prick."

While Anaïs Nin's erotica is cerebral and elegantly phrased, it was written nonetheless for the same reason as the anonymous *Men Only* excerpt was written—to stimulate readers and to sell as many magazines as possible. But we're not concerned about literary values here: only in the light that these two excerpts shed on the very different ways in which men and women become sexually excited. Those women who have creative and satisfying sex lives are those who understand what it is their men really dream about, and make sure that they give it to them.

I can't emphasize often enough that giving your partner what he wants doesn't mean that you have to do anything that you don't enjoy, or that you have to compromise yourself sexually or morally or any other way. But it may mean that you have to reconsider your present attitudes toward sex, and any inhibitions you may have. In particular, I'm talking about oral sex, which we'll be discussing in a later chapter. In the opinion of Paula Yates, the British television presenter and wife of rock star Bob Geldof, the secret of keeping a man happy is one thing and one thing only—"one b**w j*b after another."

First let's take a look at a completely different Sexual Character—Jaynie, a 23-year-old bank teller from Terre Haute, Indiana. On first sight, Jaynie doesn't look as if she needs to take on a Sexual Character in order to arouse anybody. She's five feet six, with long dark hair, high cheekbones, and a 36DD bust. In fact, her figure is so good that between the ages of 18 and 20 she posed several times for nude and beachwear photographs.

Jaynie had three "serious" relationships with men, but now she was dating a man 13 years her senior—Brett, 36, who runs an agricultural machinery business with his brother. Brett is married but estranged from his wife and two children. He dates Jaynie two or three evenings a week, and occasionally meets her on weekends. At first their sexual relationship was intense, but as the months went by they made love less and less frequently, and Brett started making excuses to break dates and to rush off early before they had time to sleep together. Jaynie sensed that Brett "isn't exactly growing tired of me ... he likes me, and he isn't going to dump me, not yet. But I can feel that the sparkle's gone out of our relationship ... leastways, as far as *he's* concerned."

So what was the problem? Jaynie couldn't figure it out. They made a good-looking couple. Brett was fit and vigorous and had no trouble achieving or sustaining an erection. They had a great many shared interests—cooking, cycling, and squash—and a taste in music that was divided generationally but didn't clash. Brett's marriage was over and he felt no need to hide his relationship with Jaynie. They regularly visited his friends, and Jaynie always made an effort to play the part of the perfect hostess. Yet Jaynie clearly felt that "something's gone badly wrong ... and if I don't do anything about it, we're going to drift apart. It's make-or-break time, I know it. I *know* it!"

Her intuition was probably right. Brett was the kind of man who was capable of loving a woman very intensely, but was equally capable of shying away from her when he felt that he was having to make a firm commitment. He had been financially burned when he had walked out on his wife—even though *she* was the one who had committed adultery—and he was extremely wary about any relationship that might break his heart or his bank balance (or both).

He was looking for a long-term sexual relationship, but not if there was any risk of emotional or financial damage.

What about their sex life? "I thought it was great," said Jaynie. "When Brett started taking me out, I was pretty damned sloppy, the way I dressed and the way I did my hair. But after he took me to all of these swanky restaurants and fancy parties, I went out and bought some real sophisticated dresses and shoes, and I put up my hair and watched the way that Brett's friends behaved, like not propping their forks on the sides of their plates, and using a separate butter knife, stuff like that."

But in spite of Jaynie's efforts to fit in socially with Brett's friends, Brett seemed to be less excited by her every time they met; and after the third date he canceled with her she wrote to me, desperate to save a relationship which, to her, was "the sun, the moon and the stars ... it's everything ... Brett is the first man I've ever loved ... I mean really loved ... and I don't think I could bear to lose him, not now."

I guessed the nature of Jaynie's problem with Brett almost immediately, and when I talked to both of them later, my guess proved to be fairly accurate. Brett had been attracted to Jaynie because she was young, because she was gauche, because she was unspoiled. He was a well-educated and sophisticated man, but he hadn't been looking for a well-educated and sophisticated woman. His experience with his first wife had shown him that he needed a woman who was pretty, young, and carefree. He hadn't wanted to change her: he wasn't Professor Higgins, trying to turn cockney Eliza Doolittle into *My Fair Lady*. He had wanted her to stay the way she was.

Their relationship hadn't deteriorated *in spite* of Jaynie's efforts to fit in socially with Brett's friends, but *because* of them. Every time Jaynie had arrived for a date, she had dressed more provocatively, and behaved in a more sophisticated manner, believing that she was fitting into Brett's circle of friends, and becoming the kind of woman he wanted. She should have had more faith in her natural, everyday self, and thought: why was he attracted to me in the first place? If he had been looking for a provocative, worldly woman, he might just as well have stayed with his wife—which he hadn't. So every time she dressed up, and used the correct knife for the butter, she was becoming more and more like his estranged wife, and further and further removed from the woman he was looking for.

His dream? "A pretty, sexy, uncomplicated girl . . . intelligent enough to talk about business and politics and theater and art . . . more intelligent than me would be nice. But relaxed, and very young, and *crazy* sometimes. A girl who doesn't mind where we fuck, so long as we fuck.

"Commitment? I'm not afraid of commitment. But I don't want baggage. I don't want somebody who's going to come trailing into my life with a whole lot of guilt or anxiety or children or old lovers. I've had all of that. I'm ready to make a commitment, but the commitment has to start on Day One, with no back pay."

In spite of what astrologers say, some of the hottest sexual relationships happen between people who seem to be totally incompatible. Sex thrives on opposites, on contrasts, on unknown quantities. A woman may make a suitable wife for a company executive, but will she be good in bed? She may dress in Chanel and be able to organize a $250-a-plate charity dinner for 500 people, but at the end of the evening, can she strip off everything except her stockings and her shoes, and sit on top of her husband's erection, and ride him like the winner in last year's Kentucky Derby?

Why do the husbands of beautiful socialites visit

prostitutes? Because prostitutes are plain, and straightforward, and very young. More than that: they don't really care what their clients' problems are. They don't care about his wife, his mortgage, his broken computer, or his mother-in-law. They don't care whether they were snubbed by J. R.'s wife at the annual company picnic.

It isn't so much the sex act that counts, when these men visit prostitutes: it's the fact that, for the first time in 10 to 15 years, *they* are the center of sexual attention. Their past lives (and with them, their present problems) are temporarily banished by a baby-oil massage and a lascivious blow job.

For the same reason, these erring captains of industry go looking for mistresses—young, impressionable women who remind them of what they used to be, not so many years ago. For a few moments during the day, they can lie back and enjoy the sexual ministrations of a naked woman and not have to answer questions about the Pacific Rim sales drive or the menu for the staff party. As we grow older, we lose many freedoms, among the most important of which is the freedom to spend all day in bed with the person you love—no visitors, no calls, no children—by order.

I asked Jaynie to try to remember what she was doing and what she was wearing on the day that Brett first asked her out. "It was a very tight black velvet dress, *very* short, so short that you could almost see my ass, and a big leather jacket, and black knee-length boots. I was dancing at a party that my friend Cindy had invited me to. Cindy's dad is in automotives, too. That's why Brett was there."

And wouldn't she consider dressing like that again? "Of course not. Brett meets all kinds of important people. He doesn't want a girl who looks like a bimbo.''

But I persuaded Jaynie that Brett had first been attracted by what she was, as much as the way she looked. Shy, young, and very awkward: a pretty girl who needed a warm and considerate man to take care of her. It was her innocence that aroused him, her lack of pretentiousness. Remember that being protective is one of the most basic of male instincts; and the more you seek your partner's protection, the more likely you are to arouse him. These days, men have learned to cope with bossy, demanding women, especially at work, but they are still excited by the vulnerable-looking waif; and don't tell me for a moment that you can't act the vulnerable-looking waif, now and again.

After talking to Brett, I reported back to Jaynie and told her that what turned him on was her youth and her beauty and her lack of sophistication. When he took her to parties, he was showing her off. She was living evidence to everyone he knew that he could still attract young women, that he was still a stud. This might have sounded like a shallow and chauvinistic reason for dating her, and in some cases it might have been. But it seemed to me that Brett cared about her deeply, and was very much in love with her; but he was almost paranoid about making the same mistake that he had made with his estranged wife.

Jaynie, however, took my advice and set about creating a Sexual Character for herself which she was sure would make Brett's wildest dreams come true. She didn't find it difficult. In fact, her "invented" Sexual Character was far closer to her true sexual personality than it was to the snobbish, soigné creature she had been trying to become so that she could fit more easily into Brett's circle of friends.

"I thought: I'm only 23, I'm going to *act* 23. I may act even younger, because I look younger. If Brett wants a relationship with no strings attached, then that's fine by me."

Since she had been dating Brett, she had worn her hair swept back, but now she let it fall loose, with just a hint of a perm to make it look casual, and to give it some body. She stopped using foundation, although she darkened her eye shadow, and painted her lips to give them a dramatic, definitive curve.

She did one thing more—"something I've always wanted to do, but never dared." She went with her best friend Irene to a tattooist, and had a lily symbol imprinted on her right shoulder blade—"because the lily is the symbol of innocence." She also had her navel pierced with a silver ring—"I love piercing . . . I would have had my nose pierced but I'd lose my job at the bank if I did."

For the first time since she had dated Brett, she let herself follow her own inclinations, and be herself. So many women try to change themselves into the kind of personality they think their partner has always wanted, without understanding that their partner really wanted someone like *them*, unchanged, the way they were. Although this book tells you how to take on a Sexual Character so that you will find it easier to communicate sexually with the man you love, it *doesn't* tell you how to change yourself so much that you are no longer the person to whom he was first attracted.

Always remember: you turned him on when he first met you, and you can still turn him on. All it takes is a little snap of the metaphorical fingers, to wake him up, to get his attention, and to show him what you want, and how he can give it to you.

In Jaynie's case, that snap of the fingers was a fresh,

innocent, but slightly kinky look (the navel ring); and some very outrageous behavior. She described her Sexual Character as "jailbait"—a kind of mischievous, provocative nymphet—"the girl they catch under the bleachers during high school football games, giving head to two seniors at once.

"I waited till the weekend before I took on my Character. I guessed that it would give Brett more time to come to terms with it; and more time to enjoy it, too. I didn't want to have a situation where I came into the bedroom and said, 'Look at me, I'm a bad, bad girl,' only to have him say, 'Sure, that's great, I have to be at the office by eight.' Another reason I waited was because I wasn't sure that it was going to work out right. Brett can be funny sometimes. By 'funny' I mean unpredictable. He can be calm and happy and sweet as pie. Then he can suddenly turn grouchy, for no reason.

"Brett was away for the most of the week in Detroit, so I had plenty of time to get myself ready. I meditated every single evening, in front of the mirror. I told myself to stop worrying; and that everything was going to be fine. I defined who I was, and what I wanted out of my relationship with Brett. I openly admitted to myself for the first time that I wanted a father-figure, a man to look after me and guide me and take care of me. A man who was going to put his arms around me and protect me.

"I'd never admitted that before. I guess I'd always thought that it was childish and embarrassing, to want a father-figure. That was one of the reasons I'd been trying so hard to behave as if I was Brett's wife, almost—or at least a woman of the world, you know. But you're right. Brett wasn't looking for another wife, and he wasn't looking for a woman of the world.

He was looking for a sexy, uncomplicated relationship with a young girl who would make him look virile and feel virile.

"Was that the kind of relationship *I* wanted? Well, yes, it was, mostly. My previous boyfriends had been very young and immature—compared to Brett, anyhow. I wanted a man who could make decisions. I wanted a man who could take me places, and buy me things, and give me some pampering.

"I found the sexual meditation incredibly helpful. Usually, you never sit down and think about yourself like that. You don't have the time or you don't have the motivation. But just to sit naked in front of the mirror and really *see* yourself, that's simple, you know, but it's so instructive. I didn't see a sophisticated woman . . . which was what I had been trying so hard to turn myself into. I saw a young girl who looked even younger than 23, with a good figure and very fresh looks, and that was what Brett must have seen when he very first met me. It wasn't just my outward appearance, either. It was the way I was.

"I didn't touch myself till the third meditation. I guess I was too shy! But that afternoon I sat naked in front of the mirror, and massaged my breasts with patchouli oil. Then I slowly masturbated, rubbing and touching my clitoris in all different ways, and sliding my fingers in and out of my cunt. I kept my eyes open . . . I liked watching myself touching myself like that. But I let my mind go completely blank . . . completely empty of everything, except the way that I felt about making love to Brett.

"I realized that both he and I wanted the same thing, sexually, but that I had been trying to change myself into another kind of person altogether, and he hadn't made it clear to me that he didn't want me to change. Maybe he was afraid of hurting my feelings. Maybe he thought he'd made a mistake about me ... and that was why he was gradually losing interest. I think if he'd found somebody younger and fresher right at that moment, I would have lost him. I'm sure of it.

"I had a long think about oral sex. I was very wary of oral sex. My very first boyfriend kept wanting me to do it, and he used to force my head down and try to push his cock into my mouth. After that, I didn't like doing it at all. It always reminded me of being pushed. I mean it was like rape, almost, except he was raping my mouth instead of my cunt.

"My next boyfriend was always begging me to do it, so in the end I gave in. The first time he came in my mouth when I wasn't expecting it. I don't mind the taste of sperm, but I didn't want a whole load of it in my mouth. I spat it out, and we had a terrible row about it. He said I didn't love him, because if I'd loved him I would have swallowed it, which was nothing less than emotional blackmail, wasn't it?

"I decided that I was going to try again with Brett—so long as I could do it at my own speed, in my own way, and so long as I didn't have to swallow—not unless I felt like it.

"Brett was due back Saturday morning. So the last thing I did, on Friday evening, was have a long leisurely soak in the tub, and shave off all of my body hair, so that I was completely smooth all over. I'd never shaved off my pubic hair before, but once I'd done it I really liked it. It felt so silky and clean. Besides, it did make me look younger, too! I took a last look at myself in the mirror and thought to myself, 'That's it, Jaynie—tomorrow you're going to be the hottest young girl he's ever met.'

"Brett arrived about ten in the morning. He'd been flying for most of the night but he wasn't tired. The first thing he noticed was my hair ... then he noticed what I was wearing. I had this short, tight white wool dress that clung to every curve. It had like a big turtleneck, so it was more like a long sweater than a short dress. Whatever it was, it only just covered the cheeks of my ass.

"I wore long ribby white socks that went right up over my knees, so I looked like a very bosomy young kid of 15 rather than a woman of 23.

"Brett loved it. He gave me a kiss and he couldn't keep his hands off me. He kept saying, 'What have you done to yourself? You look like a million. No, you don't. You look like ten million.'

"He went for a shower, and he came out the bathroom wrapped in his terry robe. He sat on the couch and I brought him a glass of o.j. He told me all about his trip, and how much he'd missed me. He'd brought me back some perfume and a cute little doll in a lacy dress. I sat real close to him and he couldn't stop kissing me and telling me how great I looked.

"I untied his robe, and slipped my hand inside, so that I could run my fingers through his hairy chest. He's very hairy, and I love it. When we make love, it's almost like being fucked by a wolf. I tugged the hairs around his nipples, and then I ran my hand down his stomach, into his pubic hair. I said, 'Oh, Brett, what a big hairy cock you've got!'—just like Red Riding Hood—and I ran my fingers deep into it, and pulled it hard. His cock was rising up hard, so I massaged it with one hand, while I rolled and played with his hairy balls with the other hand.

"I opened his robe right up, so that he could see what I was doing. He stroked my hair and touched my face, but I was in control of what we were doing, even if I *did* look like a sexy little schoolgirl. I knelt down beside the couch and masturbated him v-e-r-y slowly. His cock was rising out of that bush of black hair, all red and veiny and swollen, and the head was gleaming and purple, the same color as an eggplant, almost, and just as shiny. Brett still had his foreskin, and I love to watch it rolling up and down over the head of his cock ... one second the head of his cock is almost completely hidden, the next it gets peeled like a fruit, and it's all naked and vulnerable.

"I gave Brett the naughtiest, dirtiest look that I could manage, then I gave his cock a huge lick. Actually, I had so much inner calm that it didn't worry me at all. I licked it again, and this time I ran the flat of my tongue all the way up the underside of it, and gave it a last flick when I reached the top. I licked it again, and then again, and I found that instead of disliking it, I actually liked it. I mean I *really* liked it. I wasn't being forced to do it. It was my choice, and if I wanted to stop doing it, I could, at any time.

"The only thing was, I didn't want to stop doing it. I wanted more. I pulled down his foreskin, and then I kissed the head of his cock, planting kisses all over it. Then I opened my mouth and slowly took it right inside, so that it was pressed against my palate. I sucked it and then I ran my tongue all around it. I even chewed it—not very hard!—and all Brett could do was lie back on the couch and watch me.

"I kept on licking and sucking him, and at the same time I reached between his legs and started to pluck the hairs out of his scrotum, one by one. He winced once or twice, but he didn't stop me doing it. His cock seemed to grow even bigger, and he was clutching my left shoulder so hard that he was beginning to hurt me. In return, I started to pull out the hair around his asshole. I'd never done anything like that before in my whole life, and especially not with him. But I was acting myself now. I was naughty and provocative and it didn't matter.

"I'd never felt so free. I suddenly understood that you can do *anything,* you know, so long as it makes you happy. And sucking Brett's cock made me happy. I took it right into my mouth and sucked it and licked it and gobbled it. I took it out of my mouth and held it in my hand and wiped it all around my face. I loved it. It was mine. It belonged to me; and *he* belonged to me.

"I climbed up on the couch, right on top of him. I crossed my arms and lifted up my dress. Of course I was naked underneath, with a bare-shaved cunt and a silver ring through my navel and lily tattoo. Brett almost had a heart attack when he saw me. He said, 'When did you do that?' I said, 'Don't you like it?' He was speechless. It turned him on so much he just didn't know what to say. And all the time he'd been thinking of finishing with me, because I was too much like his ex-wife, and all of the other women he'd been dating.

"I was holding his cock in my hand and it started to pour out this clear juice, and I knew that he wasn't far away from having a climax. But I also knew that I'd changed the whole of our love life, because he really fancied me now, dressed in a much younger way. Dressed my age, really, instead of trying to be somebody I wasn't. He said, 'Did you have that done for me? That ring, and that tattoo?' Of course I had, in a way, but I wasn't going to tell *him* that. I said, 'I did it because I felt like doing it, that's all. It's the fashion.'

"He said, 'Come on, sit on top of me.' But I shook my head, and kissed him, and said, 'No ... I don't feel like it.' He said, 'Come on, I'm really dying for it.' But I wouldn't. All I did was rub his cock slower and slower. I circled my thumb around the top of it, just to tease him, and I gave him the wickedest smile that I could.

"He tried to grab me, but I twisted away from him. He grabbed me again, and this time he caught me—I wasn't trying very hard to run away! He turned me over and put me across his knees, and he slapped my bottom. I shouted out and wriggled and fought, but he held me down tight and he slapped me again, and then again. It didn't really hurt too much, we were only kidding around, but I never knew what a turn-on it was, to be spanked like that. I wriggled again, and he spanked me again. I didn't feel any pain at all, but a strange kind of warm glow all across my bottom and between my legs.

" 'Are you going to fuck me now?' he asked me. I said, 'Never!' and he slapped me again. I couldn't believe it. My heart was starting to beat faster and I was panting. I opened my legs wider, opening myself up, so that he could see everything. I knew my cunt was wet ... I could feel it on my bare skin, and against his hairy thigh. 'Now will you fuck me?' he said again, and I said 'Never, ever, ever!' For that he slapped me three times. The feeling in my bottom was amazing. It was like a hot stinging sensation, as if I'd sat naked in a bed of nettles.

"Brett opened my thighs up. He slipped two fingers into my cunt, then when it was all slippery he took one of them out, and slid it straight into my asshole. He kept on holding me down, with his left hand flat on my back, while he worked his fingers deeper and deeper inside me. He churned his fingers backward and forward, rolling the skin between my ass and my cunt as if he was rolling velvet between his fingers. I lay across his knees with my eyes closed and all I could hear was both of us panting, and the thick wet squelching noise of my cunt. I would have let him do anything, right then. I needed him so much I had tears in my eyes.

"At last he drew out his fingers and sat me up on his lap and said, '*Now* will you fuck me?' He didn't have to ask. I sat up a little, and he opened up my cunt lips with his fingers and positioned his cock head so that it just fitted snugly. He felt so big I didn't know how I was going to get him all in. But I sat down in his lap, very slow and very careful, and his cock slid up inside me, all the way up to his hairy balls. I nearly climaxed right at that moment. I swear my cunt was so sensitive that I could have described every vein and every curve in his cock as clearly as if I could see it. I could even feel his foreskin roll back when he went inside me.

"He sat me on his lap, with his cock right up inside me, and he held me in his arms and he rocked me. It was beautiful. It wasn't fierce, animal fucking. It was holding and loving—although he kept on tensing his muscles so that I could feel his cock swelling and lengthening inside me.

"He played with my breasts, gently twisting and tugging my nipples. They went incredibly stiff and tight, and the more he touched them the stiffer they went. I had such a strange feeling in them that I almost wanted him to stop; and yet I wanted him to go on, too. It was almost more than I could bear.

"He kissed me and whispered in my ear. He said I was naughty girl and I would have to be spanked and fucked at least once a day, if not more. He hooked his pinkie through the ring in my navel and said he was going to put a cord through it, so that I would have to follow him around all day and fuck him whenever he felt like it. Then he reached down and touched my cunt, sliding his fingertips around and around it, and at last touching my clitoris. I shivered, I couldn't help shivering. He said he loved my cunt shaved like that, he never wanted me to grow hair there again. He said he loved the feel of it and he loved the look of it ... he could see all of my lips and my clitoris peeping out. All the time he kept stroking and stroking my clitoris and holding me tighter and tighter. I felt small and safe and *looked-after,* even though I had his huge cock right up inside me. But I felt *myself,* too—like I wasn't under any pressure to be smart or sophisticated or anything like that.

"We kissed and we kissed until our mouths were bruised; and we held each other so tight that I hardly knew where Brett ended and I began. Then I put my hand down between his legs and gripped his balls tight, with my fingernails sticking into him. I wanted to hurt him. I wanted him to shoot his sperm up inside me. I wanted to punish him for nearly leaving me, and at the same time I wanted to show him who was boss.

"I could feel his cock expanding, and then he suddenly shook and shook; and he had a climax that seemed to go on longer than any climax he'd ever had before. He was still stroking my clitoris, though, he never stopped stroking me even when he was climaxing, and I was sitting in his arms panting and gasping, every muscle in my body as tight as a bowstring. Then his soft cock started to slide out of me, and I felt a warm wet flood of sperm between my legs. Brett's fingers were smothered in it, and as he stroked me, I was smothered in it, too. I took a deep breath and I could smell it, that incredible strong smell of sperm.

"I didn't realize I was going to have an orgasm until it hit me. I was breathing and gasping and then I found myself clinging onto Brett as if I was going to fall off the edge of the world. I'd never screamed when I climaxed before, but I did then.

"I played out the part of my Sexual Character all day ... but the longer I did it, the less you could tell the difference between my Sexual Character and the real me. We went for cheeseburgers; we went for a walk in Deming Park. I stopped trying to impress Brett with what I'd been reading in *Time* magazine, and instead of that I just gossiped and flirted and behaved like me. Oh—and I wore a very tight sweater, with my midriff showing, navel ring and all, and a very short skirt.

"It was a hard decision to make, but I made up my mind right then that if he didn't like me being young and unsophisticated, then our relationship really would be over, because I am young and I am unsophisticated, and there was nothing but heartache in trying to pretend different.

"Brett had to go to Chicago the first three days of the following week. When he came back, I met him at the airport wearing skintight jeans and a fluffy pink sweater. He looked so relieved when he saw me that I couldn't believe it. He said he'd been worried that I'd been teasing him, that's all, and that when he came back everything would be back the way it was. I said, 'No way. This is the way I am and this is the way I stay.' As soon as we reached home, I opened his pants and sucked his cock for him. I think that made the point. Oh ... and he took me to bed afterward, and it was gorgeous. Just like it used to be."

It's remarkable how many women lose sight of what it was about them that so strongly attracted their partner when they first met. I'm not suggesting for a moment that you try to turn back the clock and try to look and behave the same way you did at the very beginning of your relationship. Fashions change, people mature, and there is no more painful and fruitless pursuit than the pursuit of lost youth. All the same, during one of your sexual meditation sessions, take out your photo album and look at pictures of yourself the way you were. Try to remember what you *felt* like, way back then. Try to remember how you behaved, especially when you flirted.

Close your eyes and try to recapture the essence of what you were; and try to look at yourself from your partner's point of view.

Over the past 20 years, I've asked scores of men what first attracted them to their wives or lovers, in order of priority. The results are by no means definitive, but they will give you a clear idea of what qualities you might have lost, altered, or ignored, and which the man in your life is beginning to miss.

What first attracted you to your present sex partner?

(1) Face; (2) Personality; (3) Figure; (4) Grooming; (5) Fashion-sense; (6) Intelligence.

What was about her face that attracted you?

(1) She was pretty in a conventional way; (2) She was pretty in an unusual way; (3) She just happens to have the type of face I like (e.g., Slavic, Jewish, Oriental, African-American); (4) She reminded me of a previous girlfriend for whom I still have affectionate feelings; (5) She reminded me of a movie/TV star; (6) She wasn't pretty but there was something about her face that made me feel good.

What was it about her personality that attracted you?

(1) She was flirtatious; (2) She had a terrific sense of humor; (3) She was challenging and I like challenging women; (4) She was confident without being overbearing; (5) She was quiet but she seemed to know what she wanted; (6) She was shy and seemed to need protecting.

What was it about her figure that attracted you?

(1) Breasts; (2) Bottom; (3) Legs; (4) Waistline; (5) Good posture; (6) Height.

What was it about her grooming that attracted you?

(1) Clean, well-cut hair; (2) Smart and sexy clothes; (3) Makeup (especially eye makeup) and manicure; (4) Alluring perfume; (5) Casual and sexy clothes; (6) New and sexy underwear.

What was it about her fashion sense that attracted you?

(1) Her clothes were sexy, but they suited her age and her appearance; (2) Her clothes were striking and fashionable; (3) Her clothes always looked as if she had made an effort to look especially good; (4) Her clothes were smart but discreet; (5) Her clothes were casual but well-chosen; (6) Her clothes were eccentric, but I like eccentric women.

What was it about her intellect that attracted you?

(1) She listened carefully to what I said to her and understood it; (2) She was capable or arguing on almost any subject you could name; (3) She was obviously well-educated but she didn't make a point of showing it; (4) She wasn't intellectual but she was witty and quick; (5) She wasn't very intelligent but she was eager to learn.

Look through these "top-six" charts of what men find attractive in a woman when they first meet her.

Then—as honestly as you can—circle those attributes which you think first attracted your partner to you. Don't think about any of the attributes that you may have *now*. In some cases, you may be sexier, better-dressed, better-educated, and better at everything than you were when you and your lover first met. Nevertheless, look at those circled attributes and see which of them you might have lost, or neglected.

For example, is your figure in the very best shape that you can manage? It's surprising how many men suddenly find that their sexual interest is revived when their wives or lovers lose a few excess pounds—and I'm only talking about a few. Do you take as much care of your hair as you used to? The two most common excuses I hear are "I don't have time to spend at the hair salon any longer" and "What does it matter anyway ... he's seen me with rollers in."

Other attributes to watch are your clothes ... not forgetting your underwear. When was the last time you bought some really sexy bras and panties? Remember how important it is to give your partner plenty of visual delights to keep up his interests—and his erection.

Many women simply don't know why their partner was first attracted to them, and it's worth their while to find out ... either by the kind of self-analysis we've seen earlier, or by asking their partner outright. Claudia, a 28-year-old management consultant from Pittsburgh, told me that she hated her large breasts and that she was determined to have them surgically reduced. She thought her live-in lover Alan was being "stupid" when he protested. "They're heavy, they're ugly, I hate them."

Claudia's dislike of her breasts went right back to the age of 14, when they had first developed, far ahead of most of her classmates, and to a size that had earned her several ribald nicknames from her male classmates. "I was 38DD by the age of 18 . . . now I'm 40DD." In those days, she was deeply embarrassed. She is no longer embarrassed; but she is "incensed" by the way in which so many of the men she meets in a business context treat her—in her own words— as "a pair of fantastic breasts with a tiresome woman attached . . . they never, ever look me in the eye. They would if I had eyes instead of nipples."

I talked to both Claudia and Alan. *He* thought her breasts were very beautiful, as he was frank enough to admit that they were a major reason why Claudia was so physically attractive to him. He was concerned that if she went for breast-reduction surgery that she would lose some of her appeal. "I know that's a very selfish attitude. But it upsets me that she hates a part of her body which, to me, is so attractive. She always sits with her shoulders rounded so that her breasts won't look so obvious, and she wears big sloppy sweaters all the time."

In effect, Claudia was making Alan feel "guilty" for finding her so sexually attractive, and the constant strain that this imposed on their relationship was considerable.

Of course, if Claudia really was a suitable candidate for breast reduction, then Alan's feelings were largely immaterial. The lives of many women with very large breasts have been dramatically improved by reductive surgery, just as the lives of many small-breasted women have been improved by enlargement. But before Claudia pursued surgery I suggested she do one simple thing: talk to a professional corsetiere about having her bras specially made for her. Much of the weight, discomfort, and chafing that large-breasted women complain about is caused not by the size of their bosom but by ill-fitting undergarments. Consumer surveys have shown that more than a third of the women in the United States are wearing the wrong-size bra.

As it turned out, Claudia was no exception. She wrote later to say that, "I've been given a new life, almost. I walk taller, I feel proud of myself. My clothes seem to fit better, too, and my breasts don't seem so prominent. Alan doesn't feel guilty about paying me compliments anymore, and I can emphatically say that our love life has never been better."

You may think this "wonderbra" cure is almost too good to be true. But it really is worth a try. Custom-made underwear is expensive, but it's very much cheaper and less risky than surgery, and the difference can be even more noticeable than any surgeon can achieve.

Claudia's breasts were one of the features that had attracted her partner on first sight. What was it with you?—Your laugh? Your smile? Your face? Your hair? Try to analyze your appeal to your partner, and then do your best to enhance it. As Jaynie showed, it doesn't take very much to rekindle the flames. A new hairstyle, a new outfit, a little grooming—combined with a determination to be the sexiest woman that her partner had ever met—and she had changed her love life, and possibly her entire future, for good.

Now that we've seen how you can create and develop your own Sexual Character, let's take a look at some of the physical techniques you can use to make your lover's dreams come true.

Questionnaire
What Kind of Loving Does He Secretly Crave?

Try to persuade your partner to answer the following 40 questions about sexual touching and sexual technique. Tell him to be honest. Even if he hasn't been able to suggest any of these stimulations to you, he should try to do it now. A little honesty is the best tonic for any sexual relationship, no matter how good it seems to be. For added interest, make a copy of this questionnaire for yourself and fill in the selections *you* think he's going to make; then, when you're both finished, compare notes and see how right (or how wrong) your assessment of your partner's sexuality has turned out to be.

Just because he shows interest in a particular sexual technique, that doesn't necessarily mean that he's going to make you do it for real; or that—even if he wants to try it—that he's going to want to do it for the rest of your natural lives. What many sex "experts" seem to forget is that a majority of people try extreme sex techniques only once or twice in their lives, just to check them out—and that the memory of having tried them is often a sufficient aphrodisiac to lend excitement to many "ordinary" and straightforward acts of love. Except in cases where people develop genuine obsessions for, say, rubber or leather, most lovers find that the more extreme the sexual act, the sooner it loses its thrill.

Nadia, a 33-year-old flight attendant from Boston, told me, "Rick and I got heavily into bondage at one point. We had a bondage session almost every weekend for about two or three months. We took it in turns to be bound up. I remember we spent a fortune on bondage gear. In the last session, I had Rick wearing a full rubber helmet with eye blinkers and a ball gag. His arms were secured behind him with a lace-up leather sleeve. He was wearing a black lace-up leather corset, and a pair of rubber pants which had a hard rubber dildo inside it which went up inside his ass, and an open front so that his cock was exposed. He wore full-length rubber boots with spiked stiletto heels. Wow, we had a session that night. I was completely naked except for high heels. I made him kiss my shoes and lick the toilet clean with his tongue. I carried a thin cane and every time he did anything wrong I whipped his bare cock with it. It was an amazing evening, but somehow we never got around to doing it again. You know what they say—been there, done it, got the T-shirt. But the *idea* of it still turns me on, and I think that we might do it again one day, if we're feeling particularly horny."

There is nothing "perverted" about trying acts of adventurous sex between yourselves, provided you both derive excitement and pleasure from them. However, a real danger can arise when a single person's self-gratification graduates from straightforward masturbation into an extreme obsession for some kinds of masochistic sex, such as half-asphyxiating himself with a cord or a chain as an accompaniment to masturbation—an act that intensifies the pleasure of ejaculation, but at a totally unacceptable risk. Or mailing himself the key to a pair of handcuffs, and then lying handcuffed and naked on the doormat, in his own urine and excrement, waiting for the next day's mail delivery so that he can release himself.

People who become obsessed with potentially fatal sexual practices like these are suffering from severe disturbance, and need professional counseling.

Lucy, 24, a pretty redheaded photographic assistant from Denver, thought that she had done "the most extreme unacceptable thing ever," and although she didn't plan to do it again, she was worried because she still thought about it "and it still excites me, and

I get all flushed and hot and bothered; and yet I feel disgusted with myself, too.

"It was Saturday afternoon and we were going bowling with some friends of ours. Marty was first in the tub, and I was leaning over it, naked, running some more hot water into it, and kind of swooshing up the foam. All of sudden I thought I'd better go to the john, you know? But just at that moment Marty came into the bathroom behind me and put his arms around me and started to squeeze my breasts. I said 'Cut it out, Marty, I have to go.' He said, 'Go where?' and he kept trying to slide his hand down my stomach and between my legs. I said, 'The john, and it's urgent.' So he said, 'You don't have to go just yet, do you?' His towel slipped from around his waist, and he was naked, too. His cock was already sticking out, and I could feel it swaying against my hip. He was right up in back of me, with his arms around me, and he wouldn't let me free. I said, 'I *have* to go.' So he said, 'Go on then, the floor's only tiling . . . what's to hurt?' He was rolling my nipples between his fingers and his thumbs, and he was turning me on, but it didn't change the fact that I still had to go . . . in fact, it had the opposite effect, it made me want to go even more.

"I said, 'Come on, Marty, I don't just want to pee!' and then he realized. But instead of letting me go, he stayed where he was, squeezing me and caressing me and rubbing his cock up against me. He said, 'Come on, baby, you can do it,' and I almost screamed, '*Here?* Standing up?' and he said, 'Sure, go for it.' He had one hand on my breast and the other hand between my legs and it just happened. I peed myself, all the way down my legs and onto the floor. Then I leaned forward with my hands on the sides of the tub and my ass lifted, and, yes, I went for it. Marty held open the cheeks of my ass and I just squeezed it out, right in front of him. I mean that's the most private thing you can do in your whole life, right, and I was standing up in the bathroom with my legs wide apart, doing it. Marty said, 'Come on, babe, you're beautiful,' and I squeezed out some more. Marty took it right in his hand, right in the palm of his hand, and flushed it down the john. Then he came back over and his cock went straight into my cunt like a long smooth spear. I could smell what I'd done but somehow we were both so excited that it didn't turn us off. In a way it made it more exciting, like *dirtier,* you know? Marty fucked me over the side of the tub, harder and harder and harder, until I had an orgasm that almost made me drop to my knees, and I would have done, if Marty hadn't been holding me up.

"We both climbed into the tub together afterwards and I think we were both amazed at what we had done. It was like we had broken some terrible taboo. Marty still had a hard-on, so I made him kneel up in the tub while I rubbed it with soap. I soaped his balls, too, and right between his legs, and that really turned him on. He had a big soapy climax, all over my breasts, and so I finished up by washing myself with sperm and Dove bath bar."

In actual fact, Lucy's exhibitionistic act of excretion wasn't particularly extreme, as far as human sexual behavior goes. An erotic interest in excrement and excreting is called coprophilia, and it is well-documented in many different cultures. Several pornographic videos and books include scenes of women excreting. One of the better-known is *Sex Bizarre,* a mass-produced magazine from Sweden which regularly publishes detailed full-color pictures of young girls in the act of going to the toilet. As I mentioned in *How to Drive Your Man Even Wilder in Bed,* there is even a society in Japan where men gather to watch a woman excrete on a table in front of them, after which they all ritually consume a small piece.

But note: the drinking of a small quantity of your loved one's urine is completely harmless. Fresh urine is completely sterile, and some people even believe that it can be beneficial. But eating her excrement is a very unwise practice, which could lead to serious illness.

The reason I've quoted these two extreme examples of sexual stimulation is so that you and your partner understand that there really are no limits to what two people can do together in private if they love each other and are eager to experiment. When you start having adventures in sex, the question isn't "why?" so much as "why not?" Just because you were brought up to believe that sex was "rude" and that it was naughty to touch yourself and even naughtier to touch other people, that doesn't mean that you have to live your adult sex life by childhood rules. You really can do what you like, and more.

So—ask your partner these questions and see if he surprises you.

1. When we kiss, I prefer to have my tongue in *her* mouth rather than vice versa YES/NO
2. I like us to do plenty of kissing before thinking about more intimate caresses YES/NO
3. I like her kissing and biting my ears YES/NO
4. I like her kissing and biting my neck YES/NO
5. The more painful the love bite, the more it excites me YES/NO
6. I like having my back scratched during love-making YES/NO

7. I like it when she sucks and licks my nipples YES/NO

8. I like it when she bites my nipples YES/NO

9. I enjoy lying back while she tickles and caresses me YES/NO

10. I like it when she touches the sensitive spots at the side of my hips YES/NO

11. I wish she would caress me with her breasts and nipples more often (e.g., on the face and chest) YES/NO

12. I wish she would stroke my thighs and legs more often YES/NO

13. I would love it if she sucked my toes YES/NO

14. I would love it if she tickled or licked the soles of my feet YES/NO

15. I like it when she casually plays with my penis YES/NO

16. I enjoy her playing with my testicles YES/NO

17. I prefer brisk, hard masturbation YES/NO

18. I like having my penis scratched or pricked with her fingernails YES/NO

19. I enjoy it when she digs her nails into my scrotum YES/NO

20. I like having my anus tickled or scratched YES/NO

21. I would like her to insert a finger into my anus YES/NO

22. I would like her to insert more than one finger into my anus YES/NO

23. I would like her to massage my prostate gland, from inside my rectum YES/NO

24. I would like her to stimulate my anus with her tongue YES/NO

25. I love having the head of my cock kissed and licked YES/NO

26. I love having the whole shaft of my cock licked and kissed YES/NO
27. I would like her to take more of my cock into her mouth YES/NO
28. I would like oral sex much more often YES/NO
29. I would like her to take my testicles into her mouth YES/NO
30. I wish she would allow me to give her oral sex more often (such as by sitting astride my face) YES/NO
31. I prefer to be in a position during intercourse in which I can vary how much stimulation I receive YES/NO
32. I prefer to make love quickly YES/NO
33. Once I have climaxed, I like to have my penis caressed YES/NO
34. I like being hurt a little during intercourse YES/NO
35. It excites me to think that I am hurting my partner a little YES/NO
36. I wish I didn't climax so quickly YES/NO
37. I wish it didn't take me so long to climax YES/NO
38. When my partner gives me oral sex, she never stimulates me enough (by simultaneous hand rubbing, for instance) YES/NO
39. I wish my partner would take my semen in her mouth YES/NO
40. I wish my partner would consent to anal intercourse YES/NO
41. I would like my partner to use sex toys on me (dildos, vibrators, anal placators, etc.) YES/NO

As before, there are no "right" or "wrong" answers to these questions, but if your partner has answered them truthfully, you will have an interesting profile of what he feels he is getting, what he feels he is missing, and what he feels he would like you to do for him. If I were you, I would challenge him on one or two of his answers—especially those concerning the more extreme aspects of sexual stimulation—just to make sure that he isn't trying to make himself look like more of a saint than he really is! The way to do this is to suggest to him that *you* wouldn't mind trying, say, anal intercourse—why didn't *he* say he wouldn't mind giving it a try? You'll come up with one or two surprising changes of mind.

Now we should get on to the controversial question of oral sex. As I've said before, women are not naturally drawn to give their partners oral sex in the same powerful way that men are. Many women do it only because their partners virtually force them to; some women can't do it at all. Yet giving oral sex is one of the most potent acts of love that a woman can do for a man, and in many cases it can change a mediocre sex life into a good one, and a good sex life into a great one.

FIVE

How to Lick Your Sex Life Into Shape

"I didn't know anything about oral sex until I was 17 years old," said Catherine, a 37-year-old horse breeder from Richmond, Virginia. "Then I went to stay with my aunt in Chesapeake. One night it was so hot that I had to go the bathroom to refill my glass of water. I went past my aunt's bedroom and the door was slightly open. I couldn't see the bed itself, but I could see a reflection of it in her closet mirror. My uncle was lying back on the bed, naked, his hands gripping the sheets. He had a look on his face that I'd never seen on any man's face before. It was like complete absorption, complete ecstasy. My aunt was kneeling on the bed beside him, and she was naked, too. She couldn't see me because of the angle of the mirror. She was holding his cock in her hand and she was sucking it and licking it, her head bobbing up and down. I'll never forget the way she lifted her hair with her hand so that he could clearly see what she was doing. His cock looked enormous. I'd seen my brother in the shower, but I'd never seen a grown-up man with a full erection before. I couldn't believe that my aunt was sucking it in so far ... I could even see it swelling out of the side of her cheek.

"I felt terrible, spying on them like that, but I was totally fascinated, I couldn't pull myself away. They both looked so happy, so excited, and so much in love ... yet there she was, actually sucking his stiff penis! Toward the end, she took it out of her mouth, and began to rub it with her hand, quickly licking the tip of it with her tongue. My uncle closed his eyes, and then suddenly he shot out a great fountain of sperm ... I'd never seen sperm before, either. My aunt licked it all up like a cat who's got the cream, and swallowed it, and then she took his cock back into her mouth and gave it a long, slow, sucking, as if she wanted to suck out every last drop.

"I crept back to bed, feeling very strange and very excited. I couldn't wait to tell my best friend Sheila what I'd seen! I lay under the covers, thinking about it over and over, and playing with myself with my fingers. I kept wondering what it was like, actually to take a man's penis into your mouth. Into your *mouth*, for God's sake! And then to swallow all of his sperm!

"Although I was asking myself all of these questions, there was one thing I couldn't get out of my mind, and that was how *happy* they both looked, both of them, as if this was the secret to real pleasure, that nobody else had found out about."

Catherine soon discovered, of course, that her aunt and uncle weren't the only couple in the world who knew about the pleasures of oral sex. And these days, information about *fellatio* and *cunnilingus* is available in almost every woman's magazine, as well as in newspapers, magazines, and even television. The need to inform young people about the dangers of AIDS has had the very beneficial side effect that they *have* to be better informed about sex in general.

Nevertheless, a great many women are worried and confused about oral sex. Leaving aside the feminist arguments against it—that it amounts to an act of sexual subservience—some women feel physically repelled by the idea, because they think it's unhygienic, or because they think they may choke, or gag, or because they simply don't know what to do—"I put his cock in my mouth, then what?"

Several women have told me that they know about oral sex, "but it's what prostitutes do, isn't it?"

The reality is that oral sex is performed by millions of ordinary, wholesome, healthy, and loving couples—not just by prostitutes. Provided your partner takes the trouble to keep himself clean, there is no health risk. There are more bacteria in your mouth than there are on his cock ... so if anybody has any complaints to make about hygiene, it should be *him*. You won't choke or gag provided you know what you're doing, and you don't try to take his penis too far down your throat ... although, as you may know, "deep-throating" *can* be done if you train yourself for it.

As for not knowing what to do, most of the art of fellatio is just doing what you feel like doing, and what obviously gives him pleasure. Start by gently caressing his penis and his scrotum with your fingers ... then lick around the head of his penis with the tip of your tongue. Try a swishing, circular motion of your tongue around the ridge of his penis where the head joins the shaft. Then see how far you can probe your tongue tip into his urethra (the opening on the underside of his penis head from which he urinates and ejaculates).

Just below the urethra is a thin "bridge" of skin called the frenum (or, occasionally, frenulum). This is a very sensitive spot for most men, and some quick, delicate flicking with the tip of your tongue should give him a great deal of erotic pleasure.

Take your time doing fellatio, especially when doing it as foreplay to intercourse. Although men are much more quickly aroused than women, oral sex is usually slow to bring them to a climax, and, with practice, you can draw it out for almost as long as you like. You won't find your partner complaining!

Run your tongue all the way down the underside of his penis, then carefully take each of his testicles into your mouth, and circle your tongue around them. If his scrotum is too hairy, ask him to shave it so that you can give him the ball job he deserves. You'll have to be very careful with his testicles ... they're extremely sensitive, and if you suck too hard you could give him a dull, nasty pain that stays with him for the rest of the evening.

Return to the head of his penis and take it into your mouth. Lick all around it, and then start to "fuck" him with your mouth, gently sucking on his penis as he thrusts it in and out of your lips. Pretend that your mouth is a second vagina—but tighter, and more stimulating. You can use your tongue to press the head of his penis up against the roof of your mouth. You can "chew" his penis gently with your teeth. The most important thing about good fellatio is to start building up a rhythm ... a steady, unrelenting rhythm which he *knows* is going to make him ejaculate, no matter how long it takes.

Good sex isn't a race to see who climaxes first. In fact, it's the opposite. The longer you can draw out your sexual play, the more your partner will enjoy it—

and the more *you'll* get out of it, too. Women need much more arousal than men to reach a stage of sexual readiness, but if you perform oral sex on him *before* you get into intercourse mode, you'll have plenty of time to build up your own feelings of sexual arousal (in words and images and fantasies—"just imagine that huge slippery cock coming out of my mouth and straight into my cunt," as one young woman described it). Women who give their partners oral stimulation before intercourse almost always report that they have been able to achieve orgasm much more quickly, and that both they and their partners are "much more satisfied" with their sex lives.

Once you have overcome your inhibitions about oral sex and become adept at it, you will realize that it has several distinct advantages. First of all, let's make no mistake, it gives your partner a striking and highly erotic visual image of the intensity of your affection for him ... his cock buried deep in your mouth. It *looks* submissive, which is why it upsets feminists, but in fact it's one of the few sexual acts in which you, as a woman, are *completely in control*. It stimulates your partner as quickly or as gradually as you wish, depending on your own level of sexual arousal. If you're very turned on, you can use both your hands and your mouth to bring your partner to a high point of arousal, and then, when you're ready, have intercourse. If you're less excited, you can prolong oral sex until you *are* excited—licking and sucking him very gently, and intensifying your own arousal either by masturbating yourself, or by adopting the "69" position so that he can give you oral sex while you're giving it to him. ("Sixty-nine," of course, is the position in which partners lie head-to-toe, one on top of the other, giving each other mutual oral sex.)

You won't choke or retch if you don't take his penis too far into your mouth. However, if you're interested in trying "deep-throat" techniques—in which you can actually swallow the entire penis right up to his balls, you'll have to practice by sticking your finger down your throat until you can restrain your urge to gag. You'll have to practice breathing through your nose only. Then you'll have to ask your partner to be extremely careful while you develop the ability to take his penis deeper than it's ever been before.

"Deep throating" involves the same technique as sword-swallowing: your head has to be held back so that your throat makes as straight a line as possible. The best way to do this is to lie on your back on a bed, and let your head tilt backward over the side. Your partner can then insert his erection into your mouth, and right down your throat.

Edie, a 22-year-old art student from New York, said, "I loved it. I could feel his cock right inside my throat, and his balls were banging against my face. It was panic and excitement at the same time. The only disappointment was, when he climaxed, he rammed his cock right into my throat, and squirted his spunk into my stomach, and I didn't feel anything or taste anything or *anything*."

Gaynor, a 24-year-old cocktail waitress from Kissimmee, Florida, told me, "I love oral sex. Like you say, it gives you control over your sex life. Guys love it, but all you have to do is start doing it and then stop doing it, and you've got them eating out of your hand. I tried deep throating about twice, but I didn't like it because it changes the rules of oral sex, do you know what I mean? With deep throating, the guy's totally in charge, because if he doesn't feel like taking his prick out of your throat, then you're in trouble.

No—I say stick to ordinary oral sex. It's great—I mean, who doesn't like men's cocks, they're beautiful. I have a fantasy about sucking two cocks at once ... can you imagine that ... sitting right down and two naked men standing in front of you and you can suck this cock, and then you can suck *that* cock, and then you can cram them both in together."

Stimulation with the tongue and lips alone is not always sufficient to bring a man to climax, so while you're licking and flicking the head of his penis with your tongue, you may need to rub the shaft with your hand to encourage an ejaculation. You can do this quite forcefully, because the shaft is not as sensitive as the head.

Although the word "fellatio" comes the Latin phrase "to suck," the art of oral sex involves a lot more than sucking. Many inexperienced women take "cocksucking" far too literally, and proceed to suck on their partner's penis so hard that they cause considerable discomfort. When you are stimulating your partner's penis orally, you should use a combination of varying tongue and lip movements, but make sure that you are keeping up a steady, rising rhythm of stimulation, so that you are not constantly bringing him to a high point of arousal and then letting him down again. You will know how frustrating that can be from those times when your partner has been stimulating your clitoris with his finger, and has suddenly changed position and "lost" it for a moment.

The beauty of oral sex is that *you* can initiate it anytime you feel like making love, but it still gives you plenty of time to become fully aroused, because *you're* in charge, and you can stimulate your partner slowly or rapidly as the mood takes you. If you want to extend your lovemaking, use slow, gentle licking. If you want to speed it up, use vigorous sucking and licking and hand stimulation—with one or both hands. You can intensify your oral caresses with anal caresses, too, touching or tickling his anus, and then lubricating your fingers with your own vaginal juice and inserting one or more into his rectum. This combination of oral and anal arousal is extremely potent, when done properly, and can result in a very powerful and copious ejaculation. We'll see how in just a moment.

You can see now that the degree of control that oral sex gives you over your lovemaking with your partner negates the notion that to suck your partner's penis is somehow "subservient." Fellatio has a long and ancient history, and has almost invariably been regarded as a sophisticated and cultured sexual technique. The erotic friezes at Lakshmana Temple, in Khajuraho, India, which were carved around A.D. 1000, show women giving men the most enthusiastic fellatio, their arms entwined around their legs, their breasts pressed against their thighs.

The Devadasis women of the Ganges Valley were bought up to music and dance, and had bodies of amazing suppleness. Many of them were capable of bending over backward while still standing flat on their feet, and picking up a coin from the ground with their lips. They used this extraordinary ability to twist and twine and bend themselves to great advantage when they were making love. They could arch over backward until their hands were touching the floor, and suck the penis of one man while another penetrated them from the front.

Since they always had at least two maids or apprentices in attendance when they were making love, group sex was common, and this is where their talent for fellatio came into its own, so to speak. A maid would orally stimulate the man's penis so that it was in a fine, upright condition, ready for his principal woman.

In Japan, fellatio is often given as part of the bath-house service. In his excellent book on Japanese sexual habits, *Pink Samurai*, Nicholas Bornoff describes "the *awa-dori,* the lather dance. Thai harlotry is popularly seen abroad as the originator of body-body massage, but the Japanese claim that the invention is theirs. The therapy is provided on a king-size inflatable mattress as, assisted by a film of creamy soap suds, the naked girl massages every part of the male anatomy with every part of hers, including that softest and most arousing of scrubbing-brushes. Following a general rinse-down, the session continues with a skillful display of what is called *shakuhachi,* a poetic metaphor alluding to the classic bamboo flute."

The erotic literature of the nineteenth century also clearly shows the power that oral sex gives a woman over a man ... even an inexperienced woman, like Emily in a sexy romp called *Sub-Umbra*: " 'My love, my Emily, let me kiss you now, and it would be sublime if you would kiss me. I long to feel the love bites of your beautiful teeth in my *Cupid's Dart*.' I inclined the willing girl backwards on the soft pillow of sand, and reversing my position, we both lay at full length, side by side, both of us eager as possible for the game; my head was buried between her loving thighs, with which she pressed me most amorously, as my tongue was inserted in her loving slit. She sucked my delighted prick, handled and kissed my balls, till I spent in her mouth, as her teeth were lovingly biting the head of my penis. She sucked it all down, whilst I repaid her loving attentions to the best of my ability with my own active tongue."

Today's sexual outspokenness means that most young

women are aware of oral sex from a young age. But few of them realize that skillful and frequent oral sex can play such an influential part in improving their love lives. This is partly because many men seem to believe that they have made some sort of conquest if a woman sucks their penis. Regrettably, I have heard far too many stories about men physically forcing their partners to go down on them, which—just as Jaynie said in the previous chapter—is as serious an offense against a woman as vaginal rape. This type of assault occurs mainly in sexual relationships that are already dysfunctional, but there are plenty of instances where women have told me "I suck his penis because I know that he'll be angry and sullen if I don't" and "if I don't do it, he says I'm frigid, and makes me feel that I've failed him." In other words, they've been coerced into doing it.

Apart from the crude and oppressive way in which their partners approach fellatio, many women dislike the idea of swallowing semen. There is a locker-room joke which says that the two biggest lies in history are "your check's in the mail" and "I promise I won't come in your mouth."

Although its viscosity makes it seem like much more, the average ejaculation of semen is only about a teaspoonful, and it is a completely harmless mix of protein and simple sugars. Whether or not you wish to take it in your mouth or swallow is your own decision. Remember that. A man who tries to force you to take it in your mouth is no friend of yours—or of any woman, for that matter. If you don't care for salty-sweet egg-white, then you'll probably want to pass . . . but you can always go for some equally spectacular alternatives, such as spraying it on your breasts, or using it to massage his balls and his gradually-declining erection.

However, it's hard to make a decision about swallowing until you're actually doing it. What may seem repulsive at first may seem quite the opposite in the heat of passion. Here's Wanda, 21, a bank teller from Morton Grove, Illinois. Wanda is black, tall, big-breasted, but ever since puberty she had been having trouble with "boys getting the wrong idea." Although she looked sexually provocative, she was very shy and demure—"just a quiet family girl, really."

Wanda lost her virginity at the age of 17, and since then she has had two more lovers. Her current boyfriend, Dennis, works at Chicago's O'Hare Airport.

"Of course I knew about oral sex. I had a friend at school who used to do it with all of the boys on the football team. She wouldn't let them touch her, but she loved to give them head. Myself, I couldn't understand it. It seemed frightening to me, some guy pushing his dick into your mouth. I used to think that I'd probably choke. My friend said that she always swallowed their come, it made her breasts bigger, but I didn't believe that either. Her breasts always looked like the same size to me.

"When I first went to bed with Dennis, I knew this was going to be one of those really special relationships. He's such an amazing guy. He's cool, he's gentle, yet he's so together, too. He's amazing to look at, too. He's very tall, six feet two, something like that, and he wears a gold hoop earring in his left ear, but he has no hair on him whatsoever. His head is shaved, his whole body is nothing but smooth muscle. His chest is so hard you'd think it was carved out of wood, and he has this narrow sixpack stomach, and this ass that drives me wild, because it's so small and tight and rounded and when he's making love it just goes into *knots,* do you know what I mean?

"His cock is something else. Even when it's soft it's kind of half swelled-up. It's really big and dusky black and his balls are like huge prunes! There! I've embarrassed myself now! He doesn't have any hair around it at all, so it looks even bigger. He says he wants to have a gold ring through the end of his cock one day, but I'm not sure whether he's joking or not. Oh, no. I wouldn't mind if he had a gold ring. I could tug him around with it!

"When we first slept together, I used to love touching and feeling his cock. I used to wake up in the night and reach out for it. It was so silky and heavy and every time I touched it, it used to rise, and get hard, even when he was sleeping. Sometimes I used to kneel beside him and massage his cock between my breasts. The end of his cock was always a little bit wet and slippery, and I used to use that juice to rub my nipples. Sometimes I used to play with his cock and masturbate myself, and he never even woke up.

"One night we were getting ready for bed and I was sitting on the toilet. He walked into the bathroom naked and he had a huge hard-on. He walked up to me and stood close so that his cock was only about two inches away from my mouth. It was dark and shiny, and it had a drop of juice actually dripping from the hole. I'll never forget it. He ran his hand into my hair and he said, 'You feel like supper?' Meaning, of course, did I feel like sucking his cock?

"I took hold of his cock, and rubbed it up and down a few times. But I kept thinking of my friend at school, swallowing all of that sperm; and I didn't have the nerve to do it. I said, 'Come on, I want some privacy,' and that was it.

"He's a cool guy, like I said, and he didn't take offense. He just kissed me and walked out. But I knew that he must have wanted me to give him head real bad. His cock was so hard and a guy doesn't drip out juice like that unless he's really turned on. We made love that night, and it was sweet enough, but Dennis seemed kind of distracted ... or else it was me, because I was worried that I might have upset him. He went to sleep right after making love, and I was left lying there, thinking and worrying. I mean, what are you supposed to do in a situation like that? For the first time in my life I felt as if I was alone and ignorant. I didn't have anybody I could call and say, 'Listen, Dennis wants me to give him head, but I don't know whether I'm brave enough, of if I'm going to try it and get it all wrong, and supposing he wants me to swallow his come, and I'm sick or something?'

"Well, I lay back for a long while and then I thought of something. Maybe I could just try it, to see what it tasted like. So I put my fingers down between my legs and into my cunt. We'd only just made love about 20 minutes before, so it was brimming with Dennis's sperm. I dipped my fingers into it, and then I brought them up to my mouth and tasted it. It wasn't like I expected it to be. It wasn't like that at all. It was slippery, for sure, but it had this strange kind of taste, really strong, and dry. I dipped my fingers into my cunt again, and licked them again; and this time I licked them all clean. I couldn't describe the taste of it. If it was some kind of food, you'd say yuk, and you'd never even think of trying it again. But, like, it isn't a food, it's the actual come that shoots out of your boyfriend's cock because he loves you, and what could be more delicious than that?

"I went to sleep feeling like my problems were over. I'd tasted sperm, and I'd decided that I liked it, so long as it was Dennis's sperm. The next morning he was still asleep when I woke up, and I reached over and took hold of his cock and slowly started to rub it. He has such a great cock, he really does. It feels so thick and heavy in your hand, and when he gets a hard-on it just rises and rises like a building going up, with this big purple circumcized head on top, and this long, long, curving shaft all covered in bulging veins, and these huge wrinkled balls; and no hair anyplace at all, just smooth, smooth silky brown skin.

"I pulled back the sheet and I knelt beside him. I don't know whether he was asleep or awake. I hesitated for a moment, and then I kissed the end of his cock, and licked it. Then I opened my mouth and took the whole head of it onto my tongue, and very gently sucked and sucked it. I ran my tongue all the way down to his balls, and I loved licking his balls. I tried to get them both into my mouth at the same time, but they were too big. But I could get them into my mouth one after the other, and I sucked them and licked them. They were just like a fruit that you've never tasted before, slightly salty because he'd been sweating when he slept, and slightly pungent, too, tasting of me and my cunt, because we'd been making love the night before.

"I ran my tongue back up his shaft until I reached the head of his cock. Then I took it in my mouth, and started to bob my head up and down, sucking him in the same kind of rhythm as when we made love. He was fully awake by then. He turned right onto his back so that I could suck him better. His cock was huge. It was like a tall curved pole, you know, with this beautiful knob on the end. I rubbed it with my right hand, too, pulling his skin tight with every rub. He has all of these bobbly veins just beneath the head of his cock and I licked my tongue around them all.

I thought: if I'm going to do this, I'm going to do it so good that Dennis won't even be able to believe it. I bobbed my head faster and faster, and rubbed his cock faster and faster. My head was really flying, and so was my hand. His balls started to scrunch up, and he started panting and sweating, and his cock seemed to rise even more.

"It was *then* that I made my decision about what I wanted to do when he climaxed. I knew what sperm tasted like, but it was *then* that I made up my mind. His cock suddenly twitched and then he was spurting out sperm. He shot one spurt right onto the roof of my mouth, but then I put my head back and let him shoot the rest of it onto my lips. I could taste it. It was warm and fresh and I loved it. But do you know what my decision was? If I can taste it, then you can taste it, too. I think it's delicious; I think it's sweet. But it's something to be shared. I kissed him, with my lips all covered in his own sperm, and we shared the taste of it, every last drop of it, until I was licking his tongue and he was licking mine.

"I give him a *lot* of oral sex, yes. Before we make love, after we make love ... even when we're not making love at all, but just sitting on the couch watching TV. Sometimes I swallow, mostly I don't ... either we share it together in a real deep kiss, which is what I prefer, or else I just let it fly wherever it's going to fly. But to my mind there's no question at all. Oral sex is what guys like; but it's great for girls, too."

Wanda overcame her anxiety about oral sex by tasting her partner's semen in a nonconfrontational situation: in other words, she took it out of her own vagina when Dennis was sleeping. That gave her the opportunity to decide at her leisure whether oral sex would excite and attract her, or whether it would make her feel put-upon and used. In the end, she reached a compromise both with herself and with Dennis, whereby she would occasionally take his sperm into her mouth, provided she felt like it, and provided he shared it with her. "That sharing was the whole key to it," she said. "That was like saying, if it's good enough for me to swallow, then it's good enough for you to swallow, too. Just like my cunt juice. If he wanted to kiss me after going down on my cunt, I wouldn't object. It's only me."

These days, you have to be careful about sharing bodily fluids, and that, of course, includes the swallowing of semen. If you are not 100 percent certain that your partner has a completely clean bill of sexual health (not just HIV, but any other sexual diseases whatsoever, from herpes to gonorrhea to nonspecific urethritis) then you must use a condom. Yes, even during oral sex.

Condom manufacturers have made protected cocksucking a little more acceptable by introducing their product in various flavors. So far I've seen them in mint, chocolate, bubblegum, butterscotch, tutti-frutti, macadamia nut, marshmallow, pistachio, strawberry daiquiri, tequila sunrise, piña colada, and margarita amaretto. The best technique for putting on these condoms is to take them out of their foil packet, and then hold them in your mouth, unrolled, with the bulb on the end gripped lightly between your lips. Then bend over his erect penis, open your lips, and cover the head of his cock with the upper part of the condom. Keeping the head of his cock in your mouth, unroll the remainder of the condom down his shaft, until it fits snugly right down to his balls. You can continue cocksucking as usual ... with a loss of sensitivity, I'll admit, but with the absolute assurance that you won't be risking AIDS or any other sexually transmitted disease.

I must repeat, though: never have unprotected oral sex with a man whose medical history is unknown to you. He might be bisexual, in which case he could have exposed himself to the risk of unprotected oral or anal sex with an HIV carrier. He might have taken drugs, and used HIV-contaminated needles. He might have required a blood transfusion, like the late Arthur Ashe, and unsuspectingly acquired the HIV virus from infected plasma.

Having said that, oral sex with a man you know and love can be a huge pleasure for both of you. Once they have become skillful at it, a large percentage of women say that they like it, and a considerable number of those say they "absolutely love it." "When I'm tired, and I don't feel like making love, I can make Jim come in just a few minutes. He feels better, and I feel better because I've been able to make him feel better. Swallow? Of course. Why not? It doesn't taste of very much, and it doesn't do you any harm, does it?"

Here are some of the basic techniques of oral sex. You can try one or all of them the next time you're making love to your partner. You'll soon discover from experience which technique gives your partner the most pleasure.

Flicking the head of his penis very quickly with the tip of your tongue, concentrating mainly on the opening and the sensitive frenum just beneath it. You can flick your tongue all the way down the shaft of his penis and back up again, but don't make those downward forays last too long or the tingling sensation that you have been building up in the head of his penis will start to recede.

Sucking should be lascivious but reasonably gentle. When you're sucking, do it to a regular rhythm, moving your head backward and forward so that he also has the sensation that he's making love to your mouth. You can enhance or vary sucking by flicking the underside of his penis with the tip of your tongue. Many men find it very arousing if you make loud sucking noises while you give them oral sex ... as if you're really relishing what you're doing (as you should be!).

Blowing can be highly erotic ... flatten your tongue against the floor of your mouth, open your mouth wide and use your lips to stimulate the head of his penis while you gently huff out air onto it. Never blow directly into the opening of your lover's penis ... there is a remote but real risk that you could cause physical damage or even an embolism (an air bubble in the bloodstream).

Licking is highly visible and very stimulating. Use your entire tongue to give him swirling licks around the head of his penis ... then flatten your tongue against the underside of his shaft and lick him wetly all the way up to the head again. Lick his balls and his anus, but don't forget to keep stimulating his penis while you do so, using your fingers—or by pressing it against your face or entwining it in your hair.

Biting can be exciting, especially when you are both very aroused, but remember that his penis is extremely sensitive, and overenthusiastic biting could cause bruising or even tissue damage. It's better to take sharp little nips of the loose skin around the base of the head, followed by a series of soft "chewing" type bites all the way down the shaft. Then take the entire penis head into your mouth as if you're going to sink your teeth right into it. That's what they call a mixture of pleasure and sheer fear!

Squeezing is achieved by taking as much of his penis into your mouth as you can comfortably manage, and then pressing it rhythmically against the roof of your mouth with your tongue . . . adding to the erotic sensation by probing into his urethra from time to time with your tongue tip. You can combine squeezing with a gentle chewing motion of your jaws.

Rubbing him to a climax with nothing but your lips can be hard work, but he won't soon forget it! The easiest way is to kneel next to him while he's lying on his back, grasp the shaft of his penis firmly and take the head into your mouth, keeping your tongue flat so that when you bob your head up and down, his penis is stimulated only by your lips. Do this as quickly as you can, making sure that your lips make maximum contact with the sensitive area where the head joins the shaft. It may take a little time, but the gradually-rising feeling of excitement which this technique induces can be shattering.

Most women who give their partners oral sex tend to overestimate the sensitivity of their penises, and therefore believe that their kisses and licks are stimulating their partner much more than they really are. Of course the visual stimulus is very intense; but women should remember that men thrust very forcefully when they are making love, and that they rub themselves very briskly whenever they masturbate.

Because they do not "instantly" bring their partners to a climax, women often become bored and discouraged with a sexual act which they may not have been particularly enthusiastic about trying in the first place. They give up far too soon and are then reluctant to try it again—many of them believing that "I'm just no good at it anyway."

Another mistake they make is to keep varying their technique and their rhythm every few seconds. Just as they are beginning to produce a rising feeling of sexual arousal by rhythmically sucking, they change to flicking, and then switch to licking. While each of these techniques can be extremely pleasurable in itself, the effect of chopping and changing from one to the other is to keep delaying the buildup toward ejaculation—and therefore prolonging the whole act to the point where the man becomes frustrated and the woman becomes tired and loses interest.

Next time you arouse your partner orally, remember the way that *you* like him to lick your clitoris, especially when you're beginning to feel an orgasm on its way. You like it light, quick, and *consistent*, so that your whole being can concentrate on reaching a climax. That's the way your partner likes to be given oral sex, too. The rules of terrific oral sex are as follows:

Be demonstrative: Make a real show of sucking and relishing his penis, and while you're doing it, give him the opportunity to fondle you, too. If you kneel beside him, he'll be able to caress your breasts and nipples while you're licking him, and slide his fingers into your vagina. All sexual acts become more exciting if your partner gives you an obvious response, and if he's able to feel how juicy your vagina has become, it will stimulate him even more, and thus hasten his climax. It will stimulate you, too, so that when he's finished *his* climax, you'll be more than ready for yours.

You don't have to swallow if you don't want to, and

your partner shouldn't force you to. But there are plenty of spectacular ways in which you can spray his sperm around that will satisfy him just as much, if not more, because they'll always give him a highly erotic mental picture to remember. You may have noticed that in sex videos, men almost invariably take their penises out of their partners before they ejaculate, so that their climax is visible. Men find it both erotic and gratifying to watch themselves shooting out sperm, and if you can find a way to make that moment even more memorable, then you'll be going a long way to making his dreams come true.

Suzie, a 22-year-old receptionist from Seattle, told me, "The first time I gave Steve oral sex, I wasn't at all sure about swallowing his sperm. By the time he climaxed, I was so turned on that I think I might have done it, but somehow I held back. He said, 'I'm coming!' so I took his cock out of my mouth and gave it two or three rubs with my hand. His sperm really poured out, all over my hands. I don't know what made me do it, but I massaged it into the palms of my hands, and then I smeared it all over my cheeks and my forehead, as if it was Oil of Olay. Actually, I think it's good for the complexion, because I've done that three or four times now, and my skin's perfect."

Jennifer, a 28-year-old beautician from Houston, said, "I don't give Charles oral sex very often. I guess I should do it more, but I don't really care for it too much, to tell you the truth. I don't mind kissing his cock, I like doing that. But most of the time, oral sex is just him sitting down with my head bobbing up and down in his lap, like forever. Once or twice it's been good, though—and when it was good it was very, very good. I remember Christmas last year, we'd been to a party and we came back in a *very* good mood. Charles undressed and fell back on the bed, and I took off my dress and climbed onto the bed next to him, still wearing my black bra and panties. I kissed him and ran my hands through his chest hair, and then my hand strayed down to his cock. It kind of half-rose up, so I slid farther down the bed and I kissed it, and took it into my mouth. You should have felt the way it swelled up then—it almost choked me! But I was so turned on, I loved it. I sucked it and rubbed up and Charles was moaning because he loved it so much. Right at the end, he started pumping out sperm, and the first squirt of it I took in my mouth. I didn't swallow it, I just let it dribble out of my lips and down my chin. But then I took his cock out of my mouth and let him squirt all over my black bra, first one breast and then the other, so that there was sperm dripping off the black lace. He cupped his hands over my breasts and I could feel his warm, wet sperm soaking through to my nipples. Then he sat up and kissed me, and said that I was the sexiest woman alive. You couldn't wish your man to say much more than that, now could you?"

Twenty-six-year-old Paula, a graphic designer from Milwaukie, Oregon, wrote to tell me that "My husband Bob is a musician and he always promised me that as soon as his first record was released, he'd buy me a pearl necklace. Life has been very tough for him, and last Thursday night I tried to make him feel better by cooking him his favorite meal (rib steak with french fries) and giving him a real romantic evening. After dinner we were sitting by the fire, and I started to kiss and cuddle him. I knelt down on the floor in front of him and opened his pants. He said, 'What are you doing?' and I said, 'I'm still hungry, I need some more meat.' I took his cock out of his shorts. It wasn't hard to begin with, but when I kissed it and licked it, it started to grow. I pretended that I was this real experienced prostitute who could drive any man wild. I gave him the blow job to end all blow jobs, believe me. I sucked his cock, and every time I sucked it I ran my tongue around it, and I kind of rolled my hips so that it looked like that suck had gone all the way down me. I was turning myself on, too! His cock grew harder and bigger, and when I reached inside his shorts his balls were so tight they felt like two walnuts. I had only just started fondling his balls when he said, 'Oh, God,' and he suddenly came. I held his cock in my hand so that he spurted his spunk all around my neck, in a semicircle. Then I said, 'There, you've given me a pearl necklace already, the best there is.' After that we sat by the fire and I didn't wipe it off. I just let it dry there. I guess I wanted him to know that his love meant more to me than anything he could have bought for me."

What had often struck me about oral sex is that once a woman manages to overcome any aversion that she may have to it, and has become really skillful at exciting her lover with her mouth, her sexual relationship seems to become much more affectionate and intimate, and she feels that she has much more control over her own satisfaction. And the great thing is that men love it, and simply don't realize that once your mouth has taken charge of their penis, you have also taken control of the frequency, intensity, pace, and style of your lovemaking. Even if he does realize it, he won't care, because you'll be giving him more pleasure than he's ever had before.

Be creative: There are dozens of ways in which you can introduce added excitement into your oral sex sessions. Licking and sucking and biting and squeezing are only the beginning. You can add visual stimulation by sucking your partner's cock close to a mirror, or by having him take Polaroid pictures while you're doing it, and showing them to you while you're still doing it. Oral sex sessions make tremendous hom evi-deo, too. As Anne, 29, from Birmingham, Alabama, wrote, "When I saw myself with my boyfriend's huge Technicolor cock in my mouth, I was amazed. I watched that video over and over for a week, and each time I couldn't stop myself from masturbating. You should have seen the end of it. I'm still sucking and then sperm comes spraying out of my nose."

The "nose trick," as it's called, was popular in Ber-lin brothels in the 1930s. It's spectacular, but not rec-ommended for any woman with sinus problems. As your partner climaxes in your mouth, all you have to do is snort his semen up into your nasal cavities and blow it out of your nose. I'm making no judgments or recommendations about this particular technique: some women can do it, and enjoy it—others think it's repulsive. The choice is yours.

Heat and cold add two more dimensions to oral sex. If you fill your mouth with ice water or ice cubes before you go down on your partner, your mouth will give him an extraordinary chill. Or else you can warm up your mouth with hot chocolate, and see how he likes an extra-warm, extra-sweet sucking.

Gemma, 31, a homemaker from Rockville, Mary-land, said, "Dean and I were eating platefuls of spa-ghetti out on the porch swing one evening. Dean had been away for two weeks and he kept saying that he didn't know what he missed most, home cooking or sex. So I put down my plate and unbuttoned his jeans and took out his cock. I said, 'You don't have to make up your mind, you can have both.' And I bent over in front of that porch swing and I took his cock into my mouth and I masturbated it and sucked it, and Dean thought he'd died and gone to heaven. When he was really turned on, I stopped sucking his cock for a moment and took a mouthful of spaghetti. Then I went down on him again, and I churned all of that spaghetti all around his cock. He said that he'd never felt anything like it: it was like making love to a bowlful of live eels. He came, and I didn't even realize that he'd come, not until his cock started to shrink, and the spaghetti began to taste kind of salty. I'd never swallowed before, but I did this time. It was only food, after all, with a little sperm seasoning."

Other foods that can lend added frisson to oral sex include oatmeal cookies (the coarser, the better), Doritos, macadamia nuts, honey, and chili peppers. Bite into a jalapeño before you start oral sex, and while your mouth may blaze, his penis will, too! If you can't tolerate that much heat, masturbate him by hand with extra-hot chili powder. His cock will feel as if it has died and been sent to hell to stoke the furnaces ... but he'll have an extraordinary climax.

Try and think of unusual places and positions in which you can have oral sex. Open his pants anywhere and everywhere. Encourage him to understand that when he lives with you, he's expected to give you sexual satisfaction as and when you want it—*now,* not tomorrow morning, or next week, or next month. If he's lying on his stomach, sit astride the small of his back, facing his feet, pull apart the cheeks of his buttocks (as far as humanly possible) and start to give him an especially wriggly licking all around his anus and his balls. Before you know it, he'll be turning over and begging for it, guaranteed.

Use anal penetration in conjunction with oral sex. Men are highly responsive to anal stimulation, even the most macho of them. If you touch your own anus with your fingertips, and feel the pleasure that it gives you, then you'll have some inkling of what it feels like for your partner: delicious! Start with only one well-lubricated finger, and take it very, very easy. Your partner will probably be wildly responsive, and enjoy every minute of it, but you have to bear in mind that some men still believe that any form of anal stimulation is perverted and "wrong."

"My husband thought that when I put my finger up his ass I was trying to imply that he was gay. In fact, I just wanted to put my finger up inside a part of him where I'd never explored before. I wanted to *know* him, not only the outside, but the inside. It always sounds kind of yecch! when you talk about it cold, but it's the only way that a woman can penetrate a man without using any special kind of sex aid. He tried to twist away from me, but I said 'Ssh, and relax ... you'll enjoy it.'

"He lay back and I slowly slid my index finger up his asshole. At first he was very tight, his muscles were clenched, he was resisting me. There was my finger, halfway up his ass, and I could see his asshole clenching, trying to push me out. But when I drew my finger out a ways, and slid it back in again, his muscles relaxed, and I was able to push it in right to the knuckle. I could tell he liked it because of the way he shifted his ass around, as if he was encouraging me to push my finger in deeper.

"I drew my finger out again, right out, and waited for a moment. He said, 'Don't stop,' and that was when I knew how much he wanted it. I slid my finger inside, and then a second finger, so that I was able to stretch his asshole even wider. Once I had two fingers inside him, I licked all around his asshole, then I licked his balls, and at last I came around to licking his cock. He was so hard, and juice was literally streaming out of him. I worked my fingers harder and deeper into his asshole, then I worked my thumb in, too. He was grunting and groaning, and I knew that I was hurting him, but it was one of those hurts that he really wanted. I twisted my fingers around and around, and pushed deeper and deeper into his ass. He opened up his legs for me, like he wanted me to rape him, almost.

"It was out of this world. I mean, when you're a woman, you expect your lover to penetrate you. You don't expect to penetrate your lover. I never knew that men liked to be fingered up the ass until I read one of your books, and I guess that was when I first wanted to try it. It worked, it really worked! I was screwing his ass with three fingers and sucking his cock at the same time, and he climaxed like a flood. I didn't have time to decide if I wanted to swallow or not. He just filled up my mouth with warm, slippery sperm, and that was it.

"Now we both enjoy anal stimulation when we're having oral sex ... whether my husband is licking me or I'm licking him. I like it when he pushes four fingers up my asshole, two index fingers and two middle fingers, and stretches my asshole wide apart. Sometimes he gently blows into it, and sometimes he sticks his tongue up it. I always make sure I get my revenge! I bought a long thin vibrator and pushed it up his ass when he was least expecting it—right in the middle of making love!—and another time I opened up his asshole with two fingers, as wide as I could, and poured a whole glass of cold sparkling wine into it. I guess he was one of the first men in history to have a champagne enema!''

If you want to make your man's wildest dreams come true, never forget about oral sex and never forget about anal stimulation. If you don't feel like using your fingers, there are numerous sex aids available by mail order which are specifically designed for safe anal stimulation. Of course, almost all dildos and vibrators will fit into a willing anus, from the world-famous "Mr. Softee" (the traveling 6 inch vibrating dildo ... realistic supersoft multispeed vibrating phallus with *tingling testes!!*) To "Thin Lizzie" (8½ inches of erect phallic-shaped latex dildo, which slips into the tightest areas and throbs and reverberates through you with merciless vibrations). But there are many products that are specifically designed for safe anal stimulation, including Thai love beads, a string of vinyl beads which you insert bead by bead into your lover's anus during oral sex, and then rapidly drag out while he climaxes. Then there's the Anal Placater, a vibrator with a thin, knobbly, flexible shaft, which vibrates and oscillates inside his rectum until he's more than ready to ejaculate. There is even an anal vibrator which looks exactly like a very long finger.

Usually, anal sex of any kind is initiated by men. They have a strong natural urge to penetrate the woman they love in any way they can—and, yes, to be fair, they want to feel that they have "conquered" them. This doesn't mean for a moment that they regard them as intellectually, emotionally, or physically inferior: it's simply a powerful need to see their erect penis buried in either their vagina, their mouth, or their anus—proof of sexual possession. There is nothing aggressive or chauvinistic in this behavior (except, of course, when it is done against a woman's will). It is a perfectly normal way to express the way a man feels sexually about a woman who attracts him.

What's more, we have already seen that the reality of sexual "conquest" is very different than it first appears. A woman can exercise a tremendous amount of control over her love life through oral sex; and she can do the same with anal sex. If *you* initiate anal stimulation into your relationship before your lover does, you will make one of his wildest dreams come true. *He* will have wanted it, I can guarantee it, but if he hasn't tried it yet, that's only because he hasn't had the nerve. Let Anna, a 27-year-old journalist from Los Angeles, tell you how *she* used both oral and anal sex to change her love life "literally overnight."

"George and I had been living together for seven, maybe eight months. He was five years older than me but he might just as well have been 50. When we first dated it was great, because he knew all of the cool places to go, and we were rubbing shoulders with movie stars almost every night—well, sitting in the same restaurants, anyhow. He was a good lover, very considerate. He always made sure that I climaxed, and he always brought me a glass of wine afterward. Some women would cut off their legs for a men like George. One evening we went to the opera and then we walked by the ocean and I decided on the spur of the moment to move in with him. I loved him. I loved him so much. I really did.

"But once I'd moved into his apartment, all of the color seemed to drain out of our relationship. Instead of being this debonair man-about-town, he was just a strange guy standing buck-naked in the bathroom, brushing his teeth. He was just as considerate in bed, but I was so tired of 'considerate.' I wanted to feel that we were going someplace, that our relationship was blossoming, instead of wilting.

"I was right on the verge of leaving him. That was when my friend lent me one of your books ... and you kept saying that women have the power to change their sexual relationships. You kept saying that women have all the influence, when it comes to making love, and that men are usually too embarrassed to initiate the sexual acts they really want. You know, like BJs or backdoor sex, or whatever.

"One night I did both. He was lying back in bed reading this company report, and I crawled across the bed and opened his bathrobe. He said something like, 'Not now, Anna, I'm busy.' But then I took his cock into my mouth and I slowly, slowly started to suck it. He said, 'Anna—' but then he didn't say anything else. His cock rose up like One Century Plaza. I massaged his balls and slurped at his cock. My saliva was running down it, and dripped between his balls. His cock was standing up like I'd never seen it before—all curved and hard and flaming red at the tip. I went on sucking it, and then I reached down between the cheeks of his ass and started stroking his anus with my fingertip.

"He took a breath, and his anus tightened at first, but he didn't make any move to stop me. I could hear him panting a little, like he was jogging, and I knew that I had him hooked. It was a great feeling, to think that *I* was in control, that *I* was playing the dominant role and *he* was playing the passive role. It was a great feeling to think that I could do whatever I wanted— I could bring him to a climax with my mouth, if I wanted to, or I could climb on top of him and start fucking him, or I could simply stop in the middle and pick up a book, and leave him frustrated. *He* would never have done that to me. He was always too 'considerate.' But, like I said, sometimes you don't want 'considerate': you want passion and frustration and excitement and dirty behavior.

"I sucked his cock with long, deep sucks. I looked up at him the way he was looking back at me ... well, if an advertising agency ever needed a picture of a man who's recently arrived in heaven! I took his cock out of my mouth and gave it a really showy licking, like it wasn't a cock at all, but my favorite flavor of Häagen-Dazs. I licked my finger, too, until it was all slippery and wet, and pushed it into his anus. He closed his eyes for a moment when I did that, and just said, 'Oh—'.

"His anus was very tight at first, and it was difficult to get my finger very far inside because he kept clenching his muscles. The more I sucked his cock, though, the more he started to relax, and soon I was able to slide my finger right in, and wiggle it around. Then I slid in another finger, and wiggled the two of them together.

"He said, 'Anna ... I shouldn't be doing this ... I should be checking my report ...' So I looked up and said, 'You don't like it?' He said, 'It's wonderful, it's just that I have so much to do.' I don't know what inspired me. My Irish temper, I guess! But I took my fingers out of his anus, and took hold of his report, and rolled it up tight. He said, 'What the hell are you doing? I have to read that!' He tried to sit up but I pushed him back. I took a condom out of the Mexican dish beside the bed, and opened it, and rolled it over his report. Then I climbed astride him, so my ass was in his face, and he couldn't see what I was doing, and I took his cock into my mouth again, and rubbed it, and gave it some more good sucking because it was starting to bend ... you know, Mr. Softee! I opened the cheeks of his ass with my fingers. He was already looking red, and a little sore. But I took hold of that rolled-up report and I slowly forced it into his anus.

"His first reaction was to tighten his muscles, but then I guess he gave in to it. All rolled up like that, inside a condom, that report was even thicker than his cock, but I managed to push it into his ass, and he managed to take it. As a matter of fact he opened his legs wider to make it easier for me to push it in. I was amazed how much he could take ... it must have been six or seven inches. I actually fucked him with it, pushing it in and out. His anus was all stretched and red, so I licked around it with the tip of my tongue to wet it some more. He didn't seem to mind, though. He was clutching my hair with one hand and gripping the bedcover with the other, and his cock was so hard that I almost thought it was going to burst. I fucked him harder and harder, deeper and deeper. His balls practically disappeared up inside his body. I kept thinking: this is incredible, I'm fucking a man, rather than a man fucking me. Then he climaxed, without any warning at all, and his sperm jumped all over my face and everywhere.

"I took the report out of his ass very carefully, because he looked so sore. I unrolled the condom and gave it back to him, and kissed him, and then I said, 'There ... you can tell everybody at work that the best thing to do with this report is to shove it up their ass.' "

Anna reported that, after this incident, her sex life with George became "infinitely more varied ... infinitely more interesting." It completely broke down the barriers of sexual reticence between them, and eliminated what Anna called "the curse of being polite to each other." She didn't use any more of George's business reports to give him anal stimulation, but she did buy a long, thin vibrator specially made for "rear-entry arousal."

Her use of a rolled-up document is not as unusual as you might think. Many phone-in masturbation services recommend that callers equip themselves with a rolled-up newspaper with a wet end so that they can penetrate themselves anally during their calls. Obviously a specially-made dildo or vibrator is more effective and more hygienic, and there is less danger of tearing any of his delicate rectal membranes.

Many women are amazed to discover that their partner's anus is such an erogenous zone . . . especially since most men are reluctant to suggest that they might enjoy it. But the anus itself is richly supplied with nerve endings, and if you penetrate your partner's rectum with a finger or a vibrator, you are applying internal pressure onto his prostate—the gland that produces the mucus in which his spermatazoa swim. If you insert your finger or thumb into your partner's anus, and then press rhythmically downward toward the front wall of his rectum, you should be able to bring him to a very strong and unusual climax, in which his sperm will "flow" out of his penis rather than be violently ejaculated.

All mail-order suppliers of sex aids sell strap-on dildos—which, contrary to popular belief, and contrary to the way in which they are marketed, are used mainly by women who want to have anal intercourse with their lovers, not by lesbians. For instance, there's the "Double Cummer—a 8½ inch long latex dildo, designed to be worn by a woman to make love to another woman . . . powerful multispeed vibrating action . . . at the base is a vaginal 'wedge' covered in latex spikes which can be pressed hard into the wearer's clitoris ... the throbbing vibrating super-firm penis may then be used to mount her partner and satisfy her better than any man could." Double-ended dildos are also available—long, flexible latex penises with a head at each end, so that, during intercourse, you can insert one end into your anus and your partner can insert the other end into his.

Perhaps the most elaborate of all dildos is the Lesbian Trilogy, *three* vibrating penises in different shapes and sizes all flexibly connected together at the base—"now two or three ladies can 'get off' at the same time on the dildo of their choice ... or one lady can choose the penis she wants tonight while using one of the others for anal stimulation ... the uses are infinite." Personally I found the Lesbian Trilogy to be more of a puzzle than a sex aid, a kind of erotic Rubik's Cube, and it reminded me of the rhyme that ends *"they argued all night/over who had the right/to do what/and with which/and to whom."*

All of the devices available for female anal stimulation are equally suitable for male stimulation, too, so if you *do* want to make a strong sexual impact on the man in your life, there is no question that anal arousal will do the trick. A few do's and don'ts, though: make sure that your fingernails are well-clipped before inserting them into your partner's anus; don't insert any object that could cause laceration or that could become "lost" inside his rectum; do use plenty of lubricant—either your natural vaginal lubricant (if it's sufficiently profuse) or a proprietary brand such as K-Y; do wash your hands afterward—you are unlikely to encounter any fecal matter in your partner's rectum unless you probe very deeply indeed, but it still abounds with bacteria. Above all, do not insert your fingers directly into your vagina after anal play, and don't allow your partner to do it, either, if he's been giving you anal stimulation.

Even if you don't yet feel that you and your partner are ready for anal sex, you should try to make oral sex a regular and enjoyable part of your love life. You'll start to feel the benefits from the first moment you do it.

Elaine, a 24-year-old medical trainee from Chicago, says that oral sex is "the greatest way of having a sexual relationship without committing yourself . . . it's like play, really. If you feel like it, you can carry on and make love fully, or you can leave it as a casual blow job, it's up to you."

Elaine was vacationing in Fort Lauderdale with a female friend when she met four men—"and they were all great, I liked them all. There was Rick who was dark-haired and very muscular and neat; then there was Larry who was black and very tall and terrific-looking; then Dave who was your real blond-haired surfing type; and Gary, who was thin and thoughtful, with this beautiful dark curly hair—the rest of them called him 'Professor.'

"My friend had a date with this guy she'd met from Syracuse, so one Friday night I was left all on my own. We'd met the guys on the beach right on the first day of our vacation so we knew where they were staying. I went around to their apartment and they were all sitting around drinking big bottles of wine and watching TV, so I asked if I could join them. They said sure, they were going out later, and I could come with them. So I just sat down between Rick and Dave in the middle of this couch, and they poured me a glass of wine, and we started talking.

"I don't know how many glasses of wine I'd had—

not too many—but then Dave put his arm around me and said that I was real pretty ... the prettiest girl he'd seen in three summers. Rick started joking and saying 'Hands off, I saw her first!'—all that kind of banter. So Dave said, 'I'm going to stake my claim, I'm going to give her a kiss.' Well ... he was real handsome and tanned and I don't know many girls who would have objected to kissing him. First of all he gave me a peck, but then a peck turned into something a little more.

"Of course, Rick objected to that, so Rick gave me a kiss, too. I guess you could say that I was being too easy, but it was a hot night in Fort Lauderdale and I *was* on vacation, and all of these guys were fun and good-looking, and I *had* drunk two or three glasses of wine ...

"Anyhow, Dave wanted another kiss; and then Larry came over and said he wasn't going to miss out on any of this, he wanted one, too. He was such a beautiful kisser, it was like kissing velvet, and the things that his tongue did to my teeth, it makes them tingle when I talk about it! Gary hadn't come over, he was shyer than the other guys, but I called out to him and asked him to give me a kiss, too—like, we were living in a democracy.

"He gave me such a gentle kiss ... long and slow and lingering. But when he was finished, Dave pointed to these little blue briefs he was wearing, and said, 'You're in *love,* man, I can see it!' He had such a huge hard-on that his cock was practically coming out over the top of his waistband. They were all laughing at him and his face was so red he looked like he was on fire. I felt so sorry for him ... I took hold of his hand and said, 'Here, we can soon fix that.'

"Even today, I don't know how I had the nerve to do it, but like I say, it was vacation time, and you don't always live by the same rules when you're on vacation, do you? I pulled down the waistband of Gary's briefs, and out came his cock. It was standing straight up, and it was bobbing up and down slightly because of his pulse. A beautiful big, thick fully-hard cock, looking me right in the eye. I took hold of it in my hand, while the other guys all watched in absolute amazement, and I kissed it . . . a long, slow kiss, just like the kiss that he had given me. His cock was wonderful. He must have been swimming because it tasted of sea salt. I closed my eyes and I took the whole head of it into my mouth, and all I could hear was the other guys letting out this long, long breath and saying, 'Man . . .'

"I opened my eyes again, and Dave had opened up his shorts and taken out his cock, too. He just smiled at me and he looked so much like a little boy who's expecting a prize for being good, I couldn't resist him, and his cock was fat and bright pink, like a sugar cock. I bent down and kissed his cock, too, and sucked it, and circled my tongue around it. I gripped the head of his cock between my teeth and raised my head, so that I was stretching his cock upward, as far as it would go, and he really groaned. When I let him go, I found that Larry was standing close to me, with *his* cock out, too—this long black cock with its foreskin half-rolled back.

"I didn't need asking. I was completely into this now. I kissed the tip of his cock and then I rolled back his foreskin with my lips. I held his balls in one hand, and slowly massaged them, and at the same time I flicked the head of his cock with my tongue, really fast, so that it made him shiver.

"After that it was Rick's turn. He was so impatient that he had taken off his jeans and his shorts and he was standing right next to Larry bare-assed naked, with his cock in his hand. He had a long thin cock, olive-colored, very Italian-looking, with a dark purple head. I liked sucking Rick. His cock wasn't so fat that it choked me, I could take it right down my throat, until his pubic hair was tickling my face, and he had these beautiful oval balls with long hairs on them.

"I knelt on the couch and all four of them stripped off and stood in front of me. I had *four* cocks to suck, and it was amazing. It was like a dream. I made them stand real close together, two and two, so that I could hold two cocks in my left hand and two cocks in my right hand. I opened my lips up real wide and I managed to get two cocks into my mouth at once, just about— two hard rubbery cocks both trying to push their way into my mouth. If I was going to suffocate, that was the best way to go. Then I took the other two cocks into my mouth, while the first two guys masturbated.

"Rick tried to undress me, and said that he wanted to fuck me—he wanted all four of them to fuck me, all at once. 'Just think about it,' he said, 'two in your mouth and one in your pussy and another one up your ass, four guys all at once.' But I didn't want to do that. This was all that I wanted, you know, like a game.

"It didn't take very long before Larry said that he was coming. He was beating his cock harder and harder, he couldn't stop himself, he just needed to come. The others were close to climaxing too. So I knelt down right in the middle of them, while they masturbated, and I reached out and fondled thighs and balls and asses, until suddenly it was raining sperm. Great thick jets of it, spurting out of the ends of their cocks. They shot all over me, all over my hair, all over my shoulders, all over my T-shirt. I even had sperm dripping from my ears.

"They all collapsed after that, and lay there, with

these four wet penises gradually going soft on their thighs. I went around and I kissed all of them on the mouth, one by one, and that was the best time I ever had, as far as oral sex is concerned. You see, there was no commitment. I didn't fuck any of them. I treated them all equal. We played a sexy game and that was it. But it really made me realize how much men love having their cocks sucked ... you could do it all night every night and they wouldn't say no. And it also made me realize that women have terrific power, when it comes to sex. They should never let themselves be dominated."

That is, of course, unless they actually *want* to be dominated, which brings us to the next stage in developing your Sexual Character. Is she going to be dominant, or is she going to be submissive—or is she going to alternate between the two?

These days, more and more couples are confessing an interest in sadomasochism (S&M). They are joining S&M clubs, subscribing to fetish magazines, and practicing a variety of sadomasochistic acts such as bondage, whipping, and playing out fantasies of domination and submission.

Afraid? You needn't be. Most of the couples with whom I spoke when I was preparing this book were mild and ordinary people who had simply found a way of making some of their sexual dreams come true. There were very few "heavy-duty" sadomasochists ... and by that I mean people who needed genuine pain in order to achieve sexual satisfaction. But there were a strikingly large number of lovers who felt the need for some kind of mistress/slave play-acting, along with some remarkable dressing-up and tying-up, as well as spanking, nipple-clamping, body-piercing, and shoe-licking.

Let's see how a minority sexual taste has suddenly become mainstream, and how you could use S&M fantasies to enhance your love life ... if you dare!

Questionnaire
Is He a Dom or a Sub?

A "dom," as you'd expect, is someone who takes on the dominant role in a sexual relationship. A "sub" is the submissive partner. As we've seen, people can be both "dom" and "sub" at various times in their lives. A man who has a demanding office job that requires him to hire and fire people and to make major decisions will often prefer to be a "sub" when he comes home to his wife. He's tired of ordering his staff around; he feels guilty about all of those people he has had to hurt. He's exhausted from shouldering all of that responsibility. What he needs is a woman who's going to take charge of him, tell him what to do, and punish him for being a naughty boy.

A classic example: I spent hours touring the home of Monique von Cleef, the notorious sadomasochistic madame of the 1970s, and she showed me such apparatus as a three-legged milking stool on which a Dutch chief of police (a tyrant to his colleagues and his family) was obliged to sit while Monique told him nursery stories. In the center of the milking stool was a huge erect wooden dildo that penetrated the sitter's anus. He was not allowed to leave the milking stool until Monique gave her permission.

Some of her more extreme devices included pulleys suspended from the ceiling. Clients would be given copious enemas, their anuses plugged, and then they would be hung upside-down, their legs and arms helplessly strapped, their heads covered in black PVC hoods, until "the mistress" decided it was time for them to be let down, and to relieve themselves.

Power and the lack of power are both erotic stimuli. Although the *real* act of rape is abhorrent, many woman have highly-arousing fantasies about being raped, often in the most humiliating of circumstances. Many men have fantasies about being helplessly bound while women whip them; or being forced to lick the soles of their shoes.

Anyone who is unable to achieve sexual satisfaction unless they are dressed in a particular way, or unless they have performed a particular ritual has a clinical sexual disorder. It may not be very severe, and if they can find like-minded partners to share their fetishes and their fantasies with them—they may never need any kind of psychosexual therapy. The American masochists' rights club Eulenspiegel has managed to have S&M fantasies removed from a list of pathological behavior in a medical textbook, and has won a ruling from a Brooklyn judge that "bootlicking, dominance and submission for money" do not constitute prostitution. All the same, many extreme sadomasochists live an extremely difficult and lonely existence, relying on fantasies and masturbation in order to achieve some semblance of sexual fulfillment.

But the sadomasochistic feelings that most people have are nonobsessive. There are thousands of completely normal people who belong to S&M clubs or who subscribe to S&M magazines and newsletters. They do it because it excites them, and there's a hint of something "forbidden" and "dirty" about it, but in reality they're more often concerned with coffee klatsches than nipple clamps. It's a way in which couples can socialize and mingle with other couples who are more sexually adventurous than most.

Niki, a 32-year-old editor of *Fetish Times* said, "Sadomasochism is extremely common—it's just that people don't realize it. Many people do it during sex as a matter of course—even holding onto someone's wrists is a mild form of S&M.

"I switch, which means that sometimes I'm submissive, sometimes I'm dominant. When I'm in a submissive mode, it means the responsibility for my sexual pleasure is in someone else's hands. But when I'm dominant, I get off on leading someone else through a sexual experience.

"Just because you're into S&M doesn't mean you don't have normal sex. For me, S&M is something special, like an exotic meal, it's not the center of my life.

"What I love most about S&M is the freedom—I can be anyone I want to be. It's like being a child again, playing 'let's pretend.' I can be turned on by pretending to be a divine goddess who demands to be worshipped or I can be a trembling slave girl."

S&M can bring imagination and experimentation back into your love life. It doesn't have to be painful. It doesn't have to be extreme. It depends on how far you and your Sexual Character feel prepared to go. As Niki said, "S&M relationships are extremely intense because you must have complete faith in your partner. Everybody has limits and it's the submissive person in an S&M relationship who sets the limits."

First, however, any couple who is interested in an S&M relationship or even just an S&M-*ish* relationship have to decide what they're going to do and how they're going to do it—"you don't just start whipping."

So here's a list of questions that will help you build a profile of your partner's sexual fantasies. Count how many D's he scores (for dominant) and compare them with how many S's he scores (for submissive). Then compare *his* fantasies with what you'd love to do, or like to do, or tolerate, or hate.

1. I would like to try tying up my partner during sex (YES - D; NO - S)

2. I would like to blindfold my partner during sex (YES - D; NO - S)

3. I would like my partner to spend the day completely naked while I remain clothed (YES - D; NO - S)

4. I would like my partner to play the part of a slave, fetching and carrying for me and obeying my slightest whim (YES - S; NO - D)

5. If my partner is disobedient, I would like to spank her or whip her (YES - S; NO - D)

6. I would like my partner to dress up in erotic clothing for me, such as short skirts, stockings, G-strings, split-crotch panties (YES - D; NO - S)

7. I would like my partner to dress up in rubber or leather clothing, especially restrictive clothing, such as high leather dog collars, tight corsets, and stiletto boots (YES - D; NO - S)

8. I would like my partner to give me oral sex whenever I demand it (YES - D; NO - S)

9. I would like my partner to submit to anal sex whenever I demand it (YES - D; NO - S)

10. I would like my partner to give me a sexual "show"—dancing and exposing herself (YES - D; NO - S)

11. I would like my partner to masturbate herself to orgasm in front of me (YES - D; NO - S)

12. I would like to play the part of my partner's master, disciplining her whenever she displeases me (YES - D; NO - S)

13. I would like to show other people that I am completely in charge of our relationship by disciplining her in front of other people—such as, by attaching a dog collar to her neck (YES - D; NO - S)

14. I would like my partner to decorate her body with jewelry, such as navel rings or nipple rings (YES - D; NO - S)

15. I would like my partner to wear a tattoo saying that she belongs to me (YES - D; NO - S)

16. I would like to try putting my partner into bondage—blindfolding, gagging, and tying her up (YES - D; NO - S)

17. I would like my partner to display herself to me while she urinates (YES - D; NO - S)

18. I would like to urinate over my partner's sexual parts (YES - D; NO - S)

19. I would like my partner to urinate over me (YES - S; NO - D)

20. I would like my partner to tie me to the bed during sex (YES - S; NO - D)

21. I would like to my partner to force me to walk around naked while she remains fully clothed (YES - S; NO - D)

22. I would like to be a slave to my partner, cleaning and running errands and doing everything she asks me (YES - S; NO - D)

23. I expect my partner to whip me if I disobey her or contradict her in any way (YES - S; NO - D)

24. I would like to lick my partner's shoes (YES - S; NO - D)

25. I would like to give my partner oral sex when-

ever she demanded it, day or night (YES - S; NO - D)

26. I would like to dress up in women's underwear and serve my partner as a maid (YES - S; NO - D)

27. I would like to dress in rubber or leather bondage clothing (YES - S; NO - D)

28. I would submit to wearing restrictive straps on my sexual parts (YES - S; NO - D)

29. I would wear nipple rings or other intimate jewelry if my partner demanded it (YES - S; NO - D)

30. I would submit to being completely subservient to my partner in public, allowing her to order meals in restaurants, and giving me a tongue-lashing whenever I displeased her (YES - S; NO - D)

31. I would wear a tattoo declaring that I was my partner's property (YES - S; NO - D)

32. I would like my partner to put me into total bondage, with helmet, blindfold, gag, and other restrictive clothing (YES - S; NO - D)

33. I would like to give my partner an open display of masturbation to climax (YES - S; NO - D)

34. I would submit to my partner giving me anal sex with a dildo or similar object (YES - S; NO - D)

35. I would submit to my partner giving me a limited amount of pain during sex—such as sticking needles into my nipples (YES - S; NO - D)

36. I would like to inflict a limited amount of pain on my partner during sex—such as attaching clamps to her nipples (YES - D; NO - S)

37. I would like my partner to dress in dominant

clothing (such as high leather boots, leather straps, and chains) (YES - S; NO - D)

38. I would like to play a sexual game in which I am a victim in a torture chamber and my partner is the torturer (YES - S; NO - D)

All of these questions relate to very common S&M practices that are done every day of the week by perfectly ordinary men and women. On the whole, they are not sexually disturbed—they simply have discovered what they call the "freedom" of being able to act out their erotic fantasies quite openly.

Sadie, who runs a mail-order fetish catalog with her partner Steve, said, "S&M is great for a couple's relationship and sex life because it introduces imagination and respect, and sex becomes more than just a quick bonk."

She herself said she'd been into S&M so long that "we've had enough of dressing up ... but Steve and I still have a sub-dom relationship. He calls me madam."

There is something of the sadist and the masochist in every one of us. Most of us don't feel the need to act out full-blown S&M games, complete with whips and rubber stockings—but, in a way, all of our relationships have some ingredient of domination or submission, or a complicated combination of the two.

If your partner was *very* honest when he answered the preceding questions, you should now have an accurate picture of the kind of man he is, sexually speaking. Remember, however, that these questions are all hypothetical, and just because he says he likes the idea of seeing you in nipple clamps, that doesn't mean he's serious about doing it for real (By the way, the economy-minded *Fetish Times* recommends clothespins instead of professional-quality nipple clamps ... they're less expensive and less embarrassing to buy.)

In most S&M relationships, the woman is the dominant partner. The reasons for this are psychologically complicated, but one of the major underlying causes is that men derive emotional relief and sexual pleasure from abandoning their career- and their decision-making responsibilities for a while and becoming completely submissive. Women, on the other hand, are able to express their sexuality and the depth of their imagination in an S&M situation without their usual fear of embarrassment or criticism.

Quite honestly, women are better at S&M than men. Many dominant men see it as an excuse for abusing their partner in a way they wouldn't normally dare. But as Sadie said, "There's a caring way to dominate someone; it may not be a sexual turn-on but it's not necessarily about sexual acts. Women are better at dominating men without it being sexually based."

With a little mild S&M, you can certainly make your partner's wildest, *wildest* dreams come true. But remember the golden rule: *never do anything against your will*. That's not what S&M is all about. S&M is about discovering new and exciting dimensions in your sexual relationship, about role-playing and self-expression and freeing yourself completely from your inhibitions.

Let's see how two different couples found that S&M whipped up new enthusiasm in their love lives.

SIX

Would You Be Bound to Please Him?

Right from the very beginning, I should make it clear that the kind of "therapeutic" S&M we're discussing here isn't the heavy-duty sadomasochism that you can find in some big-city clubs and private circles of those who share particularly extreme tastes in sex.

We're not talking about nailing your partner's scrotum to the chair he's sitting on; or dripping hot candlewax on your nipples. In fact, we're not talking about anything that could cause any kind of injury or lasting physical damage. Even if you're interested in the idea of erotic body jewelry, there are nipple chains and clitoral decorations on sale that don't require piercing to wear them—a little decorative item for weekend masochists, as it were.

The nipple chains are nothing more than gold chains with loops at each end. The loops can be tightened around your nipples so that even when they are not erect, the chains stay in place. They are described as giving you "lascivisious thrills through your nipples" when you're wearing them, but I haven't yet had a field report on that. You can also buy pearl and gemstone chains to dangle between your breasts.

The "clit clip" is simply a gold-plated clip that fits onto your vaginal lips, and from which dangle two short chains, with ruby-colored crystals on the end.

Real nipple- and navel-piercing has become increasingly fashionable in recent years, for both men and women, and a form of body decoration that was once considered a sexual perversion is now completely unremarkable, which shows just how liberal sexual attitudes have become in the 1990s. I have found scores of young women with pierced noses, lips, tongues, nipples, navels, and vaginal lips. Some of them are running out of places to pierce. I have also found young men with "mouth jewelry," bull rings through their nostrils, pierced nipples, and rings through their penises.

In Japan, incidentally, it has long been a recognized sexual practice for a man to have a pearl sewn into the shaft of his penis. Not only are pearls considered to have sexual "aura," the feeling of the pearl rubbing against the inside of her vagina is supposed to give a Japanese woman an extra erotic delight. Some men have rows of pearls inserted all the way down their penises, which intensifies sexual pleasure for both of them, and certainly gives a new definition to "pearl diving."

Piercing is one of the most obvious manifestations of S&M. It has very strong sexual connotations, as does tattooing, because it shows that you have marked yourself irrevocably in order to attract or arouse your partner. It also has strong social connotations, too—young people wear nose and lip jewelry to create a shock effect: those who are shocked by it should remember the same shock effect caused by young men wearing their hair over their collars for the first time.

Personally, I think that if sexual piercing is professionally done, there is no harm in it whatsoever, and some people derive a great deal of erotic excitement from it. Don't forget the "professionally," though: piercing and tattooing should both be done by qualified practitioners with sterile needles. You don't want to avoid HIV by making sure that your partners always wear condoms, and then put yourself at risk because you want a diamond stud in your vagina.

Rita, a 33-year-old singer from St. Louis, had been divorced from her first husband Don for more than two years before she met her second live-in partner Jeff, a 35-year-old auto dealer. Rita is a very vivacious and attractive woman, with curly dark hair, and a figure about which she says "eat your heart out, Dolly Parton." Her first husband was a depressive, and after he lost his job he began to drink. "I sent him to AA but he met another woman there and never came back. I cured him, but I lost him." She married Jeff in the belief that she had found "a real, solid reliable man."

She had. But the qualities of reality, solidity, and reliability soon began to bore her—especially at bedtime.

"You couldn't say that Jeff wasn't a kind lover, but he was such a *staid* lover. The trouble was, I respected him because he was so decent and upright and I didn't know how to say to him, 'Jeff, that was great, you lying on top of me and fucking me like that, but how about you get hot with me, give me some lovebites, suck my nipples, go down on me, stick your fingers where you shouldn't, that kind of thing?' I was even afraid to go down on him myself. I mean, I wasn't actually *afraid,* but I didn't have any kind of signals from Jeff that he wouldn't mind if I went ahead and did something like that, and that he might even do something back to me.

"It reached the point where we were arguing all the time. Most of the arguments were my fault, but the reason was that I was sexually frustrated. I think Jeff gave me one orgasm in 18 months, and that's not enough for a growing girl."

Rita's problem was that she was waiting for Jeff to initiate interesting sex. Her first husband may have been a depressive and a drinker, but he had always taken the lead when it came to lovemaking, and his taste in sex had included plenty of "romping around" and oral intercourse. Jeff simply didn't know how to do that; and what was more to the point, he didn't have the inclination to do it. He worked at his dealership from 6 A.M. until 7 P.M., directing a staff of 45, and by the time he came home in the evening the last thing he felt like doing was taking responsibility or initiating anything, including sex.

I suggested to Rita that Jeff's sexual interest *could* be aroused if she made the best of her existing difficulty rather than trying to meet it head-on. She should go with the flow, as it were, and make Jeff's submissiveness a *positive* part of their sexual relationship, rather than treating it as a problem. Rita's experience is shared by millions of women who live with a hardworking man, and in too many cases the relationship ends in separation or divorce, when it could have been revived by a little more understanding of what it is that men are *really* looking for when it comes to bedtime.

Women's point of view: Handsome, hair-chested

hunk emerges from bathroom, his teeth minty-fresh, his cock sticking out of the fly of his red-and-white-striped pajamas. He bounds across the room and takes his fragrant woman into his arms, and remembers to compliment her on her lacy negligee.

Man's point of view: He's lying flat on his back in bed when she stalks into the room wearing nothing but a skimpy outfit of leather straps and thigh boots. She snaps the end of his cock with her riding crop, and then she climbs on top of him, her boots squeaking, and demands "fuck me."

Rita decided that she *did* have a dominant streak in her sexual personality. She would take on a Sexual Character that could probably give her the confidence to introduce new and varied sexual acts into her relationship. She would play "Ms. Domina," and *tell* Jeff what she wanted in bed rather than waiting for him to suggest it—which probably would have been, she said, "when hell froze over."

She knew that it might not be easy to enliven her sex life, but in the guise of "Ms. Domina" she was prepared to give it a try. Even if the full S&M paraphernalia didn't appeal to Jeff, there was a good chance that he would find much in her positive, uninhibited approach that would give him satisfaction and relief, and help him to "unlock" his own fears about sex. And, believe me, men do have fears about sex, just as as women do, particularly when they're stressed or preoccupied, and everything depends on their performance.

Rita said, "I did some of that meditation that you suggested. I took off my clothes and sat in front of the mirror and looked at myself. I asked myself what I was and who I was and what I thought of myself. My first impression was a tired-looking woman with

messy hair and breasts that were far too big and heavy
. . . not to mention a waistline that could have used
some aerobics. I realized that I'd let myself go. Not
badly, but I'd slipped. There was a time when I always
used to make sure that my hair was perfect. There
was a time when my nails were always polished and
my makeup was always fresh. I used to be proud of
my breasts instead of thinking that they were some
kind of encumbrance.

"But you were right . . . sexual meditation sure
helps. I sat on my own and I thought about *me*—
what I wanted—not what anybody else wanted. And
I thought . . . I can do this, I can take charge of this.
If Jeff can't manage it, then I will. Because what's
the alternative? Watching your relationship gradually
falling apart, watching yourself growing older and
older and you're *still* not having any fun?

"I went to have my hair done. I had it cut short,
and quite severe, because that's the way that Ms. Domina would have her hair. I plucked my eyebrows, I
polished my nails, I shaved off all of my pubic hair.
I've been dying to get rid of that silly little bit of
brown fluff for years, and I never had the courage!
You don't walk around with hair under your arms, do
you? So why should you walk around with hair between your legs? Anyhow, I shaved it all off, and it
never felt better. Clean, free—and really *naked!* I have
to admit that after I'd done it, I masturbated, and
watched myself masturbating in the mirror. I have to
admit that I loved it, especially with a totally naked
cunt! I really wished that I'd bought a vibrator. I
would have loved to have seen that sliding in and out
of me.

"It's so liberating to think about sex and the kind
of loving you want . . . I mean to sit down naked and

do it deliberately. When I think of my mother's attitude toward sex ... she would never talk about it openly. I didn't realize that my parents even *had* sex until I accidentally walked into their bedroom and caught them doing it. Under the covers, of course. I can't imagine my mother doing it *on top* of the covers, not for a moment. I think the only intimate thing she ever told me was that it took her years to pluck up enough courage to use her first tampon, because she was always afraid she was going to lose it 'up there,' and that the string would get twined around her heart! No, I'm serious! A whole lot of women of my mom's generation were completely ignorant about 'down there.' I think a whole lot of women still are. I didn't know myself where I peed from until I saw myself in a mirror.

"I've always had fantasies about dominating a man, telling him what to do. It's strange, really, because I've never been very dominant in my personal relationships. I was so meek and submissive with Don. He only had to snap his fingers and I'd be there. I guess the reason is that I haven't been too lucky in love. I was in love with a guy called Michael before I met Don, seriously in love, but he was married, with two kids, and when he went back to his family that knocked all the confidence out of me. It was bad enough trying to take a married man away from his wife and kids, but when he actually turned around and said that he didn't want me anymore ... well, it doesn't do much for a woman's self-esteem.

"Maybe that was why I had fantasies about being totally in charge of my sexual relationships. Some of the fantasies were pretty mild—like ordering a man to kiss my hand; or opening up my robe and ordering him to kiss my nipples. Some were stronger, like telling a man that he *had* to make love to me, or else he had to strip off all of his clothes and jerk off in front of me. Actually, I'd really like that, I'd really like to see a guy jerking off, just for me. When I was about 16 I was walking our family dog in the woods and I came across a guy standing completely naked, jerking himself off. He was pretty young, only 18 or 19 years old, and he was very thin. But his cock was huge, and tilted right up, and he was whacking at it for all he was worth. I stood behind this bush watching him, and I was *fascinated*. He was rubbing himself so fast, and all his balls were crinkled up. I'd never seen a guy naked before, not like that. I was frightened but I was really attracted to him, too. I almost felt like going up to him and asking him if he wanted *me* to jerk him off, except that I was too shy and I didn't dare. In any case, he suddenly shot out these big loops of white stuff that dropped onto the leaves. That was the first time I ever saw sperm.

"Afterward he stood there for a while, squeezing his cock with his hand. Then he got dressed and left, like nothing had happened. That made such an impression on me, I fantasized about it for weeks.

"Anyhow, after Michael left me, I started having fantasies about domination. I wanted to have a sexual relationship in which *I* was in charge. If I wanted to be fucked, then the man would have to fuck me. If I wanted him to stay the night, he'd have to stay. If I wanted him to go down on me, he'd have to do it. If I wanted him to lick my ass clean after I'd been to the bathroom, he couldn't say no. If he disobeyed, I'd whip him.

"It took a long time to build up this fantasy; but then I saw some pictures of old-style underwear in a fashion magazine, believe it or not, and the whole fan-

tasy kind of came into focus. I could just imagine myself wearing high black leather boots, with thousands
of laces, and a tight black basque that left my nipples
bare, And a whip, you know, one of those cat-o'-
nine tails.

"It was a fantasy, and that was the way it stayed
until I wrote to you asking for advice. When you said
live your fantasy, I was scared, to tell you the truth.
Thinking about it inside your head is one thing. Doing
it is something else. Besides, I didn't even know where
I was going to get hold of whips, and boots and
basques, and stuff like that. I was amazed when you
told me that I could buy it all mail order—even whips.
And more! I couldn't believe some of the merchandise
in that catalog—whips, chains, handcuffs, turkey-trussers,
gags, masks—it was just incredible.

"Anyhow, I sent off my $125 for the things that I
wanted, and for three weeks I had to make sure that
I was the one who went to collect the mail every day.

"No question about it, the first time was the hardest
time. Jeff came home from work. He was tired, and
all he wanted to do was eat his evening meal, open a
beer, and sit in front of the television. I was so scared
that this wasn't going to work. I was going to dress
up like 'Ms. Domina' and look like a fool. If there's
one thing worse than not looking sexy, it's looking
like a fool.

"Well, I fed him, and he watched TV for a while.
While he was watching, I went into the bedroom and
changed into the clothes I'd bought. Black stockings,
black PVC thigh boots. The heels were so high I could
hardly walk in them! And of course my black satin
basque. It left my breasts completely bare, but it made
them jut out like they did when I was 16.

"I took one last look at myself in the mirror, and I

said to myself, 'This is it. This is where you become Ms. Domina,' and if he won't do what he's told, then you'd better start thinking seriously about finding yourself another man—either a man who obeys you, or a man who doesn't need to obey you.

"But your advice made me feel powerful. For the first time ever, I felt like I was in charge. I was just hoping that Jeff wouldn't feel threatened or upset, or that what I was doing was some kind of criticism. It wasn't meant as a criticism. It was meant as a way of showing him that he *could* satisfy me, and satisfy me good, if only he used his imagination.

"I stood in front of the bedroom mirror admiring myself, and then I plucked up courage and called Jeff to come see me. It seemed to take him an age. When he came into the room, he stood there staring at me and I don't think he could believe his eyes! He walked all around me, shaking his head, and for one moment I thought it was all going to go wrong. But then I said, 'What are you staring at?' in a real snappy Ms. Domina voice.

"He said, 'You ... you look amazing. Where did you get all of that stuff?'

"I said, 'If you want to find out, you'll have to grovel for it.'

"He said, 'You're kidding me, right?' But I said, 'I was never more serious. Get down on your knees and kiss my cunt and then I'll tell you.'

"That was more than he could resist. He hadn't said anything about it, but he hadn't taken his eyes off my bald cunt since he'd walked into the room. He knelt down, and he kissed it, and then he gave it a lick, too, right in the slit, between my lips. Well, that was a chance for Ms. Domina to get angry. Your slave should do what he's told but *only* what he's told ...

no improvization. I said, 'That's it, you don't get any more. I said kiss, not lick, don't you know the difference, you imbecile?'

"Jeff was really getting into the spirit of it. He said, 'I'm sorry, I didn't realize.'

Of course I corrected him. 'You should say, "I'm sorry, *Ms. Domina,* for taking advantage. It won't happen again.'"

"I punished him by ordering him to take off all of his clothes and clean my boots with his tongue. I never saw him undress so fast! When he took off his clothes his cock was red and swollen and sticking right up. I put one foot up on the stool in front of my dressing table, and he licked all around it. He even kissed the heels. Then he did the same with the other foot. After that, I ordered him to polish both boots with his penis. He was pretty juicy already so it did give a little extra shine! He pressed his cock all around the soles and the heels, and rubbed it up and down the sides, right the way up to my thighs.

"Before that evening, he had never, *ever* done anything kinky ... not with me, anyhow. It was amazing how much he was enjoying it, and how much it was turning him on. The odd thing is that you hear about all of these S&M couples, and you think *ugh,* that's not for me, but when you actually do it, when you actually have this mistress-slave relationship going between you, even though it's only play-acting, kind of, it's so exciting and sexy. You feel you can do absolutely anything you want.

"When he was finished licking my boots, I looked down at them, and said, 'Not good enough ... you'll have to be whipped.' I told him to bend over the dressing-table stool, and I gave him three lashes with this special whip that I'd bought. It's like a cat-o'-nine-tails, you know, with flat leather tails. It doesn't hurt like a cane or a real thin whip, but it smarts, and it leaves a red mark. By the time I'd finished, his bare ass was crisscrossed with red, like somebody had been playing tic-tac-toe on it! He started to sit up, but I told him to stay where he was. One of the main things about this whip is that the handle is a big black dildo. I ordered him to take the jar of night cream from my dressing table, open it up, and smear it all around his asshole.

"He said, 'What are you going to do?' but I gave him another lashing and he said he was sorry for talking out of turn. His cock was just enormous. I could actually see it throbbing and there was this long drip of juice dangling from the end of it.

"He opened the cheeks of his hairy ass and smeared night cream all around his asshole. I told him that he wasn't allowed to resist or to cry out, and he had to hold his ass open as wide as he could. Then I turned the whip around, and forced the dildo into his asshole. I really had to screw it in, but he didn't cry out and he didn't say a word. I was amazed how submissive he was. I forced it in as far as it would go, until there was nothing but the whip hanging out of his asshole like a black tail.

"I went and sat on the chair by the window, and I told him that I would give him permission to lick me now, but he had to crawl on all fours all the way across the room. He did it, with his tail waving with every step he took. I sat right on the very edge of the chair and opened my legs up wide. He put his head down between my legs and started to lick my cunt. Every now and then I pretended to get angry with him, and slapped his face or pulled his hair. I said things like, 'Lick my clitoris now! Not so hard!' or 'Stick your tongue in my hole!'

"Of course I was turned on, too. I was more turned on than I could ever remember. Sitting in my chair with my legs open like that, watching my naked husband obediently licking and sucking my naked cunt ... I started to squeeze my breasts and twist my nipples around with my fingers, which is what I always do when I masturbate.

"All the same, I told him he was useless at licking my cunt, he'd have to have more punishment. I made him lie back on the bed, then I blindfolded him tightly with a black silk scarf. I had six or seven crocodile clips which I'd bought from our local hardware store—it's surprising how many instruments of torture you can find in your local hardware store! I clipped one to each of his nipples, and I clipped the rest to the skin of his balls. Believe me, they really pinch, these clips.

"I climbed on top of him, took hold of his cock, and rubbed it all around my cunt, but not actually *in* it. I said, 'What will you do for me, if I allow you to put your cock inside me?' He said, 'Anything—absolutely anything!' I said, 'Will you suck my dirty panties every day?' and he said, 'Anything.' I said, 'Will you sleep naked on the floor every night, handcuffed to the end of the bed?' and he said, 'Yes ... you know I will.'

"It was only then that I opened up the lips of my cunt and guided his cock inside me. It was totally rigid, and it was so big that it made me shiver so that I couldn't stop shivering every time I went up and down on it. I fucked him harder and harder, I couldn't help it, I really needed it by then. All the crocodile clips were rattling between his legs, and of course he still had that enormous whip handle up his ass. I reached around behind me, and I gave the whip a few hard thrusts, so that it went even further up.

"When he climaxed, he doubled-up like he'd broken his back. I'd never actually felt him coming before, but I did this time. Of course, 'Ms. Domina' was furious with him for coming first—a terrible act of disobedience. I made him lie facedown on the bed. Then I pulled the whip out of his ass and gave him six lashes with it, on his shoulders and his bottom. After that, he had to kneel on the floor with his hands clasped behind him while I stood over him, and he had to lick me to an orgasm, no matter how long it took. He kept having to stop licking to swallow, because his own sperm kept sliding out of my cunt and down his throat. Every time he stopped I promised him another punishment, and by the time I was almost ready to climax, his cock was standing up again. That was another first for me—having an orgasm standing up, although I did have to hold onto the brass rails at the foot of the bed.

"We talked almost all night about what we'd done, and we made love twice more before morning—in the conventional way, you know. We both agreed that we'd like to try it again, and we went through two of the catalogs that I'd sent for, and chose three or four more things. One was like a black leather lace-up corset called 'Peter's Hell.' It fits tight around a man's cock, leaving only his balls and the head of his cock exposed. Another item we chose was a pair of ankle cuffs, with padlocks and a connecting chain. I wanted this wide studded leather belt, too, with a tight chrome chain that goes down between my legs."

What was Jeff's reaction, when he first saw her dressed up in her basque and her boots?

"At first he was shocked, but only for a few moments. Then he said he had a huge feeling of relief, that *I* had actually taken the first step, and lifted all of the responsibility off of his shoulders for once. He didn't have to make any decisions; all he had to do was play the part of the slave and do exactly what I told him to do.

"He also said that he felt completely free, because I was showing him that I wasn't inhibited about anything to do with sex. He'd never tried S&M before, but he'd wondered about it from time to time—you know, what it was really like. He'd never realized how exciting it was, to be submissive like that."

How often do they have S&M sessions now?

"Weekends, mostly . . . at least twice a month. But sometimes Jeff will come home and I'll be ready, dressed in my belts and chains and my spike-heel shoes."

And the effect on their sexual relationship?

"Very, very good. There's always a feeling in the back of our minds that we have this secret between us. We go to parties, and I can look across the room at Jeff and think, only a couple of hours ago, that man was kneeling in front of me, all chained up, while I bent down in front of him and made him lick my ass. And he looks across the room at me and thinks the same. Two people couldn't share more than we share now. We share *everything*."

Sadie, a 28-year-old jeweler from Santa Fe, had a very different problem than Rita. She had been brought up as the oldest of five children but the only girl. Ever since she was small she had been obliged to take care of her brothers and to help her mother with cooking and cleaning and running the household. Consequently she had found very little free time in her teenage years to meet boys and develop full sociosexual relationships with them, as most of her friends had.

Her brothers often brought home friends, but most of them, of course, were much younger.

Although Sadie appeared on first meeting to be very confident, almost dominant, it quickly became clear that this was little more than a facade. She had learned to act in a strict and dominant way when she was taking care of her brothers, but in reality she was extremely shy and unsure of herself, and up until the age of 21 her sexual knowledge was limited to what she had learned in school and what she had picked up from teenage magazines. This sort of information is well-meaning but does very little to prepare a young woman for the complexities of a mature sexual relationship, and does nothing at all to show her how adventurous sex can be.

A typical example is this (true) excerpt from *Your Sexual Self,* a 50-page booklet on sex written for girls of 19: "There are sexual positions that can increase the chances of an orgasm when you're bonking. One— the missionary position with a pillow under your bum will raise your clitoris and increase the friction. Two— if he enters you from behind with you kneeling on all fours, he can also use his hands to bring you to orgasm. Three—get on top and straddle his hips and squat or kneel down over his willy, grinding your clitoris over his pubic bone. He can also use his hands to stimulate this area."

Apart from the evasive language, this is the only mention of intercourse in the entire book, which principally concerns itself with information about breast size, premenstrual tension, toxic shock, and itches in a girl's "nether parts." Although there is much more explicit information about sex in women's magazines such as *Cosmopolitan* and *New Woman*—and although it's true that *any* mention of a clitoris and a "willy" would have been unheard of a decade ago in a magazine for teenage girls, and that some information is better than none at all—it's sobering to think that a young girl could enter into a marriage or a long-term sexual relationship with no more idea about adventurous sex than putting a pillow under her "bum."

Sadie had only three boyfriends before the age of 21, despite the fact that she is blond, petite, and very pretty. "Each time they wanted to get serious, I'd turn all cold and angry. I was so scared of sex, I didn't know what to do and I was sure it was going to be messy and a big disaster. My panties would be wet after I'd been kissing, and I never wanted any boyfriend of mine to see *that*.

"In the end I lost my virginity on my twentieth birthday to a boy named Tom. We were both quite drunk and I don't honestly remember much of what happened, except that we lay on top of all the coats that people had left in the spare bedroom and my panties were still around my ankles when we'd finished. I never dated Tom again. I was ashamed and confused about what had happened, but of course I acted in my usual way which was to freeze him out. The boys at my vocational college used to call me Ms. Amana because they said I was an icebox ... get it?

"Then I met David, and that was when my real trouble started. David's tall, and dark, and incredibly good-looking. He came from Austin, Texas, originally, and he has this fabulous lazy accent that sent goosebumps down my spine the very first time he spoke to me. We met at my friend's twenty-first birthday party and the minute he walked in the door I knew that he had to be mine.

"He liked me, too. I mean he liked me a whole lot. He spent most of the evening talking to me and dancing with me, and after the party was over he asked me back to his place for breakfast. Champagne, orange juice, eggs Benedict. Doesn't that sound *romantic*? And it *was* romantic ... he had a beautiful apartment with a fantastic view, and all these Puye Indian relics on the walls. He made perfect eggs Benedict, and we sat out on the deck on a swing and drank mimosas, and he told me all about himself and I told him all about me. He's a designer ... he designs interiors for airplanes, and corporate livery, and stuff like that. I mean it's very commercial work but he's very artistic.

"He kissed me and told me how pretty I was, and I knew what was coming. The stupid part about it was that I wanted him just as much as he wanted me. He unbuttoned my dress and slid his hand into my bra and it made me feel so breathless, I wanted him, I wanted him. He laid me back on the swing, and he stripped off his shirt and took his condom out of his pants pocket. He pulled down his pants and his shorts, and he was actually rolling the condom onto his cock when I said, 'No, I can't do it ... I just can't do it. I've only just met you, what kind of girl do you think I am?'

"He sat down and tried to make me feel better about it, but the moment was gone. The poor guy was just sitting there with his pants around his knees and a half-unrolled condom hanging from the end of his cock, and the whole thing was so uncomfortable and awful.

"I went home, and I really didn't expect to hear from him again. But three days later he called me and asked me if I wanted to go to an art exhibition with him. I went, and we had a wonderful afternoon, but when it came to the evening, the same thing happened. I couldn't stop myself acting all icy and unresponsive. I was *afraid,* that was the truth of it. I was afraid that David would find out that I was no good in bed. I was afraid that his cock was going to be far too big for me. I'd heard all of those stories about men and women getting locked together when they were having sex, and having to call the paramedics to pry them apart. I didn't know how you were supposed to touch a man's cock ... somebody had told me something about it hurting if you did it the wrong way. Supposing I hurt him and looked like an idiot?

"It all sounds ridiculous, when I think about it now. But I was afraid and I was confused and I panicked. David dropped me off home. He didn't say more than two words on the way, and I thought, 'now I've really blown it.'

"I was very depressed about David for two or three weeks. Well, not so much about David—more about myself. I tried to talk to some of my friends about sex but all they said was, 'don't worry about it, let it happen,' and the trouble was I couldn't let it happen.

"Then I had a call from my brother John—he's the second oldest, after me. He was coming to Santa Fe to visit some of his old college friends and he had no place to stay. I said sure, if he didn't mind sleeping on the couch. Out of the whole family, John and I were always the closest—close in age, and close because the two of us had always had to look after the other kids. I really love John a whole lot. He's quiet, and good-looking, and he always has time for people ... which is more than I do.

"Anyhow he came the same afternoon. I cooked dinner for us, and then we spent the rest of the evening drinking wine and catching up on all of the news. One of the reasons he'd come back to Santa Fe was because he'd split up from his fiancée, Ellen. He wasn't too sad about it. I guess he'd seen it coming. All the same he was feeling pretty lonesome and strange, the way you do when you break up with somebody you really like—the way *I* felt about David.

"We were almost ready for bed when the doorbell rang. It was an artist friend of mine called Guy. His car had broken down about two blocks away and he wanted to know if he could sleep on the couch till the morning. He had some crazy kind of hot rod and it needed special parts or something, I don't know. I told him the couch was already booked, but John said, 'that doesn't matter, we can share the same bed, we are related, after all.' So we opened another bottle of wine, and talked for a while longer. Then Guy crashed out on the couch and John and I went to bed.

"Usually I sleep naked but that night I wore a nightshirt. John wore a T-shirt and undershorts, and we were all very decent and made sure that he was sleeping way over on one side of the bed and I was sleeping way over on the other side.

"I'd drunk so much wine that I went to sleep as soon as I switched off the light. But around one or two o'clock in the morning, I woke up. I guess I wasn't used to have somebody else in bed with me. I listened, and I could hear John panting, like he was running or something, and the whole bed was subtly kind of shaking. I switched on the light and said, 'John . . . are you okay?' and of course he *was* okay, only I was too naive to realize what he'd been doing. I said, 'Oh, my God!' He was lying there with his shorts pulled down and his cock sticking out, masturbating. His cock was enormous. He was gripping it tight in his right hand and it was purple like a plum.

"He was so embarrassed he went red and then he

went white. He tried to drag the covers back over him, but I said, 'Sorry, I'm sorry. It was my fault. I should have known.'

"After a while, he managed to say, 'I miss her, that's all. I shouldn't have been doing it, not in your bed. You're my sister.'

"I said, 'I'm still a woman. I can try to understand, if you'll let me.'

"He said, "Look, I'm frustrated, that's all. I shouldn't have been doing it.'

"I said, 'Why don't I help you? You don't want to feel bad.'

"I knew what I was saying. I knew exactly what it was that I was offering to do. He was my brother and everything, for sure; but I wasn't planning on having intercourse with him or anything like that. But I'd never been so close to a man before, not sexually, without being frightened, without turning all stiff and cold and behaving like Ms. Amana. I wasn't frightened of John, he was only my brother John, and I knew for sure that he wouldn't hurt me, not for anything. But I wanted to know what it was like, feeling a man's cock, and I wanted to know what I was supposed to do.

"I reached out and touched his arm and said, 'What do you want me to do?'

"He said, 'You can't do anything. You're my sister.'

"I said, 'Of course I can do something. I want to. I don't know anything about it and I want to find out. I don't want to marry you. I don't want to have babies. I just want to make you feel better.'

"I put my hand down and tried to take hold of his cock, but at first he pushed me away. I said, 'John . . . let me feel it. Let me try. I've never done it before.'

"He didn't say anything, but slowly he took his

hand away. I reached around and felt his pubic hair and his balls. I touched them really gently. I said, 'Does this hurt?' and he said, 'Why should it hurt?' I held his balls tighter, my brother's balls, I could feel them moving around inside his—scrotum, is that it? It was fascinating. I pressed them and squeezed them and at last he said 'ouch!' and I knew that was too much. I said I was sorry. He said, 'Just be more careful.'

"I took hold of his cock and it was very big and hot. It seemed to radiate heat. I moved my hand right up the shaft until I reached the head and I recoiled for a second because it was wet and slimy. He said, 'Go on, rub it, that's what I want you to do, rub it.' So I started to rub it, up and down. He said 'harder,' so I did it harder. He said 'faster,' so I did it faster. Then he said, 'too fast,' so I slowed down. At last I was gripping his cock so hard that his veins bulged out, and slowly massaging it up and down. There was so much slimy stuff coming out of it that my fingers were slippery, and so was his cock, but it was so beautiful, here was my own brother and I was making him feel, like, out of this world.

"I said, 'Tell me, how does this feel? Do you really like it done like this?' and he said, 'It's perfect, it's heaven ... nobody ever rubbed my dick like this before. Nobody.'

"Then he suddenly turned toward me and said, 'Suck it for me.'

"I knew about oral sex. I knew some girls who had done it. But I'd never done it myself ... and with John, my own brother?

"I said, 'I don't know. Maybe we shouldn't be doing this.'

"But he said, 'Who can it hurt? It's just play. It's

just brother and sister playing together, that's all. Anyhow, how will you ever know what to do, if you never do it?'

"He lay back on the bed, holding up his cock in his hand. I knelt beside him, and looked at his cock for a long time. I said, 'I don't know what to do. I really don't know what to do.'

"He said, 'Lick it, bitch. Suck it. Take it in your mouth and suck it dry.'

"I don't know what it was, but when he called me 'bitch,' that kind of triggered something off. I guess I'll have a whole horde of feminists after me, but when he called me 'bitch,' it turned me on. It was like I'd been waiting all of these years for a man to insult me, a man to curse me, a man to tell me what to do. I wasn't the cold, angry person that everybody imagined I was. I wasn't 'Ms. Amana.' If I was anything, I was 'Ms. Bottled-Up Passion.' I needed a man to take charge of me. I needed a man to fuck me and fuck me and never let me breathe in between fucks.

"I don't care how wrong you think that might have been, but it was what I needed. I'd already spent most of my teenage years taking care of my brothers, cooking my father's dinner when Mom was too busy, going to the market, making beds, being in charge. I wanted somebody to take charge of me, body and soul. Not forever, perhaps, but as long as it took me to learn about loving and making love ... as long as it took me to blossom, as a woman, because I'd never had the chance to blossom. I was like a tight bud, that never let anything in, and never let anything out. I needed to open out. I needed to be fucked.

"I licked John's cock and it tasted salty. Then I licked it again, and again, and it tasted beautiful. It tasted like young man. I pushed his thighs farther apart so that I could feel his balls properly, and then I took the whole head of his cock into my mouth, and sucked it, not too hard.

"He was rude to me and he was cruel to me. He made me lie on my back while he forced his cock into my mouth. He sat astride my face so that I could hardly breathe. He called me a slut and a bitch, and the more he swore at me, the more I loved it. I was his sister, and I had his stiff cock halfway down my throat! I would have done anything for him, then; or any man. I just wanted to be taken, and taken, and taken, in every possible hole.

"He made me kneel on the bed and bend over, and he pushed three or four fingers up inside my cunt, and finger fucked me until I almost fainted. I was mad, I know that! But I needed so badly to know what a man wanted from me, and what I was supposed to do. And now I understood! You just gave yourself, that's all. You didn't worry about technique or style or positions—you just gave yourself.

"John whispered in my ear that he wanted to fuck me, but I knew that he couldn't. He was my brother, I didn't mind play, but not real fucking. 'Between your breasts, then,' he said, and that was something else I learned that night. He sat astride my chest, squashing my breasts together, and he fucked my cleavage. Toward the end, he gripped my breasts and pulled my nipples and said I was a whore and a slut; but he didn't want any other kind of sister, only a slut sister. He was still talking dirty to me when this thick warm flow of sperm poured out, all over my chest, all over my breasts, and my nostrils were filled with the smell of it. He sat astride me, massaging my breasts and my stomach and my underarms, kissing my breasts and biting my nipples, kissing my mouth and biting my tongue. He ran his hands into my hair and pulled my hair. He rubbed his soft cock against my lips and all over my face. He said 'suck it,' and I obeyed him and sucked it.

"In the end we lay side by side holding each other. I said, 'Why did you treat me that way? Why did you call me all of those names?'

"He said, 'That was what you wanted, wasn't it? You won't want it next year. You may not want it ever again. But you needed it once. You needed to give everything, just once.'

"He was right, you know. There's no room in any relationship for coldness, or ignorance, or ignorance hiding behind coldness. If you don't know, you have a duty to your partner to admit that you don't know, rather than trying to hide it, don't you think? Openness, that's what it's all about. Open minds—open bodies, too.

"I talked to John about David and John suggested that I call him. Maybe I should invite him for dinner, and show him that I wasn't cold and I wasn't angry, just shy, just protecting myself. David didn't know how to react to me at first, but after a while he said okay, he'd come along, although he might have to leave early because he had a business breakfast the following morning.

"I cooked my best meal, *tajine msir zeetoon*, which is Moroccan chicken, and John bought some good bottles of chardonnay. My relationship with John had been very strange all day. We were like lovers, but we knew we couldn't be lovers. We kept holding each other and kissing each other, but it was almost like saying good-bye, rather than saying hello. John came out of the shower after Guy had left, dressed in his bathrobe, and said, 'Open my robe,' which I did. His cock was half-erect, and he said, 'Touch it, hold it,' which I did. It was beautiful. I would have died for his cock, right then. I was in love! I knelt down and sucked it, right there in the middle of the living room, but he pulled himself away and closed his robe and said, 'No, we can't.'

"Right after that, though, he said, 'Take off your clothes, let me look at you.' I undressed, and stood in front of him naked, and there was a moment when I thought he was going to say, 'Live with me forever ... let's forget about the fact that we're brother and sister, let's be lovers.' But he didn't say it—and, even if he had, I wouldn't have done it. Do you know what he did for me? He demystified sex ... he taught me, and he showed me. He might have treated me like a slut but that's what I needed to be. I wish it could have been any other man except him, but when you think about it logically, it *couldn't have been any other man but him.*

"David came around that evening and the atmosphere was good. I lit a log fire and the food turned out great. I could tell that David was cautious ... and I guess he had every right to be. I'd already rebuffed him twice; and I don't think he would have stood for it a third time. But after we'd drunk some wine and played some music, everything relaxed. We sat on big cushions in front of the fire and David told this long, wild story about dancing girls he saw in Thailand who could extinguish lighted candles up inside their vaginas. We drank some more wine and I guess you could say that the atmosphere went from good to mellow, and then from mellow to very mellow.

"We started talking about sexual relationships and I told David that I was sorry about acting so cold. John held my hand all the time that I was talking, and encouraged me, and in the end I was able to tell David how fearful I'd been, you know, that I was afraid of sex. John started to kiss me, and this time they were real deep kisses, and I think that David began to get the message. He came and sat next to me, too, and started kissing me, and then he fondled my breasts through my blouse. John fondled them, too, and there I was with two men playing with my breasts.

"John said, 'You'll do anything, won't you?' and I said yes. He said, 'You're not afraid of sex anymore, are you?' and I said no. And it was true. I wasn't. I wasn't afraid of anything. I guess I'd discovered the big secret about sex, the big secret that your parents never tell you ... the big secret that always makes you feel guilty. And the secret is, sex is great, and wonderful, and fun, and never did anybody any harm. The only time it ever does you any harm is if you feel guilty about it ... or, of course, diseases like AIDS. But you don't have to get AIDS if you're sensible and wear a condom, and you don't have to be guilty if you're sensible, either.

"David and John unbuttoned my blouse and took it off. I felt like I was in a dream. The fire was crackling and all these shadows were jumping on the ceiling. They kissed my breasts and they bit my nipples. Then John took out his cock and massaged my left breast with it ... so David took out *his* cock and massaged my right breast with it. I took a cock in each hand, two of them, and rubbed them around my breasts and my nipples, and then I massaged their two cocks together.

"John unfastened my wraparound skirt, and took it off. I was only wearing a thong underneath, a little white lace thong. He tugged that off, too, and passed it to David, and said 'Smell ... that's a woman in heat.' David stripped off his shirt and pants, and knelt on the couch beside me. This time, I rolled his condom on his cock for him, and smoothed it right down— down to his pubic hair, so that it fitted his cock perfectly. Then I rolled another condom onto John's cock.

"David sat on the couch, with his cock pointing upward, and John helped me up so that I could sit on it. He even reached around and opened up my cunt with his fingers so that David could slide up inside me. I sat on David's lap, slowly fucking him, while John stood behind me, squeezing my breasts, and I never, ever knew that sex could feel like this.

"After a while, David started to fuck me quicker and harder. I leaned forward, kissing him and biting him ... anything I felt like. I felt John's fingers touching my anus, and my first thought was, he can't do that, he's my brother! But he kept on tickling and stroking, and after a while he pushed a finger up my anus, straight up, stiff, and it felt so erotic that all I could do was wriggle myself around, and enjoy every inch of it.

"John took his finger out, and I was disappointed for a moment, but then I felt something wide and wet, all the way down between the cheeks of my ass, and it was John's tongue. As soon as he'd licked me, he pushed his cock up against my anus—slowly to begin with, because my anus didn't want to let him in—then right up inside, all tight and rubbery.

"I had two cocks inside me now, my brother up my ass and my lover up my cunt, and their cocks were fighting and jostling each other for space. I reached down between my legs and I could feel their balls banging together as they both fucked me.

"I never really knew what an orgasm was, but I had

one. I thought I was blacking out. I couldn't feel anything except these two enormous cocks up inside me, fighting each other, you know, invading my body, like all they cared about was filling me up. Then everything went blank and I was holding onto David so tight that I almost strangled him.

"We didn't stop there. We slept on the cushions in front of the fire, and then I woke up and saw these two beautiful naked men lying next to me. I kissed David's cock, and then I kissed John's. Then I started to masturbate both of them, and it wasn't long before their cocks stiffened up, and I had one in each hand. I kissed and sucked both of them. They were heavenly, they were out of this world. Such wonderful cocks.

"I opened another condom and rolled it onto David's cock. He was so sleepy he hardly knew what I was doing to him. Then I turned John onto his side, and spread his legs, and guided David's cock toward his ass.

"David said, 'Hey, I'm not gay . . .' but John reached around and took hold of his cock and helped him to fit it into his anus. I said, 'This isn't anything to do with being gay . . . this is to do with giving in.'

"David didn't argue anymore. He pushed his cock into John's anus, and I helped him by holding the cheeks of John's ass wide apart. He pushed his cock in so far that their balls touched. I put my head down between their legs and I could kiss and suck two pairs of balls—four balls, all jumbled together, it was fantastic!

"The two of them were groaning and sweating and pushing. David had never fucked a man before, and neither had John. I wormed my way between John's thighs and took his cock into my mouth. I didn't suck it but I just held it there. David kept on ramming him and ramming him, and in the end David said, 'Oh, no—!' that's all he said, and he must have come. John came too. He poured the whole lot into my mouth and I swallowed all of it. It was sweet and sticky and to me it was nectar. My brother's come.

"I think it was even sweeter because I knew that we would never do this again, ever.

"I don't know if David really understood what had happened to me. I don't think I really understood it myself. Sometimes, I guess, you have to give in to your instincts. Maybe it was wrong of me to make love to my own brother. But he was there, and he was sympathetic, and he showed me that sex isn't frightening or wrong ... so what more could you ask than that?"

For the record, Sadie and David were married four months after their "threesome" with Sadie's brother, and they're showing all the signs of a very satisfied and sexually creative couple.

In spite of the cold facade which she presented to most of the men who were sexually attracted to her, Sadie was a naturally submissive lover. She wasn't at all prudish. She was quite prepared to go to the outer limits of sexual adventure, as many women are—even those who seem to be "frigid." What they need, however, is a lover who is prepared to guide them and teach them—a confident, masterful man who won't often take no for an answer.

Because such lovers are, unfortunately, few and far between, women like Sadie have to adopt a far more submissive role in order to bring out their dominant streak. David had two opportunities to make love to Sadie—opportunities that he "blew" because he was obviously too impatient. In the end, it was Sadie herself who showed him that she could be submissive if he treated her strongly and gently (as her brother John had), and that her submissiveness could lead to very exciting sex.

"Submissiveness" in sex has nothing to do with "inferiority." A woman who is capable of being creatively submissive is a talented lover. A man can be creatively submissive, too—allowing his partner to take control of love play, intercourse, and any inspirational variations she can think of (such as whips or Saran Wrap or cross-dressing.)

S&M has as many different manifestations as the number of people who practice it. It can amount to nothing more than one partner dominating the other, on a day-to-day basis—such as where they shop, what they do, which side of the bed they sleep on—right through to whips and chains and darning needles stuck through the nipples. Every couple finds their own way of acting out their sexual fantasies and expressing their sexual personality. All that counts is that they do it freely and openly, and never hide any secrets from one another.

If you really want to make his wildest dreams come true, think what his wildest dreams might be. Even if they shock you—even if you find them frightening—remember Sadie and Rita, who did things that they never imagined they would ever do—and emerged not only unscathed, but satisfied, fulfilled, excited, and looking forward to more.

The only limits to your sexual experience are your imagination and your common sense. Some of your fantasies will obviously be so extreme that you can never act them out in real life, and you probably wouldn't enjoy them if you did. But you can still share them with your partner by talking about them.

A book that discussed *all* the excitement that you and your partner could enjoy in bed would be a hundred times longer than this one. But I'd like to conclude with an A–Z of sexual tips that should give you plenty of information and lots of arousing suggestions.

SEVEN

A Sex-Dream Dictionary

A is for Autoerotism or masturbation. Autoerotism can help with focusing on your sexual feelings during meditation, and one or both partners can use it to excite and instruct each other during lovemaking. Despite the old wives' tales of the past, autoerotism is completely harmless for both men and women, and is a useful outlet for pent-up sexual feelings when you have no partner to give you relief. Many sex-toy companies market autoerotic devices for both sexes, including "Little Miss Lucy's First Time"—an extremely tight masturbatory sleeve for men, which is supposed to simulate a virgin's vagina.

A is also for anal play. The anus is a highly erotic area for both sexes. It can be stimulated with the tongue (anilingus) or tickled with the fingers. It can also be penetrated (but carefully, please, and with a great deal of lubrication!) by finger or fingers, penis, dildo or even—for very extreme anal sex—by a whole fist and arm. Always use an extra-strength condom during anal penetration, for fear of the last of our

'**A**'s'—AIDS. AIDS is a communicable disease transmitted in blood and body secretions, and one of the easiest ways to contract it is to indulge in unprotected anal sex, during which sensitive tissues can be torn and the bloodstream exposed to infected semen.

B is for Breasts. Whether your breasts are small or large, remember that your partner loves them; therefore give him every opportunity to see them (and feel them). More than 85 percent of the men I talked to about visual arousal rated seeing their partner walking around the house topless as one of their favorite turn-ons. Try giving him glimpses of your breasts at unusual times (when you're out walking the dog, maybe, or at a dinner party). Go without a bra when he's least expecting it, or buy yourself a quarter-cup or "peephole" bra. When you're making love, encourage him to slide his penis into your cleavage, then squash your breasts together so that he can actually have intercourse with your breasts.

C is for Clitoris. If you haven't tried it already, locate your clitoris in a mirror and watch the way you stimulate it when you're trying to arouse yourself. Next time you make love, show your partner how you like him to touch it. Guide his fingers, and don't be afraid to tell him when he's got it just right (or when he's missed the spot, or when he's rubbing too hard or too gently). He wants to please you, but he's not psychic, and he won't be able to arouse you to the very limits of pleasure unless you tell him how.

D is for Dildo ... an artificial penis with or without a vibrator inside it. These days, dildos are available in a bewildering array of shapes and sizes, and with all kinds of attachments, including anal stimulators and ejaculating testes. At least one vibrating dildo makes an exciting bedtime companion for him to use on you (especially after he's climaxed, and his erection has died) or for you to use on him ... but don't forget that lubricant!

E is for Erection. Sometimes, your partner will find his erection fails him. There are all kinds of reasons for this—stress, financial worries, career problems, alcohol or drug abuse—but if you're thoughtful and understanding and continue to have sexual petting sessions then it's likely that the problem will gradually resolve itself. In serious or persistent cases, a visit to your doctor is called for, but today there are several highly successful treatments for loss of erection, and the chances are that he'll soon come bouncing back.

F is for Fellatio, or oral sex. Up until now, you may have been too shy to suck your partner's penis, but a majority of men regard it as "the one sexual act I most want my partner to do to me." Read the chapter in this book on licking your love life into shape, then see if you can add some variations of your own, such as smothering your partner's penis in your favorite ice cream before licking it, or giving him oral sex while he's engaged in a completely different activity, such as watching TV or working or driving the car.

G is for Glans, which is the technical name for the head of the penis. This is where your partner's most sensitive nerve endings are located, and this is where you should concentrate your licking and (gentle) sucking during oral sex. A majority of American men have been circumcized, leaving the glans permanently exposed, but it is becoming increasingly common for parents who do not have religious reasons for doing so to leave the foreskin intact. This foreskin peels back when a man becomes erect, leaving the glans bare. There is no difference in the sexual sensitivity of a circumcized or an uncircumcized man.

G is for G-Spot, a collection of highly sensitive nerve endings supposedly located deep inside the vagina on the front (or stomach side). There are conflicting opinions about its existence, but some women say that stimulation of the G-Spot gives them very wet, flowing orgasms of great intensity. Whether or not the G-Spot exists, you and your partner can have hours of innocent fun trying to locate it.

H is for Hair (the pubic variety). These days, with high-cut swimsuits and lingerie, many women already shave off most or all of their pubic hair. The sight of a hairless vulva can be extremely arousing for many men, however, with all of its implications of sexual display and readiness to make love. Try it on your partner tonight. If he prefers you hairy, it won't take long to grow back.

I is for Intercourse, and especially for different positions. Many of the positions in classic erotic literature such as the *Kama Sutra* are impossible for all except professional contortionists, and some of the ancient Chinese positions are so veiled in metaphor and subtle language that you can't really tell what you're supposed to do. But do try changing positions, such as making love on all fours, or sitting on his lap. You'll also find that a change of location (making love in the living room, or in the bathroom) can suggest a whole variety of new positions (over the backs of chairs, for example, or over a table.)

J is for Jism, or the male ejaculate. Seeing himself ejaculate can be very exciting and satisfying for a man, and occasionally you can arrange for this to happen by drawing his penis out of you when he climaxes, and rubbing the head of his penis around and around your vulva, or by aiming his climax into your stomach. Alternatively you can masturbate him and/or give him oral sex, directing his climax wherever takes your fancy. Men ejaculate only a teaspoonful of semen when they climax, and it is composed of nothing more than a few simple sugars, acids, and proteins. Contrary to high school rumor, swallowing it has no effect on the size of your breasts.

K is for Keeping Fit. You can improve your love life dramatically by making sure that you exercise regularly, and that your partner exercises, too. Not only does fitness help you to adopt more strenuous and more erotic sexual positions, it actually extends your partner's staying power. Sex therapist Barbara Keesling has come up with what she seems to believe is a "secret" technique for improving a man's ability to keep on coming all night, which is for him regularly to flex the muscle that extends from the pubic bone to the base of the spine, the pubococcygeus, or PC muscle. She's quite right, of course, although sex therapists have been saying for many years that exercising the PC can help staying power. He can do it anyplace—even while he's sitting at a desk. All he has to do is pretend that he's trying to shut off a flow of urine, then relax, then flex, and so on.

L is for Language. I'm still amazed by now many couples make love in total silence. Language can be arousing, suggestive, lustful. When you're alone together, you can talk as dirty as you like. People often ask me how I manage to persuade so many respectable men and women to describe their sexual experiences in such a frank way. It takes a lot of coaxing, believe me, but once you've discovered that you *can* say the words "cunt" and "cock" without blushing or being struck by lightning, sexual conversation becomes much freer and easier. Failing that, you can always invent your own euphemisms or pet words. In Japan, for instance, they call a man's penis his *nagachochin,* meaning his long lantern, or else his *tenggu no hana,* referring to the outside nose of the demon Tenggu. A woman's vagina is called *shita-kuchi* or lower mouth; or *hotategai,* meaning scallop. Her clitoris is *mame,* or bean.

M is for Medication ... and taking a look into your partner's bathroom cabinet could reveal why he may have been having problems with his sex life. Although very few doctors mention it to their patients, some prescription drugs have a sexually debilitating effect, both for men and for women. Chief among these are tranquilizers and sedatives such as Xanax and Valium, as well as many different sleeping pills; antidepressants such as Prozac and Tryptizol; blood-pressure drugs such as Inderal and other beta-blockers; ulcer drugs like Tagamet, which can cause loss of erection; appetite suppressants; migraine medication; and a score of over-the-counter products for allergies and nasal congestion. If your partner has been suffering an inexplicable loss of sex drive, talk to your doctor. Dr. Theresa Crenshaw, from San Diego, the coauthor of

Sexual Pharmacology, says, "There are many common drugs that can cause sexual impairment that I call 'sex offenders.' "

N is for Nipples. You know that *your* nipples are sexually sensitive, but so are his. You can stimulate your partner's nipples in a whole variety of ways, from licking and tickling to pinching and biting. As we saw in Chapter 5 on S&M, you can add to his sexual stimulation by attaching clips or clothespins to his nipples when you make love, or you can stiffen them with ice cubes. Some men love having their nipples pulled out as far as they will go, and then twisted.

O is for Orgasm. Many women become extremely introverted as their orgasm approaches: all of their attention is concentrated on their own rising sexual feelings and their inner selves. This is understandable when women find it difficult to achieve orgasm, but it also can confuse their partner, who is stimulating them and looking for some signs of sexual response. More movement, more panting (even if it's simulated) will help to return the favor that your partner is doing you with his fingers or his tongue or his penis. You will make him feel like a better lover, and you will also excite him more ... which can only benefit you.

P is for Penis. Don't be shy about touching or holding or squeezing your partner's penis at every possible opportunity. Unlike most women, who dislike being "touched up" or "goosed," men rarely receive a flirtatious fondle. Try asking him to wash the dishes for you, and then slip your hands into his fly while he's doing it, and gently masturbate him. Try reaching across the bed in the middle of the night, when he's fast asleep, and seeing if you can rub him into an erection. Try it anyplace, at any time. Sex doesn't begin at bedtime and end with the *Star Spangled Banner*. If you keep on touching him, you'll find that you get more sex than you know what to do with ... and he'll think that you are a dream come true.

Q is for Quickie. Although leisurely, luxurious sex is obviously more rewarding, don't forget to encourage him to have hasty sex sessions whenever you can find the time ... preferably when you're expecting guests at any minute, or when he's going to be late for work, or at any other time when urgency is everything. Don't bother to undress: just lift up your skirt and pull your panties to one side. Talk dirty to him while you do it.

R is for Rubber. Until recently, rubberwear was considered to be a turn-on for "fetishists only." But these days, rubber dresses and skirts have been exhibited at mainstream fashion shows, and you can buy them almost anywhere. Try a clinging rubber mini-dress, or a rubber miniskirt, and see how your partner reacts. You can also buy black rubber panties with no crotch. Be adventurous: rubberwear can be so hot when you're wearing it that you might even lose some weight, too.

S is for Sexual Self-Confidence. One of the best ways of improving your love life is to reassure yourself that you are sexually attractive to your partner, and that you are a skillful and exciting lover. That's why it's so important to learn as much as you can about sex and different sexual acts, even if you have no intention of actually performing them all. Don't forget to allow yourself regular time to meditate about your sexual feelings and your sexual desires, and to figure out what *you* want from your sexual relationships. By getting everything that *you* want, you will be going a long way toward giving your partner everything that *he* wants.

T is for Testes. It's surprising how many women ignore their partner's testes when they're making love. Usually, they're worried about hurting them, and it's true that a hearty squeeze of his scrotum will bring tears to the eyes of the toughest. But do pay attention to them, particularly during oral sex, when you can "bobble" them in your mouth with your tongue, or very gently suck them. A complainant to the *Playboy Adviser* said that she wanted to suck her lover's testes but his scrotal hairs were too long. You are perfectly within your rights to demand that he shave them off.

U is for Underwear. Even the most prudish men will respond to erotic underwear. I know that market research has shown that women put comfort before titillation, but you will reap great sexual rewards if you occasionally dress up in G-string, garter belt, and stockings. Go for blacks, scarlets, purples—and tassels, too, if you wish. It doesn't matter if you think you look as if you've just stepped out of a Nevada brothel ... vulgarity can be a terrific turn-on. Most good sex is about game-playing, and there are few raunchier parts to play than that of the prostitute-cum-stripper. Think about it: if men weren't excited by sexy underwear, strip clubs would have closed down years ago.

V is for Vulva. Don't be shy about displaying your vulva to your partner. He loves you and it excites him to see it, especially if your exposure is "accidental." Lie on the couch wearing nothing but one of his shirts, reading a book ... and make sure that he can just see between your legs. Bend over when you're not wearing panties.

W is for Water Sports, which is a euphemism for sex games involving pissing. Water sports vary from the very mild (watching each other urinate) to the very extreme (urinating over each other's genitals and faces and even drinking each other's piss). Water sports are harmless, and many couples indulge in them when they are showering together. Fresh urine is completely sterile and there is no harm in drinking a small quantity ... in fact some health gurus even recommend it.

X is for X-rated videos, which can do a lot to liven up a dull evening at home. Don't wait for your partner to suggest that you rent one—there's no doubt that he'd love to, but he doesn't want you to think that he's dirty-minded. Just say, "I've always wondered what those porno videos are like—do you think we could see one tonight?" You'll surprise him, but chances are he won't say no.

Y is for You—the new sexy you. From tonight onward, you're going to show your partner your real Sexual Character, and you're going to make up your mind that you're never going to look back.

Z is for ZZZ ... and may your wildest dreams come true!